Creative Writing

Creative Writing

A Guide and Glossary to Fiction Writing

Colin Bulman

polity

© Colin Bulman 2007

The right of Colin Bulman to be identified as Author of this Work has been asserted in accordance with the UK Copyright, Designs and Patents Act 1988.

First published in 2007 by Polity Press

Polity Press
65 Bridge Street
Cambridge CB2 1UR, UK

Polity Press
350 Main Street
Malden, MA 02148, USA

ISBN-10: 0-7456-3687-X
ISBN-13: 978-07456-3687-0
ISBN-10: 0-7456-3688-8 (pb)
ISBN-13: 978-07456-3688-7 (pb)

A catalogue record for this book is available from the British Library.

Typeset in 11 on 13 pt Scala
by Servis Filmsetting Ltd, Manchester
Printed and bound in Malaysia by Arden Press Ltd

For further information on Polity, visit our website: www.polity.co.uk

Contents

Introduction

Creative writing has blossomed at all levels of education. Twenty-five years ago it was rarely, if ever, found in British university English courses; it was neither part of A level English studies nor even many GCSE courses. Now it is popular in all these areas. In addition, writing creatively has become a favoured activity for many people not in formal education perhaps but attending evening classes or for the lone writer labouring not in a garret but at the kitchen table. Some writers seek publication; others simply enjoy the process of writing and the struggle to create a good piece of fiction. This book is for anyone who wants to know the techniques used by fiction writers and to improve their own. An understanding of how stories are constructed, the techniques used in writing and the elements stories typically contain will assist aspiring writers and help them to avoid those mistakes that lead to less successful fiction.

Creative writing has, like most subjects, its own vocabulary. It is not as mysterious to the layperson as the jargon of the sciences, and some of the terms are frequently used but often inaccurately. For example, few people can explain the difference between plot and story. Other terms such as intertextuality or fabula are less familiar and even aspiring writers may be uncertain about some of the names given to elements of their craft.

This book has a dual purpose. It sets out to define the key terms used in creative writing (fiction). It also acts as a guide and source of suggestions on how to use the techniques of fiction writing to improve the writer's work. It might also be used as an aid to improving a story which has been thought to be unsuccessful but is not ready for the waste-paper basket.

The entries in the book are of three kinds:

1   Simple definitions of basic terms without any instructional or advisory elements where these are deemed unnecessary.

2   Some contain definitions together with suggestions that may provide a spur to writers to try techniques or types of fiction that they had not previously considered and to recognize these techniques in their reading of fiction.

3   Others, in addition to defining terms, have suggestions on how to achieve specific effects or convey subject matter in an appropriate or effective way. Examples of these include conflict, dialogue, hooks, inciting incident, plot and story, suspense, and twist ending stories.

The book can be used in at least four ways: (1) the glossary element will provide an explanation of any terms about which the reader is uncertain; (2) browsing through some of the entries may spark off an idea or enable a writer to develop an idea they had been considering; (3) having got a firm idea for a piece of fiction, the writer can check out if their plot is satisfactory and how it may be improved. They might get ideas for introducing conflict or suspense; they may need to improve or introduce an inciting incident, or check on which is the best point of view for their story and revise ideas about writing dialogue; (4) in their reading and analysis of fiction (and aspiring writers should read a lot) they can check a published author's techniques against the techniques described in the book.

It is important to note that while the entries are discrete, in any story the various elements work together in subtle ways. Thus the plot of a story cannot be seen in isolation from the characters and it will possibly contain conflict and suspense. Cross-referencing enables the reader to consult closely related techniques.

No book or teacher can make anyone a great artist, but most great artists are masters of basic techniques. Giants of the literary world like James Joyce and Samuel Beckett are supreme innovators. It is useful to remember that they understood and used (or reacted against) traditional fictional techniques. Whether using them or reacting against them, they had to *know* them. This book is largely about basic fictional techniques; no book can show the reader how to be an innovator in fiction.

Many of the entries in the book cite particular works of fiction which illustrate good practice in the techniques. For a survey of nineteenth- and twentieth-century fiction to supplement the many books mentioned in the entries, see the section Literature surveys in Further Reading and Websites at the end of this book.

Guide and Glossary

ABSURD LITERATURE

Absurd literature is mainly theatrical but some novels fall within this category. The chief dramatists labelled absurd include Samuel Beckett, Eugene Ionesco, Jean Genet, Harold Pinter, Edward Albee and N. F. Simpson. Novelists include Albert Camus, Jean-Paul Sartre, Günter Grass, Friedrich Dürrenmatt, Max Frisch and from an earlier age Franz Kafka.

Most absurdists were active in the 1950s and inevitably were affected by the Second World War and its aftermath. In addition to the war itself, the discovery of German concentration camps and the dropping of the atomic bomb on Japan led many to wonder at the sanity of the human race.

The term absurd is used in two ways. Primarily it means that human existence is regarded as meaningless, irrational and purposeless and human beings are alienated. It has much in common with, and is usually regarded as part of existentialism. The other meaning of absurd is related to the comic and grotesque. In spite of the seriousness of most absurd drama and novels there are often comic touches and interludes. It may be that writers are suggesting that things are so bad that in the end all one can do is laugh.

Albert Camus, dramatist, novelist and essayist, wrote a seminal work on the absurd, *The Myth of Sisyphus* (1942). In the following passage he states vividly what the state of the absurd means:

> A world that can be explained even with bad reasons is a familiar world. But . . . in a universe suddenly divested of illusions and lights, man feels an alien, a stranger. His exile is without remedy since he is deprived of the memory of a lost home or the hope of a promised land. This divorce between man and his life, the actor and his setting, is properly the feeling of absurdity.

The title of Camus' book is also significant. He recounts the Greek myth of Sisyphus and how as punishment for angering the gods he is condemned to roll a huge stone up a mountain. As soon as he reaches the top, the stone rolls down and he must start all over again. The myth for Camus is indicative of the life of human beings – a struggle that has no end except death. In spite of this, he concludes the story 'One must imagine Sisyphus happy'. Perhaps it is because he knows nothing other than the rolling of stones. Living life distracts most people from contemplating some significant purpose. We accept the absurdity of existence without knowing it.

Camus' novel *The Outsider* is a brilliant evocation of an absurd and alienated life. The protagonist has murdered someone for no apparent reason and at his trial he is completely disengaged from the proceedings and displays no regret for what he has done or anger at his own predicament (which will lead to his execution). His only display of emotion is when a priest tries to persuade him to repent and believe in the Lord. He cannot do this; it means nothing to him. His only hope is that he goes to his execution laughing, presumably at the absurdity of it all.

Samuel Beckett is the most acclaimed absurd dramatist and his play *Waiting for Godot* is regarded as one of the greatest of the twentieth century. *Breath*, a drama (if it can be called that), reduces the absurd to its essence. The play lasts only a couple of minutes. The curtain rises on a huge pile of rubbish. After about a minute, a birth cry is heard and then there is silence. After another moment, the curtain comes down.

Few authors write now within the absurd tradition but the work of Camus, Sartre, Beckett and Pinter among others is still read and performed.

See also EXISTENTIALISM

ACQUIRING EDITOR *SEE* COMMISSIONING EDITOR

ACTION

Action is a term used for what happens in any story. If a remark such as 'The action takes place in a city' is made, it simply means that all the events happen in a city. Action in no sense suggests that the events are fast and furious. The term in fiction does not have the same meaning as it does with reference to an action film.

See also PLOT AND STORY

ADAPTATION

Adaptation is simply the changing of one literary or artistic form to another. Many films are adaptations of novels and stage plays. Occasionally popular original films may be novelized. It is common for classic novels to be adapted into TV plays and also into films. While adaptations usually try to keep to the spirit of the original, it should be acknowledged that an adaptation is a different work. In the case of adaptations of novels to a film or play, the authorial or narrative voice is almost bound to disappear.

Occasionally authors adapt their own work but more frequently a specialist in the target media will be used. Many novelists cannot or prefer not to dramatize their own work. Adaptations are almost always commissioned by a film or TV company (or by publishers in the case of films which become novelized). They will have bought an option on the work if it is in copyright. It would be inadvisable for an unknown author to spend time adapting a work on the chance that it may be accepted.

See also COPYRIGHT; OPTION

ADVANCE

An advance or 'advance on royalties' is money paid to an author before the book has been published and sold. An advance is paid when the author may need expenses during the period of writing the book. Any advance paid will be deducted from subsequent royalties.

See also ROYALTY

ADVENTURE AND QUEST STORIES

Most people crave excitement and want to do extraordinary or adventurous things, they would like to take chances but they also want to avoid the danger such escapades involve. These opposing attitudes account for the popularity of adventure literature. Readers get their thrills vicariously. Adventure stories are one of the most popular genres of fiction, next only to romance and crime. Novels by authors such as Ken Follett, Wilbur Smith and Tom Clancy usually become instant best-sellers. While there are some serious literary adventure stories most are unashamedly escapist.

The emphasis in adventure stories is on plot and action rather than depth of characterization. The protagonists are mostly heroic although many have to overcome weaknesses in order to carry out their mission. The protagonists must act decisively and quickly.

The plots of adventure stories are also fairly uncomplicated. The plot pattern outlined in the entry on plot is almost always used. The protagonist will have an objective or aim or some task to perform that is explained in the exposition; or some inciting incident will get the story going. Pace is necessary in the adventure story, readers want action. There will then follow a series of obstacles, setbacks and problems that the protagonist will eventually overcome. Invariably in these stories, success is the outcome.

The quest story is a subgenre of the adventure story. The aim or object referred to above involves a quest for something. Some of the principal subjects of the quest are as follows: treasure; a lost child/wife/parent/friend; a lost city; the Holy Grail; a missing person; a hidden bomb or other danger; Atlantis; utopia; ghosts; a sunken wreck; a person who has done you or someone a wrong. Sometimes the quest is for something less tangible such as: justice; human rights for someone or a group; truth; fame; knowledge; freedom for oneself or others.

Very often a natural as well as a human hazard may be a central element in the story and provide further problems for the protagonist's realization of the aim. These could include disaster in the air, floods, fire and drought. The settings for adventure stories range from contemporary urban scenes to stories set in the desert, the jungle, at sea or in snowy wastes. Often the stories cross the boundaries of countries, even continents, providing a variety of landscapes and dangers. Historical adventure stories also have a considerable following.

There is nothing new about the adventure story. The earliest examples were in the form of narrative poems such as the ancient Greek story, *The Odyssey* by Homer that concerns, in part, Jason's search for the Golden Fleece. The legends and stories of King Arthur are great adventures and include the quest for the supposedly magical Holy Grail. Written in the fourteenth century, *Sir Gawain and the Green Knight* is a story of adventure.

The novel, of course, proved an ideal vehicle for the adventure story and one of the earliest novels was *The Life and Adventures of Robinson Crusoe*, a familiar story of inventive attempts to overcome hardships and sustain life on a desert island.

One of the most remarkable adventure phenomena of the early twentieth century were the novels of Edgar Rice Burroughs (1875–1950) about Tarzan. *Tarzan of the Apes* was published in 1914 and was followed by twenty more novels which have sold in their millions in nearly sixty countries. The appeal of the Tarzan stories is probably not only to do with the adventure element but also with the popularity of animals and the appeal of a character who is more 'natural', having rejected civilization. Another phenomenally successful adventure story from the late nineteenth century is Robert Louis Stevenson's *Treasure Island* (1883). H. Rider Haggard's *King Solomon's Mines* (1885) and John Buchan's *The Thirty-Nine Steps* (1915) are still popular. The work of all three writers has never been out of print. Some of the most successful adventure stories of more recent times are *The Hobbit* (1937) and *The Lord of the Rings* trilogy (1954–55) written by J. R. R. Tolkein. In these books fantasy, quest and adventure combine.

Adventure stories for some readers will never go out of fashion. For the writer who can devise ingenious and imaginative problems for protagonists and equally inspired means of overcoming them, it is a genre with a multitude of possibilities, subjects and settings.

See also INCITING INCIDENT; PLOT AND STORY; STORY AND NOVEL CATEGORIES

AIM

It is very common as part of the structure of a story for the protagonist or central character to have an aim, goal or purpose which is delineated near the beginning of the story in the exposition. The story then centres on how the aim is eventually achieved, or not. The obstacles which have had to be overcome provide the interest of the narrative. According to the genre of the story, the aim may be to bring a criminal to justice, to find the perpetrator of a murder, to find treasure or some valued object, to find love, to achieve social justice or to right a wrong, to explore space, to cure an affliction either spiritual, physical or mental, to wreak revenge and so on. The possibilities are as infinite as have been the aims in the stories already written.

In creating the plot for a story, the aim must not be too easily achieved. Obstacles must be created if the story is to have any interest and suspense. If the aim is not achieved, the story may be tragic but not necessarily. It could be that the character discovers in the course of his or her search that the aim was not worth pursuing. The aim is an essential part of plot.

See also EXPOSITION; PLOT AND STORY

ALIENATION

To be alienated is to be divided from some person, state or thing. Karl Marx and Max Weber contended that workers' lives were made meaningless because they were alienated from their work and the fruits of their work under capitalism which required many workers to undertake soulless, routine and repetitive tasks. In literature (as in life) the alienated character may be divided from any meaning in life, from family and friends, from other people and also feel a sense of power-lessness and a lack of control over his or her own life. The individual's desires are thwarted by society, its rules and conventions. He or she feels an outsider, not at home.

Franz Kafka's novels and stories invariably contain characters in extreme states of alienation. In *The Trial* (1925) and *The Castle* (1926) the central characters find themselves in a world they cannot under-stand or enjoy or control and they feel that society and other people are opposed to them. In his short novel, *Metamorphosis* (1915), the central character Gregor is alienated from his father, his work and fellow workers to the extent that he feels like an insect – and in the story he duly becomes one. Kafka seems to be saying, among other things, that if people treat you like an insect, you may as well be one. In the twentieth century particularly, many people experienced this sense of alienation and hence the acclaim afforded to Kafka, Albert Camus, Jean-Paul Sartre and Alberto Moravia among others.

Alienation is likely to take different forms depending on the type of society and historical period in which people live. In the nineteenth century many people became alienated when Darwin's discoveries about evolution undermined religion and the idea of God, and this led them to lose the faith on which their lives had been based. John Fowles's novel *The French Lieutenant's Woman* (1967, film 1981) clev-erly explores both nineteenth- and twentieth-century alienation. Unusually the author has both female and male characters that are alienated.

Sometimes an alienated character has no idea why he or she feels the way they do and writers do not always give cut and dried answers. The reasons for alienation, however, are usually religious, political, social, economic, sexual, familial, or a mixture of these. Institutions or the people connected with them afford no fulfilment to some indi-viduals. An inability to control life and a sense of powerlessness is almost always associated with alienation. Novelists who write about alienated characters are usually implicitly making some criticism of the society or institution in which they live.

See also ABSURD LITERATURE; EXISTENTIALISM (EXISTENTIAL NOVEL)

ALIENATION EFFECT

Escapist fiction often engages the reader to the extent that at least while reading, they get lost in the fictional world of the characters and story. To a lesser extent this can happen with more serious literature.

The German dramatist and essayist Bertolt Brecht (1898–1956) felt that the escapist element in fiction worked against the possibility of the audience fully considering any serious issues raised by the author. Thus, in his own later plays he employed what he called alienation effects to remind the audience not to get too emotionally involved in the characters and action. He would remind them they were just watching a play. Characters as narrators might address the audience directly as the character or as themselves, the actors. The mechanics of the stage scenery would be visible to the audience so they were constantly reminded that this was a stage set. Settings would not represent any known place. Songs were sung in a serious play that clearly was not, nor was meant to be, a musical. Brecht wanted the audience to take a critical and active attitude to what was represented and it would appear that he hoped this might lead to political action (he espoused communism himself) or at least a change in the attitudes of the audience. The novelist can similarly remind the reader he or she is simply reading a novel by addressing them personally, although this is rarely done.

John Fowles's extremely entertaining and popular novel, *The French Lieutenant's Woman* (1967) successfully uses an alienation effect throughout and the novel is given three possible endings so that the reader must choose which is appropriate in the light of preceding events. Fowles may be implicitly asking why he, the novelist, should have the responsibility of suggesting a conclusion. A film version in 1981 used a different alienation effect to the novel. The nineteenth-century historical story which provided the basis of the film and novel was juxtaposed with a story of the actors who were in this historical version, so the audience gets one story which constantly reminds them that the other is merely a story.

See also ALIENATION; COMMITTED LITERATURE (LITTÉRATURE ENGAGÉE)

ALLEGORY

An allegory is a fictional work which tries to express some truth by using symbolic characters, actions and objects. A character will often represent some abstract quality, for example truth, virtue, beauty. The action may represent another, for example a journey from one city to another may represent a journey through life. Encounters on the journey will stand for something other than the obvious.

One of the best-known and immensely popular English allegories is *The Pilgrim's Progress* (1678) by John Bunyan (1628–1688). This is a religious allegory endorsing a Puritan form of Christianity as a road to salvation. The central character is called Christian and the book follows his journey through life as he encounters difficulties, temptations and some joys.

George Orwell's *Animal Farm* could be categorized as a twentieth-century political allegory. The animal characters represent identifiable figures in Russian Communism of the early twentieth century. The allegory form, however, is not very popular now although Orwell's allegorical novel is one of his most popular works, probably because it is so finely crafted.

See also FABLE; PARABLE

ALLITERATION AND ASSONANCE

Alliteration is a figure of speech used to foreground or highlight an important subject or idea in verse or prose. It does this by repeating consonants of a similar sound. It is used most often by poets but prose writers use it selectively and it is common in journalism, advertising and everyday speech.

Samuel Taylor Coleridge in writing of a river describes it in *Kubla Khan* as 'five miles meandering with a mazy motion'. The 'm' is a comparatively soft sound and the repetition of the 'm' sounds in the line give the impression of a slow-moving 'meandering' stream or river with frequent bends, 'mazy'.

Alliteration makes a phrase, sentence or passage more memorable, hence advertisers frequently use it in slogans. For example: 'Top people take *The Times*'; 'Naughty but nice (of cream cakes)'; 'Good food costs less at Sainsburys'. Product names that use alliteration are catchy: Coca Cola, PrittStick, KitKat.

The novelist Vladimir Nabakov used alliteration extensively in some of his novels, as did Anthony Burgess. The following is from Burgess's *A Clockwork Orange*. The anti-hero, Alex (who speaks and writes a strange kind of slang) is carried away as he listens to a piece of music by Geoffrey Plautus:

> Then brothers, it came. Oh, bliss, bliss and heaven. I lay all nagoy to the ceiling, my gulliver and my rookers on the pillow, glazzies closed, rot open in bliss, slooshying the sluice of lovely sounds. Oh it was gorgeousness and georgeousity made flesh. . . .
>
> [nagoy = naked, gulliver = head, rooker = arm, glazzies = eyes, rot = mouth]

In everyday speech expressions such as 'dead as a doornail', 'back to basics', 'pretty as a picture', 'boom and bust', 'the more the merrier', and 'live and learn' are common but note these are also clichés.

Even criticism can be made more memorable by the use of alliteration. The novelist and dramatist John Mortimer has commented how he remembers sixty years after the event an unfavourable review by Val Gielgud of an early work and in particular one sentence which went: 'This writer indulges in the sort of piddling around the skirts of sex which passes for sophistication in suburban minds.'

Assonance is closely related to alliteration and the two are often used together. Assonance is the repetition of vowel sounds. One of the most memorable political slogans in America was that of Dwight D. Eisenhower, an ex-soldier who became president of the United States in 1953. His slogan was 'I Like Ike'. Undoubtedly the mixture of alliteration, assonance and brevity made it effective. Sometimes the effect can be gained not just by repetition of a vowel sound but by using a series of different vowel sounds. For instance, in the Coleridge line quoted above, the series of vowel sounds is:

Five miles meandering with a mazy motion
'i'   'i'   'e' 'a' 'er''i'   'i' 'a' 'ay'   'o'

These have an effect as well as the 'm' sounds. In alliteration, the consonant sounds come at the beginning of words.

See also CLICHÉ

ALLUSION

If we allude to something we refer to it, usually to make some point of comparison or to enhance the meaning of the subject or person under discussion. Allusions are made to people, to things, to events, virtually anything. Everyone knows what is meant if we say of a place 'it was Blackpool on a rainy day'.

In literature allusion is used by an author to illuminate his or her own text or meaning. The allusions may be to things such as those mentioned in the first paragraph but writers frequently allude to parts of other works of literature. T. S. Eliot in *The Waste Land* alludes to dozens of other literary texts to illuminate his poem.

The following example illustrates everyday allusion to literature as used by ordinary people. In 1990 the BBC showed a four-part television play, *House of Cards*, that became immensely popular. It was based on a novel by Michael Dobbs and concerned a ruthless Conservative Party

Chief Whip. He would rarely give a straight answer to anyone, especially to journalists. He never wanted anything attributed to him. But if a journalist suggested some possibility to him which he clearly agreed with he would invariably say: 'You might think that, but I couldn't possibly comment'. People still make this remark when they do not wish to commit themselves to a straight answer or opinion. Those who remember the play will make the connection and recognize the allusion.

The following is a simple example of literary allusion. Kurt Vonnegut Jr's novel *Cat's Cradle* begins: 'Call me Ahab. My parents nearly did. They called me Jonah. . . .' Vonnegut, an American novelist and satirist, knows that most readers will recognize his short first sentence as alluding to the American classic novel *Moby Dick* by Herman Melville. *Moby Dick* is a very serious work whereas the flippant follow-up to Vonnegut's first sentence suggests that his novel is going to show the comic and absurd potential of American life and manners. This is also an example of intertextuality.

Allusion enables a writer to make a point succinctly. No one will miss the meaning if a character is referred to as a Samson or a Judas. Allusions are rarely put in quotation marks even if a phrase or sentence is quoted from the source. It is assumed that most readers will recognize it. In no sense is the user of the allusion plagiarizing or trying to pass something off from another writer as his or her own. The only danger is that readers will not recognize the allusion.

It is not something to be over-used.

See also INTERTEXTUALITY

AMAZON

Amazon.com (Amazon.co.uk) is an online bookshop that was started in 1995. It is now claimed to be the biggest bookshop in the world. It makes available almost all books in print, and some no longer in print, through subsidiary booksellers. Books are sold at a discount so it has become a serious rival to high street bookshops. Recently Amazon has branched out into selling other goods such as CDs, cameras, audiovisual equipment etc.

AMBIGUITY

Ambiguity can be both a fault or an asset in writing. It is a fault when it refers to vagueness in expression. This sentence is ambiguously vague: 'The girl was showing her mother how to do it when she fell.' It is unclear whether it was the girl or her mother who fell. Constructions that are ambiguous in this sense should be avoided.

Ambiguity in literature, however, can have a legitimate purpose. It can enrich an idea as many words and expressions in English have more than one meaning and a writer may wish to exploit this in order to introduce nuances into a statement. So in some cases the context may support simultaneous interpretations. The following is an example from Shakespeare's *Romeo and Juliet*. Mercutio has received a fatal sword wound and he plays down the seriousness of the wound to his friends by remarking jocularly 'Ask for me tomorrow and you shall find me a *grave* man'. He is implying by the ambiguous use of the word 'grave' that he will be more serious later, but also probably 'in his grave'.

The ending of a story may be left deliberately ambiguous by a writer. Did they or didn't they marry? Did he die? Was he or she successful? Some readers do not like this kind of ambiguity. The writer may wish however to reinforce the undoubted truth that life does not always offer easy solutions or closure to problems.

Ambiguity has always been used in poetry but its importance was enhanced by the publication of a book called *Seven Types of Ambiguity* by the poet and critic William Empson in 1930. Empson goes into the subject in great detail. His first two types of ambiguity are (a) when a detail has an effect simultaneously in more than one way and (b) when two seemingly unconnected meanings work together. Empson's book clearly repays study by anyone interested in the subject.

See also CONNOTATION AND DENOTATION; PUN

ANACHRONY

Anachrony is concerned with the chronological order of a narrative and usually refers to deviation from everyday chronology. Flashbacks, flash forwards and foreshadowing are examples of anachrony. It is used by the fiction writer in the construction of a plot that may be better served with something other than a straightforward delineation of the events in time sequence.

See also PLOT AND STORY

ANALEPSIS *SEE* FLASHBACK

ANECDOTE

An anecdote is a brief account of a single incident, event, character or animal. Anecdotes may amuse, illustrate some abstract quality or emotion, convey an idea or say something about character. They often illustrate some general point or truth through a single, specific example. Frequently, people who relate anecdotes do so using personal experience. Anecdotes are often true but some writers make them up. An anecdote is not a story, it is rather too short and it lacks plot or character development. It may make a point about character but usually only one. Anecdotes may be told by a character in a story.

The following anecdote illustrates some of these points. It is amusing and makes a single point about character although it could be regarded as illustrating a stereotype of old people.

> An old lady had two dogs. She had been fond of them for some years and called them Jill and John. Regrettably Jill caught a virus, infected John and they both died after a short illness. Wishing to preserve their memory, the old lady called a taxidermist and requested that her dogs be stuffed so they could still be pets, albeit silent ones. She was rather shocked when the taxidermist asked her if she wanted them mounted. 'Dear me, no, of course not!' she said. 'Touching noses will be fine.'

Anecdotes have long been popular and in 1791 Isaac Disraeli, the father of Prime Minister Benjamin, published a collection entitled *Curiosities of Literature, consisting of Anecdotes, Characters, Sketches, and Observations.* Nowadays anecdotes are more likely to appear as fillers in newspapers and magazines.

See also PLOT AND STORY

ANGRY YOUNG MEN

The term 'Angry Young Men' referred to a group of writers in the 1950s who in general expressed anger or dissension with the established values of their society and time. The term was popularized by journalists although it is said to have come from Leslie Allan Paul's autobiography of 1951, *Angry Young Man*. John Osborne's play *Look Back in Anger* (1956) revived and publicized the idea. The movement was an unusual instance in British literature of writers becoming the subject of news reports. This was partly because, although their political anger was somewhat muted, they occasionally got angry with each other and were involved in brawls. One was horsewhipped by his father-in-law.

The writers associated with the group included, William Cooper, John Wain, John Braine, Kingsley Amis, Arnold Wesker, Alan Sillitoe and Colin Wilson, as well as Osborne. Most of these writers rejected the term while at the same time making use of the publicity it afforded them. Their rejection is understandable because although most of their early works contained some critique of British society, their interests and styles were very different. Most of them were on the left politically (with the exception of Wilson) but they mostly veered towards the right as they became older and more successful. The settings of their work tended to be provincial.

ANTAGONIST

The antagonist is the character who is opposed to the protagonist. He or she usually represents negative things while the protagonist espouses positive values. The existence of the two in a story creates conflict, an essential ingredient of plot. The protagonist and the antagonist at their most extreme will be hero and villain. Examples are Hamlet and Claudius in Shakespeare's *Hamlet*; Antonio and Shylock in *The Merchant of Venice*. The two character types need not be so extreme as these. In *Romeo and Juliet*, the eponymous lovers are the protagonists and their antagonists are their parents and family members and the latter are not so much villains as misguided, foolish and unsympathetic. In *The Catcher in the Rye*, the protagonist is the teenager Holden Caulfield, the antagonists are almost everyone else in the novel except his sister and two nuns as he finds almost all adults and most of his school colleagues phonies.

The antagonist of the protagonist is not always another person. In *Hamlet* Claudius is the antagonist, so is Hamlet's indecision. Perhaps it is his conscience. Quite frequently in fiction conscience is the protagonist's antagonist.

The antagonist may be society's rules or conventions that prevent someone from behaving in the way they wish. In adventure stories it may be forces of nature such as storms, earthquakes, the desert or the sea. Only occasionally is the antagonist an out-and-out villain.

See also ANTI-HERO; CHARACTERS; CONFLICT; HERO; HEROINE; PROTAGONIST

ANTICLIMAX

Anticlimax is a figure of speech that describes the situation where something appears as if it is going to be important or significant and it turns out to be the reverse. The following is a simple example of anticlimax: 'John S. Smith is the most astute political philosopher in Ashby Street, Croydon'. The first part of the sentence suggests Smith is someone special. Unless Ashby Street is a hotbed of political philosophers, the second part suggests the remark is humorous or sarcastic.

It is sometimes called an anticlimax when someone has shown great promise in some field when they were young but in fact have very mediocre later careers. A possible future prime minister of Britain had shown political flair and promise even as a schoolboy – but it is an anti-climax that he never won an election.

Satire sometimes makes use of anticlimax, often in the way the dignity and self-importance of public figures is punctured.

There is another kind of anticlimax which has a bearing on fiction. This is when the plot builds up with tremendous tension to an expected climax and then the resolution proves a complete letdown – or anticlimax. Because the writer is in control of what happens, this is not likely to be a frequent occurrence and it should certainly be avoided. It would only occur if the writer had not planned ahead sufficiently and could not devise a climactic ending.

See also PATHOS AND BATHOS

ANTI-HERO

A hero is said to have the positive characteristics of courage, bravery, enterprise, integrity and both physical and moral strength, or at least some of these qualities, which will eventually help him to overcome any weaknesses he possesses.

The anti-hero is quite simply the opposite of the hero. He or she (most of the anti-heroes of literature are male) is ineffectual, passive, negative, petty and often ignominious. They are strangers in a strange land, wherever that may be. One of Aldous Huxley's anti-heroes in *Antic Hay* says: 'I glory in the name of earwig'. The student Raskolnikov in Dostoevsky's *Crime and Punishment* (1866) does not believe in God and attempts to make his life meaningful through acts of murder and, of course, fails.

The 1950s and 1960s saw an upsurge of anti-heroes of varying kinds. The most extreme were probably characters created by the dramatist Samuel Beckett. In his seminal *Waiting for Godot* (1956) the refrain of his two main characters is 'Nothing to be done', by which they mean nothing is worth doing. In fact they do only one thing, which is to wait. What they are waiting for is unclear and he, she or it never comes.

Another kind of anti-hero is portrayed by John Osborne in *Look Back in Anger* (1957). Jimmy Porter does little except carp vociferously but the play is a social critique and Osborne seems to blame Jimmy's negativity on the inadequacies of the political and social changes of the post-war era. In Kingsley Amis's *Lucky Jim* (1954) the anti-hero is a university lecturer who believes in none of the traditional values. The social satire is less sharp than Osborne's but the novel is notable for being a humorous take on the anti-hero. Neither author offers anything very positive. An example from American literature is the character Yossarian in Joseph Heller's *Catch-22* (1961). He is used by the author to demonstrate the utter futility and absurdity of war and human behaviour in general.

Critics have maintained that anti-heroes began as early as *Don Quixote* (1605) and *Tristram Shandy* (1767) but there is no doubt that the phenomenon gained momentum in the mid-twentieth century, possibly because many people felt a sense of alienation and purposelessness in the years after the Second World War.

See also EXISTENTIALISM; HERO; HEROINE; VILLAIN

ANTITHESIS

Antithesis is a figure of speech which involves the placing of words, ideas or sentences in opposition in order to make a point. Apparent contradictions reveal truths – or opinions. The structure of phrase or sentence complements the ideas that are often in parallel. A saying of Samuel Johnson (1709–84) illustrates the notion of ideas in opposition supported by a parallel structure: 'Marriage has many pains, but celibacy has no pleasures' (*Rasselas*, 1759).

In the Biblical book of Revelation utopia or heaven is envisaged as a place where 'The lion will lie down with the lamb'. The wit of these two examples of antithesis is helped by the use of alliteration.

Great writers and thinkers often seem to utter a thought in antithetical form. Here are a few examples:

Life is long, art is longer. (Anon)

Without Contraries there is no progression. Attraction and Repulsion, Reason and Energy, Love and Hate are necessary to human existence. (William Blake, 1757–1827)

> Man is a rope, tied between beast and Superman – a rope over an abyss. (Friedrich Nietzsche, 1844–1900)

> We live in stirring times – tea-stirring times. (Christopher Isherwood, 1902–86)

There are no rules for the use of antithesis. It may be that a character is given to coining such expressions or the narrator may occasionally make a point by the use of antithesis but it should be used very sparingly in fiction. An excellent example can be taken from Charles Dickens' *A Tale of Two Cities* (1859) set in the late eighteenth century during the French Revolution. This is the opening of the novel:

> It was the best of times, it was the worst of times, it was the age of wisdom, it was the age of foolishness, it was the epoch of belief, it was the epoch of incredulity, it was the season of Light, it was the season of Darkness, it was the spring of hope, it was the winter of despair, we had everything before us, we had nothing before us, we were all going direct to Heaven, we were all going direct the other way – in short, the period was so far like the present period, that some of its noisiest authorities insisted on its being received, for good or for evil, in the superlative degree of comparison only.

See also OPENINGS

APHORISM

An aphorism is a generally accepted truth expressed succinctly and memorably. If it is not absolutely true, it is thought-provoking. Some writers are adept at including the occasional aphorisms in their work. The following are a few examples:

> There are many reasons why novelists write, but they all have one thing in common – a need to create an alternative world. (John Fowles, 1926–2005)

> Experience is the name everyone gives to their mistakes. (Oscar Wilde, 1854–1900)

> Cynicism is humour in ill-health. (H. G. Wells, 1866–1946)

> In art economy is always beauty. (Henry James, 1843–1916)

> A lover without indiscretion is no lover at all. (Thomas Hardy, 1840–1928)

> Is not life a hundred times too short for us to bore ourselves. (Friedrich Nietzsche, 1844–1900)

Oscar Wilde was very adept at thinking up aphorisms which he scatters throughout his plays. This gives them an air of artificiality because too many of his characters are given the facility for making witty remarks and in reality very few people are as quick-witted. Clearly an interesting character with an ability to create aphorisms could be created but it depends, of course, on the writer's own ability to come up with them.

See also EPIGRAM

APOSTROPHE

Apostrophe is a figure of speech referring to the way in which an actor may turn to and address a single member of the audience (not usually, an identifiable member of the audience) or it could be that the narrator in a novel addresses a single person (even though clearly all readers will get the message). The addressee could be God, a dead person or even an inanimate object. It is a device that is seldom used, particularly in the novel. It could provide an alienation effect in dramatic work.

See also ALIENATION EFFECT

ARCHETYPE

There are a number of meanings of the term archetype. Plato posited that archetypes were ideals or ideal forms of things like beauty, truth and goodness that only partially exist in the real world. We have a notion of beauty but even the person or landscape or thing which we regard as beautiful will not live up to the archetypal or ideal beauty.

The psychologist Carl G. Jung, in the early twentieth century, described another but related view of archetypes, suggesting they were ideas or concepts which are buried in the unconscious of all human beings and are inherited from the previous generation. Examples of these kinds of archetypes are: the god who dies and is reborn (found in many religions), the journey underground, the ascent to heaven, the scapegoat, the femme fatale, the damsel in distress, the struggle between children and parents, and family life.

All of these are found in literature from the earliest times until today. Some critics have dismissed Plato's notions and Jung's ideas of a collective unconscious and contended that they are unnecessary explanations. Certain concepts or archetypes such as those listed above simply have been and are universally important in human life.

The writer need not study archetypes to use deliberately in fiction; they will almost certainly choose themselves.

Another use of the term archetype is in expressions such as the following: 'The Edwin Porter film of 1903, *The Great Train Robbery*, is the archetypal Western'. This was the first ever Western and it contained elements which appeared in literally hundreds of later Westerns.

Archetype is also used sometimes to refer to recurring objects or symbols in literature such as the cross, dove, sword, water.

ATMOSPHERE AND SETTING

Atmosphere and setting are frequently indivisible but not necessarily or always. For instance, a setting of a dark, night-time forest will be useful in creating an atmosphere of fear if the character is a child alone, less likely if it is a poacher. Fear can also occur in a bright, urban setting.

The key elements of setting are place, time, historical events (a story set against an important happening), social circumstances, political climate, religious belief, atmosphere.

Accuracy with regard to all of these is important and accuracy will be achieved from personal experience or by research (particularly with regard to historical setting). Small details are important; especially details that the reader may not be familiar with, but they must not become a 'catalogue'.

Setting with regard to place can contribute to an understanding of character. The kind of place the character inhabits will say something about them. Is it opulent, shabby, fashionably furnished, tidy or untidy, how is it decorated, which part of town is it in, is it cared for, what things dominate the place, has it a view that is important?

It is not always necessary to be absolutely specific. A writer who wishes to show the impact of city life on a character may set the story in London, Manchester or New York – or the city may be anonymous in order to make the place universal; but in either case, detail must be provided. In some stories a specific location is essential. James Vance Marshall's *Walkabout* could not be set anywhere but the Australian outback, otherwise the story of abandoned children meeting an Aborigine boy would not make sense. In *Walkabout* the outback is not only the setting but it helps to create the atmosphere of the novel and the mood of the characters who at first are on the verge of despair because they are lost as well as oppressed by the heat. However, when they realize they will be saved by the Aborigine their mood lightens and the setting seems less oppressive.

In his book *A Passion for Narrative*, John Hodgkins lists seven functions of setting, one of which is atmosphere. He points out that a story may have an overall atmosphere or different scenes may reflect changes in a character's mood. Occasionally powerful effects can be created by providing details which suggest a mood different from that usually associated with the setting. For instance, a circus usually has a happy atmosphere but if reference is made to the routine life of the artistes, the brevity of their active lives or the pain they endure for their art, the atmosphere can be changed. Franz Kafka did this in his story *Up in the Gallery*.

Hodgkins' other six functions of setting are as follows: (1) the setting simply provides background for the story which is plausible but has little or no effect on the action; (2) a generic background is where the setting is totally undefined or the action could occur anywhere; (3) local colour is provided to add authenticity but the story could have occurred in other places; (4) the historical and geographical background is essential to both the plot and characters; (5) the setting is a crucial part of the story such as when a character is lost in the desert or exploring equatorial Africa – setting becomes almost another character; (6) the setting is symbolic of something in the story, for example in Graham Greene's *Brighton Rock*, the 1930s seaside town represents sleaze, downmarket values and criminality.

Atmosphere or moods such as joy, fear, hope, despair; happiness, horror, etc. fortunately never have to be described abstractly or in isolation. They are always the outcome of the behaviour of characters and the turn of events and, of course, sometimes the setting. There is, in effect, an objective correlative. Thus fear may occur in a particular place, partly because of the place itself, but also because of the predicament of the protagonist or because of the actions of another character towards the protagonist.

The following are superb examples of the combination of setting and atmosphere but remember that this occurs in almost all good fiction:

Great Expectations (1861) Charles Dickens. Childhood terror and atmosphere of lonely marshland in the opening pages.

The Return of the Native (1878) Thomas Hardy. Desolate opening description sets atmosphere of the novel.

Dracula (1897) Bram Stoker. Fear and horror.

The Turn of the Screw (1898) Henry James. Low key psychological fear and menace.

Metamorphosis (1915) Franz Kafka. Absolute helplessness and fear.

The Plague (1947) Albert Camus. Confinement and helplessness.

The Heart of the Matter (1948) Graham Greene. Guilt and shabbiness.

Lord of the Flies (1954) William Golding. Idyllic desert island turns to terror.

Cider with Rosie (1959) Laurie Lee. Joy and carefree atmosphere of childhood.

First Love, Last Rites (1978) Ian McEwan. Dark and erotic side of childhood.

See OBJECTIVE CORRELATIVE

AUTHOR

Author is the name given to the writer of any book whether fiction or non-fiction. It may also be used of the writers of shorter works but journalist or poet indicate specialisms. The attributes of an author are twofold: authors must have mastered the techniques of their chosen type of writing and, in the case of the novelist, they must have the capacity to invent stories and create plots and characters. They are usually attributed with vivid imaginations, inventive powers and creativity but modern literary theorists (e.g. Roland Barthes) have pronounced 'the death of the author' claiming that novelists knowingly or unknowingly pillage earlier literature (and life) for their work. In addition these theorists argue that the reader contributes much to the effect gained from the work because each reader brings different experiences to it and therefore gets something slightly different from it. This may or may not have been the intention of the author. This claim is explored in more detail in the entry on intertextuality.

See also INTERTEXTUALITY

AUTHOR INTERVENTION

In fiction, whether it is written in the first person or third person, for the most part the author is not in any way personalized or present in the story. In a first-person narrative, the narrator is usually one of the characters in the tale. In a third-person narrative, the teller of the story is frequently an omniscient narrator who knows all and thus can tell all. Rarely is the actual author identified as the narrator. For the reader there is in both styles an illusion that the author is anonymous or hidden. Needless to say, whichever style of narration is chosen, the reader is, or should be, aware that it is an illusion; that the author, the person whose name is on the cover of the book, has written and is responsible for everything in the novel or story. The reader and author collude in a kind of illusion.

Very occasionally the author *does* intervene as the author. In a number of nineteenth-century novels it is not unknown for the author to actually address the reader with the words 'And now dear reader . . .' and to follow this with some comments on the characters or story. Sometimes a moral judgement may be made.

The twentieth-century novelist E. M. Forster in *Howards End* (1910) remarks of his central character:

> To Margaret – I hope this will not set the reader against her – the station at King's Cross had always suggested Infinity. . . . If you think this ridiculous, remember that it is not Margaret who is telling you about it: and let me hasten to add that they were in plenty of time for the train.

The technique is less frequent in twentieth and twenty-first century novels. The reason that author intervention is not popular is probably because readers prefer, when reading a story, to be immersed in it. They do not want to be reminded that it is the product of the author, even though after reading the story they will be quite aware of the author's part in their experience.

See also ALIENATION EFFECT; INTERTEXTUALITY; SUSPENSION OF DISBELIEF

AUTOBIOGRAPHICAL NOVEL

It is fairly obvious that the autobiographical novel is one that is based on the life of the author. The key word here is based. These novels are not all based on fact, as autobiographies claim to be; they are as much fiction as autobiography. Most people's lives do not have a neat plot in the fashion of novels and this is likely to be one of the changes which the novelist will make as well as possibly introducing fictional characters and events which may or may not be based on real people and real events.

The majority of autobiographical novels published are about the childhood or early life of the novelist simply because, in most cases, the autobiographical novel is the novelist's first attempt at fiction or an early one. Another possible reason for this is that the budding novelist, if they are young, has not a great deal of experience and they may feel that their lives provide ready-made material. It is one thing they know well. Of course, there must be something singular about an autobiographical novel. No one wants to read about a mundane life unless it is told with extraordinary literary panache. The main thrust of the story, on the other hand, does not have to be something bizarre or melodramatic. From the novels mentioned below, the success of Jeanette Winterson's *Oranges Are Not the Only Fruit* is due in considerable part to the conflict of two remarkably self-assured and strong characters, the young girl based on the author and her fanatically strong-minded and religious step-mother. In Louisa M. Alcott's *Little Women* the amusing and sad events in the lives of a fairly ordinary family make an engaging story; but the central character is in strong contrast to the personalities of her siblings.

While the first-person narrative method may seem an obvious choice for this kind of novel, it could be helpful for the novelist to use the third person simply because this encourages objectivity.

Some notable autobiographical novels are as follows:

A Pair of Blue Eyes by Thomas Hardy (1837). The hero is an apprentice architect and when he goes to survey a church he meets the woman who is to become his wife (based on Hardy's first wife).

Of Human Bondage by W. Somerset Maugham (1915). A powerful novel based on Maugham's early life as a medical student prior to his becoming one of the most successful novelists of his time.

The Bell Jar by Sylvia Plath (1963). An account of a college student suffering a breakdown and attempting suicide. It was based on Plath's own experience.

A Quiet Life by Beryl Bainbridge (1976). A popular novelist's early autobiographical work about a troubled family.

Empire of the Sun by J. G. Ballard (1984). Ballard's boyhood experiences as a prisoner of war in Japan during the Second World War.

Inconceivable by Ben Elton (1998). A humorous treatment of the problems of a couple who cannot have a baby.

One Hundred Strokes of the Brush Before Bed by Melissa P. (2003–4). A teenager's sexual awakening and search for love.

See also STORY AND NOVEL CATEGORIES

AVANT-GARDE

Avant-garde (French for 'vanguard') refers to movements or artistic works that show innovation or experimentation. In literature the innovation is usually to do with technique but it can also relate to subject matter.

After considerable stability in the form of the novel during the nineteenth century, the movement known as modernism (roughly 1910–30) produced writers such as James Joyce, Virginia Woolf, T. S. Eliot and Franz Kafka who questioned the objectivity of writers and the idea of an omniscient narrator. Subjectivity and questioning replaced the certainties of the Victorian age. The use by Joyce and Woolf of stream-of-consciousness technique and the interior monologue are examples of innovation and experiment. The modernists were the avant-garde of their time.

After the Second World War postmodernism replaced modernism as an avant-garde movement. Although they have features in common, postmodernism celebrated the fact that the world was fragmented and sometimes absurd. Novelists associated with postmodernism include Vladimir Nabakov, John Barth and John Fowles.

Avant-garde and experimental movements in literature have never entirely replaced the traditional forms. Most novelists today, both popular and literary, work within the traditional novel form, although innovators probably change attitudes and practices in small ways.

See also EXISTENTIALISM; INTERIOR MONOLOGUE; NOUVEAU ROMAN; STREAM OF CONSCIOUSNESS

Backstory

Vladimir Nabokov's *Lolita* is a novel about the middle-aged Humbert Humbert's fatal obsession with a teenager. An incident in the novel concerns Humbert when he was himself a teenager and how he fell in love with a girl his own age while on a seaside holiday in Europe. The girl died of a fever shortly afterwards. This traumatic tragedy, we are led to believe, has partly been the cause of Humbert's arrested emotional development and has led him to pursue entirely unsuitable relationships.

This incident is an example of backstory, which can be defined as an account of a significant event in the past of (usually) the main character and which explains subsequent events or behaviour in relation to that character. It could also concern an important subsidiary character. Backstory is most likely to occur in a novel or film; short stories would become unwieldy if the technique was used in them.

In some cases the backstory incident may be kept a secret from the reader until late in the fiction, but it can occur at any point. It is not an example of the writer withholding important information because it is information the character may suppress or not even realize its significance at the time. In some cases they may have forgotten it.

Pip's fear when he encounters an escaped convict at the beginning of Dickens' *Great Expectations* leads him to help the convict by giving him food and a means of breaking his shackles. Later, as an adult, Pip gets money from a benefactor he believes to be Miss Havisham but it is actually Magwitch, the convict who is repaying an act of kindness. Pip's early encounter is the backstory to Magwitch's later behaviour. Both Pip and the reader do not realize the significance of the early encounter until late in the novel, but it explains a number of important events.

Backstory incidents echo the way many people in real life are influenced by things which happened to them in the past. Common examples are the death of a parent or sibling; schoolday traumas such as bullying; sexual abuse; imprisonment; accidents; an experience in the armed forces; unrequited love; a criminal act; a huge disappointment leading to loss of faith in human nature; a win on the lottery.

Note that the backstory usually concerns and refers to a single significant event; it is not the entire previous biography of the character concerned.

See also FLASHBACK

BEAT LITERATURE

In its non-musical sense, beat describes a literary movement or a literary technique. The term beat generation is also used. The latter does not describe a whole generation of people because a relatively small number of younger people espoused beat. The term 'beat movement' would be more appropriate.

The movement began in the 1950s in Manhattan but moved to San Francisco, and the term beat is said to have been coined by its central figure, the writer Jack Kerouac. The word is linked to others with religious connotations, for example 'beatitude' or 'blessedness'. A small group of novelists and poets was associated with Kerouac, the most notable being the poet Allen Ginsberg.

Kerouac called his style of writing 'spontaneous prose' and his novels do have a spontaneous, free flowing, fresh and unedited feel about them. Most are autobiographical. *On the Road* describes a car journey Kerouac and his friends took. The friends are given fictitious names. The novel lacks a conventional plot and concerns the adventures the group have and the people they meet. Although the beats were regarded as part of the counter-culture of the 1960s and 1970s, Kerouac was largely a romantic rather than overtly political.

The chief names associated with the movement are William Burroughs, Gregory Corso, Gary Snyder and Michael McClure. The beat movement was very much of its times, although its members still have a following.

BERNE CONVENTION

A convention held in Berne, Switzerland in 1886 aimed at protecting the copyright of authors in all countries which signed the convention. The countries which signed are part of the Berne Copyright Union. The convention has been modified at various times and in various countries since 1886. Countries who are not part of the Union occasionally publish authors from other countries without paying them royalties.

BILDUNGSROMAN

Bildungsroman is a German term meaning 'formation novel' or 'education novel'. The word 'education' is used in the sense of education for life rather than formal school or college education, although the school and college period experiences of the central character will often be important in their development. The *Bildungsroman* deals with decisive events and the people who help to form the adult from the child and adolescent. Frequently there are mental and spiritual crises on the way. The novel usually takes the character only as far as his or her early twenties, by which time he or she has usually gained some stability and/or found his or her place in the world. The characters in most of the novels will rarely have felt at home or happy in their surroundings and may have to escape from them in order to find fulfilment. A happy childhood does not usually make for a successful novel.

Frequently the writer of the *Bildungsroman* will use his or her own experiences, in fictional form, as the basis for the novel. The *Bildungsroman* is not, however, an autobiographical novel but it could be seen as a kind of autobiography of a character and will probably be partly, at least, based on experiences or interests of the author. Jane Eyre is not Charlotte Brontë but the character has some characteristics in common with the author.

The first *Bildungsroman* is usually considered to be Goethe's novel *Wilhelm Meister* (1794–96). Nineteenth century examples include Charles Dickens' *David Copperfield* (1849–50) and *Great Expectations* (1860–61); Charlotte Brontë's *Jane Eyre* (1847) and Flaubert's *A Sentimental Education* (1869). Twentieth-century *Bildungsroman* include Thomas Mann's *Buddenbrooks* (1901); Samuel Butler's *The Way of All Flesh* (1902); Somerset Maugham's *Of Human Bondage* (1915); James Joyce's *A Portrait of the Artist as a Young Man* (1916); Graham Swift's *Waterland* (1983) and Jeanette Winterson's *Oranges Are Not the Only Fruit* (1985).

The characters in all these novels have to struggle to make their way in the world. This quality gives the novels their interest. The *Bildungsroman* is an attractive genre for novelists who may not wish to create a complicated plot with many characters because the structure of this kind of novel is simply dictated by the early life of the central character.

The *Künstlerroman* is similar to the *Bildungsroman* but it is concerned with the development and education of an artist or novelist. Strictly speaking, Joyce's *A Portrait of the Artist as a Young Man* would be considered a *Künstlerroman*. Knut Hamsun's *Hunger* (1890) and Thomas Wolfe's *Look Homeward Angel* are other examples.

Bildungsroman are sometimes called '*apprentice novels*'.

See also STORY AND NOVEL CATEGORIES

THE BITER BIT

The idea of the biter bit is an element in some popular stories, sometimes it is central. These are stories where the protagonist (the person who has been 'bitten' – or had some hurt perpetrated on him) manages to turn the tables on the other main character (the person who 'bit' first) and the situation is reversed so that the original aggressor becomes the victim and gets his or her just reward.

One of the first story films to be made (1900) was called *Biter Bit* and concerned a boy who was watering the garden with a hose. He stopped the water flowing with his hand, caused increased pressure, let the water burst out and soaked an adult gardener. The adult chased the boy and soaked him. Thus the 'biter' gets 'bitten'. The biter bit story is usually more sophisticated than this example. The person who is first bitten may plot an elaborate revenge on the biter. An example of a more subtle biter bit story is *The Verger* by Somerset Maugham.

The idea of the biter being bitten often plays a part in novels but it will usually be part of the story rather than the main element on which the story depends. Sometimes it *is* central. Clearly villains in stories often get their come-uppance after perpetrating some wrong on the hero or heroine. It could also be a case of the hero being bitten by some anonymous organization or government quango and subsequently getting his revenge. The notion of the biter bit is also very common in popular films.

A reason for the popularity of the biter bit element is that it appeals to the reader or viewer's sense of justice. We long for the biter to get their just reward. An analysis of a selection of popular stories, novels and films will almost certainly reveal that the biter bit element is quite common.

Some of Aesop's fables are biter bit stories. *The Bird and the File* is an example of a rather sinister and gruesome fable.

See also IRONY; TWIST ENDING STORIES

BLACK HUMOUR

Black humour or black comedy basically gets its humorous effects from subjects which would not generally be thought of as either humorous or something to be made fun of. The subjects which have traditionally been those of tragedy become the stuff of humour which is often cruel and sardonic. These include war, murder and other serious crimes, cruelty, drug taking, injury and illness, disability, the elite and other generally revered institutions. The black humorist must almost inevitably view the world and human behaviour as largely absurd.

Black humour does not have a long tradition but it certainly comes to prominance in the twentieth century. This is probably because in an increasingly democratic society, there is less respect for those in authority and those who have gained their positions through birth rather than merit. Increased freedom of speech means that virtually no subject is off limits and anything can become a target of disrespect, vituperation and humour.

Clearly black humour can also be related to an almost universal human response or failing, call it what you will. It is very common for people to laugh when they see someone fall over or have some minor accident. It is not funny for the subject but many viewers find it so. The old music hall comedian falling when he skids on a banana skin is not black humour in the current sense but it is not unrelated.

The unexpected also causes us to laugh sometimes. When someone falls flat on their face, it can be amusing because it is accidental and unexpected.

There is also a sense in black humour that sometimes human behaviour is so grotesque and irredeemable that the only response is laughter as those with the power to prevent disaster do not have the will and the ordinary citizen is powerless.

Black humour has been employed by serious literary artists such as Samuel Beckett, Eugene Ionesco, Joseph Heller, Kurt Vonnegut Jr and John Barth among others and also by popular playwrights such as Joe Orton and the novelist Tom Sharpe. Sharpe uses black farce to gain his effects.

Dickens was aware of how the tragic could be humorous. This passage from *The Pickwick Papers* (1873) is a good example. Mr Jingle frequently gossips and his description of a tragic accident becomes humorous, partly because of his clipped delivery:

> Terrible place – dangerous work – other day – five children – mother – tall lady, eating sandwiches – forgot the arch – crash – knock – children look round – mother's head off – sandwich in her hand – no mouth to put it in –

Black humour is sometimes referred to as 'sick humour'.

See also INTERIOR MONOLOGUE

BLURB
The blurb is a brief description of a book usually found on the back of a paperback or on the flap of the dust jacket of a hardback book. Its function is to give the browser in a bookshop an idea of the content and it serves as an advertisement of the book for the publisher.

BOOK CLUB
Book clubs sell books by direct mail at prices lower than those usually found in book shops. The member of the club then has to agree to buy a set number of books in a given period. Some clubs require that a book per month or a book per quarter be bought, although more recently a few clubs have sprung up which require no set number of purchases. While most clubs have an extensive list of books available, they do not rival bookshops with regard to choice. Some clubs specialize in genres such as thrillers or romances. Clubs can sell books

more cheaply because their membership list enables them to calculate with some accuracy how many books of a particular title need to be ordered.

Book Jacket

The book jacket (sometimes known as dust jacket) is the paper cover that protects hardback books. It is usually a protective glossy laminate and pains are taken to make it attractive so that it stands out in a shop. Book collectors attach importance to a book that has a jacket in good condition.

Book Proof

A book proof is an advanced copy of any book that is sent to reviewers or shown by sales teams to bookshops. It is often an uncorrected version of the book. It is also known as a 'bound proof'.

BookTrack

BookTrack is an organization that monitors the sale of books in order to compile the best-seller lists which feature in many newspapers and magazines.

Bowdlerization

Bowdlerization is a process of censorship whereby the whole work is not banned but potentially offensive words or passages are deleted. These include swear words, words connected with sex, matters relating to drug taking and references to religion. Frequently in the past bowdlerization was practised on texts for children (including school books) and family reading. In the twenty-first century there is more tolerance for references to sex, drugs and swearing even in children's books although bowdlerization still occasionally occurs. Some of the incidents in fairy tales (especially those by Hans Christian Andersen) are extremely horrific and these incidents are still often removed.

The term *bowdlerization* derives from Thomas Bowdler (1754–1825) an English doctor and later editor who published a *Family Shakespeare* which was, as the title suggests, for family reading in other words with the bawdy bits deleted. But not just the bawdy bits, for instance it is hinted that Ophelia's death was accidental rather than suicide which is what is generally assumed. Bowdler got his blue pencil out to work on other classic texts such as the Old Testament and Gibbon's *Decline and Fall of the Roman Empire*. Bowdler would have endorsed T. S. Eliot's line 'Human kind cannot bear very much reality'.

Scholars scorned Bowdler for his efforts but his editions were popular. The phenomenon to which he gave his name existed before he gave it his name, and it persists until today, more perhaps on TV than in written fiction. Many films shown on television have potentially offensive violent and sexual scenes removed. How a writer writes on sensitive subjects depends on his or her judgement and an awareness of the potential audience. No subject is taboo in serious literature today.

See also Obscene Publications Act

British Library

The British Library is the national book collection. It is held at St Pancras in London. Publishers in the UK and the Republic of Ireland have a legal obligation to send one copy of each of their publications to the British Library. All published books are available in their reading rooms.

See also legal deposit

Camera-ready Copy

Camera-ready copy is material ready for photographing for reproduction looking exactly as it should appear when published.

Campus Novel

Campus novels are mostly written by university or college lecturers turned full or part-time novelists. This is simply because they more than anyone else are familiar with college life from the point of view of staff and students – for this is what campus novels are about. Campus novels are frequently comic, witty and satiric. University academic staff seem only too enthusiastic to see their colleagues fictionalized as incompetent, unworldly, often promiscuous and incapable of dealing with everyday emotional and practical problems.

Campus novels have enjoyed considerable popularity even with those who have not attended college. Perhaps it seems an attractive existence and readers may like to see that clever people can be as silly in some areas of their lives as anyone else. Another reason for their popularity is that fiction set in institutions provides ready-made arenas for conflict, intrigue and romance. Campus novels and fiction set in other institutions will be partly judged on the authenticity of the background – so thorough research is necessary.

Notable authors of campus novels include Malcolm Bradbury, David Lodge, Tom Sharpe, Howard Jacobson and Ann Oakley.

THE CANON

The idea of a canon of books was first used with regard to those Biblical books which were authorized as part of the Bible as opposed to the books which were excluded because they were considered less authoritative. The latter became the Apocrypha.

In literary terms, the canon refers to a collection of literary works that are endorsed as the best by university departments of English. The university's endorsement creates the idea of classics and has an effect on the kinds of texts studied on college courses, in schools and for examinations like GCSEs and A levels. Popular novels would never be regarded as canonical or as set texts although over the last twenty years a much more liberal approach has been taken to the texts studied in universities and schools.

The problem with a canon is that there is no objective way of establishing which texts should be included and which left out. In the nineteenth century a writer, teacher and schools' inspector virtually appointed himself to establish the literary work that should be canonical. He was Matthew Arnold (1822–88). He believed that great literature should be morally uplifting. The great writers for Arnold were Homer, Dante, Shakespeare and Milton. Acceptable but lesser writers included Chaucer, Dryden, Pope, Gray and Burns. Mathew Arnold's *Culture and Anarchy* (1869) is still a readable account of his ideas on literature.

In the twentieth century literature teachers at Cambridge University were most influential in re-establishing a canon and the most important of these was F. R. Leavis (1895–1978). Leavis believed that great books should uphold moral values and a superior way of living which would be passed down from the educated by their influence even to those who were not scholars and did not read extensively. Leavis and his group were vigorously opposed to the products of mass or popular culture; mass production and advertising were similarly abhorred and seen as the enemies of a rich life. Leavis's touchstones of great literature included the poets John Donne, Keats, Wordsworth and T. S. Eliot and the novelists Jane Austen, George Eliot, Joseph Conrad, Henry James and D. H. Lawrence. Some of Dickens' novels eventually gained his favour.

The notion of a canon of literature, while it still affects English studies, has diminished in influence. English as a world language and post-colonial literature of a high standard has made the Englishness endorsed by Leavis seem somewhat parochial. America has produced many great writers and America has created its own canon. Also, recent critical theories of literature have diminished the influence of so-called practical criticism that the Leavis school espoused. The current idea that there can be multiple readings of texts is one which would be alien to Leavisites. A general liberalization in life has made a canon chosen by a self-appointed elite of critics something which finds little favour today.

F. R. Leavis's main study of great poets is *New Bearings in English Poetry* (1932), his study of novelists is *The Great Tradition* (1948), and also of interest is his study of *D. H. Lawrence: Novelist* (1955).

CARICATURE

A caricature is traditionally a drawing, usually of a well-known person, which exaggerates and distorts some of their features but which enables recognition of the subject. The purpose is invariably a mixture of satire and humour but occasionally caricatures are so grotesque that they indicate an element of cruelty on the part of the caricaturist. Caricatures are mainly found in the political cartoons published in newspapers and some magazines.

Occasionally the term caricature is used of literary descriptions and, as with drawings, the description will exaggerate undesirable features and omit the good points of the subject. The purpose, again, will be satire or invective. The writer of farcical novels, Tom Sharpe, has created many caricatures in his fiction. In his novels *Wilt* (1976), *The Wilt Alternative* (1979), and *Wilt on High* (1984) Mrs Wilt is portrayed as a grotesque woman – and she is not the only character to be portrayed in this way.

Literary caricature is unlikely to be found in serious novels unless they are told from the point of view of a first-person narrator who does not like the other character.

See also INVECTIVE

CASE

The case is the cover of a hardback book. It is usually made of cardboard covered in leather, cloth or synthetic material.

CATHARSIS

It is impossible to prove that the phenomenon of catharsis in art exists. It derives from the ancient Greek philosopher Aristotle (384–322 BC) in his writings on drama and tragedy. While it is usually discussed in the context of drama, it could presumably also apply to the reading of fiction and the viewing of films. In Aristotle's time, drama was thriving but there were, of course, no novels.

The word catharsis means 'cleansing' or 'purging'. In its medical sense it might refer to the purging of the bowels or stomach. With regard to drama, Aristotle contends that a tragic play can have the effect of purging and purifying the audience of negative emotions such as terror, pity or fear. Members of the audience transfer their negative emotions to a character in the play and get rid of them. The cause of the character's negative emotions need not be exactly the same as those of members of the audience. Audiences would be unlikely to share exactly the same problems as Hamlet, Lear, Macbeth or Oedipus.

But does this actually happen? It remains after many centuries a theory in dispute. One thing, however, is certain and interesting. On the face of it we would expect audiences of drama and fiction to be attracted to plays and novels which are upbeat and have happy endings. Works of this kind *are* popular but there is no doubt that audiences are also attracted to tragedy. They appear to get something from tragedy and it does not generally depress them or make them unhappy. Surveys which have asked members of the public to name their favourite plays or novels often indicate that tragic works head or come high up in the results. Whether this is because tragic works have a cathartic effect or not it is impossible to say but perhaps it goes some way to endorsing Aristotle's theory.

See also EMPATHY; SYMPATHY

CHARACTERS

Fiction is made up of many elements which vary in importance in different stories. The various elements interweave to create an imagined world. You cannot have plot without conflict and conflict creates suspense. These three elements are crucial and they all depend in turn on characters. If one were to choose the most important elements of fiction these four would be mentioned and character may well be the most popular choice. Interesting characters appeal to readers. They account for the success of novelists like Dickens and J. K. Rowling. Many children want to be like Harry Potter.

Readers identify with characters, empathize with them, are fascinated by them, like them and are also sometimes repelled by them. They evoke the whole gamut of human emotions. We choose our friends from people we like but we are usually interested in those we do not. We may not like a murderer but he may intrigue us. Similarly with characters in fiction; they evoke in us the whole spectrum of feelings from love to hate. The one thing they must not be is boring.

A fictional character is a representation of a person just as a photograph is a representation of a person, both give a partial portrayal of the whole. The photograph mainly represents appearance, of course, whereas a fictional representation concentrates on personality, emotions, behaviour and the speech and thoughts of the character. The fictional representation can probably never have the fullness and complexity of a living person and, in fact, some writers deliberately limit the characteristics they describe. For example, some neglect descriptions of appearance almost completely.

In Henry Fielding's novel *Tom Jones* (1749) the physical attributes of a young lady called Sophia are of great attraction to the hero Tom among others. She is described thus:

> Sophia . . . was a middle-sized woman, but rather inclining to tall. Her shape was not only exact, but extremely delicate, and the nice proportion of her arms promised the truest symmetry in her limbs. Her hair, which was black, was so luxuriant that it reached her middle before she cut it to comply with the modern fashion, and it was now curled so gracefully in her neck that few would have believed it to be her own. If envy could find any part of her face which demanded less commendation than the rest, it might possibly think her forehead might have been higher without prejudice to her . . .

The writer goes on for over a page about her virtues. Fielding wants the reader to know what Sophia looked like and his description is detailed. In contrast, Charles Dickens' portrayal of the Artful Dodger in *Oliver Twist* (1838) gives the reader an equally vivid picture but it also suggests something of the nature of the boy as well:

He was a snub-nosed, flat-browed, common-faced boy enough, and as dirty a juvenile as one would wish to see; but he had about him all the airs and manners of a man. He was short for his age: with rather bow-legs, and little, sharp, ugly eyes. His hat was stuck on the top of his head so lightly that it threatened to fall off every moment – and would have done so, very often, if the wearer had not had a knack of every now and then giving his head a sudden twitch: which brought it back to its old place again. He wore a man's coat, which reached nearly to his heels. He had turned the cuffs back, half-way up his arm, to get his hands out of the sleeves, apparently with the ultimate view of thrusting them into the pockets of his corduroy trousers; for there he kept them. He was, altogether, as roistering and swaggering a young gentleman as ever stood four feet six or something less, in his bluchers.

Elements of Character

In essence, a character is created from the following: actions; speech and thoughts; beliefs and viewpoints; relationships (friends and enemies); and appearance (including clothes). Different kinds of novels and stories will dictate their relative importance. Usually the protagonist of a novel will have the most detailed character portrayal. The adventure story may often not be concerned with the protagonist's beliefs except in the sense that they may oppose some attitude on the part of the villain that is considered reprehensible.

In almost all stories, action is important and relates to a suggestion which all writers are usually advised to practice: it is better to show than to tell. For example, rather than describing a character as envious or brave, it is better to dramatize an incident which demonstrates these qualities. Similarly, a character with strong beliefs should not be described as having these beliefs but they should be shown to affect the character's behaviour or relationships. One of the most powerful exponents of how beliefs (in this case Roman Catholic beliefs) affect a character's behaviour and relationships is the late Graham Greene. In a number of his novels he writes about the conflict between human desire and beliefs which render these desires wrong or sinful and the consequent agony for the characters concerned. The best examples of this in Greene's work are the novels *The Power and the Glory* (1940) and *The Heart of the Matter* (1948).

Types of Character

It is useful to consider the various ways in which some literary critics have classified characters. Fictional characters are representations of people and are never as complete or complex as people in real life. Possibly the most complex fictional characters are those portrayed by writers who employed the stream-of-consciousness technique and the interior monologue. These writers including Virginia Woolf, James Joyce and Dorothy Richardson tell us what their characters do but also provide us with their inner life in tremendous detail.

Nonetheless, the protagonist of any novel should almost always be portrayed in detail. E. M. Forster made a distinction between what he called 'round' characters and 'flat' characters. Round characters include all the major characters in a novel as well as the protagonist. They emerge as almost human because the reader knows a great deal about them and the author portrays them in terms of the five elements of character outlined earlier.

Most novels also contain a cast of flat characters, characters who, according to Forster, are portrayed in terms of a single idea or quality. They are minor characters, 'extras', who are necessary to the story but not important. The fact that they frequently have a limited number of characteristics makes them easily recognizable after they have been first introduced. The reader does not want a detailed description. It is not a criticism of an author that they create flat characters. If every person who appeared in a novel were given detailed characterization the reader would end up confused and overloaded with unnecessary information. In a sense they are the equivalent of flat characters in our everyday lives. We may pass the time of day with a newsagent when we get our daily paper but probably we know very little about him. Sociologists talk about 'significant others', people in our lives who are important to us. These people are the equivalent of round characters. Flat characters are less significant. Someone else could just as easily sell us newspapers. Forster's notion of flat and round characters is, perhaps, rather cut and dried. It might be better to see that there is a continuum between the protagonist portrayed in the round and the flower seller, a flat character, from whom the protagonist buys a bouquet for his mistress. In between may be some characters who are not major but play some quite important role in the story. These characters will deserve more comprehensive characterization than the flower seller.

Some critics refer to dynamic characters and static characters. These are not the same as Forster's round and flat characters. A dynamic character is one who grows and changes in the course of a novel. The experiences they have undertaken or endured have affected them in some way. The static character, on the other hand, remains the same at the end as they were at the beginning. There is not necessarily any virtue in either of these types of character. Some people in real life are changed by experience; some are not. Some travellers go abroad and have their horizons extended; some go abroad determined to confirm their prejudices – and do so. On the whole, though, the great classic novels tend to have protagonists who change in the course of the novel. The heroes and heroines of Dickens, Jane Austen, Charlotte Brontë and George Eliot nearly all learn and change, certainly the main ones. Pip in Dickens' *Great Expectations* changes and develops in the course of the novel, Mr Micawber does not. Raskolnikov in Dostoevsky's *Crime and Punishment* goes from respectable student to murderer, to repentant.

The Character Profile

It goes almost without saying that the author of a fiction should know all about all their characters before setting out to write. It is a good idea, therefore, to create a character profile for each of the main characters. This can also be used as a reference to see that inappropriate deviations are not made. A profile can be created for each character using the following checklist. The information can be kept on file.

- Age and sex.
- Main personality traits.
- Habits – good or bad?
- What are the important features of his/her looks?
- Are looks important to the character?
- What is his/her job? Do they enjoy it?
- What is his or her educational background?
- Is he/she ambitious?
- What is the character's domestic situation? Married/single/partner? Living alone?
- Are they a city or rural dweller?
- Does the character have strong religious/political views?
- Is the character capable of changing behaviour/opinions?
- Do they want to change?
- What are their interests outside work?
- Do they get on with people?
- Are they extravert or introvert?
- Have they a strong or weak sense of morality?
- Are they self-centred?

- What is their family background and is it important to them?
- Has anything in their family background or past affected them in the long term?
- Are they afraid of anything? What?
- Are they proud or humble, arrogant or self-effacing?
- What is their status in life with regard to job/social class?
- Have they any mannerisms?
- Are they generally happy or unhappy, satisfied with life or dissatisfied?
- Are they steady or unpredictable?
- How do they speak?

The list can easily be extended. Fairly detailed notes should be made on what is considered essential and if necessary research should be done. If it is important that a character has gone to university as part of his education, give details of which one and what he studied there. If the writer decides he wants to create a witty character, the idea should be abandoned if the writer cannot create witty remarks. It is simply not enough just to say the character is witty. A great deal about character can be revealed through dialogue.

The items listed in such a profile should not be mechanically delineated near the beginning of a story. They should have been absorbed and kept in the back of the mind of the writer and then the character will be more consistently portrayed. Some of these characteristics might be an important part of the story, others may never be used at all. Making a profile on these lines is similar to creating a backstory for a character.

The author should also ask what the protagonist's main motive is in the story. It will say a great deal about the character. People's motivations come under one of the following categories. In any story, of course, the general will become specific; for instance, love will be love for a particular person – or thing.

Love	Riches
Power	Revenge
Praise	Self-fulfilment
Survival	Justice
Jealousy	Greed
Social equality	

Small details are important in character portrayal. People sometimes behave in unexpected ways and characters should reflect this. It is not advisable to make a hero figure all good or a villain all bad. Heroes some-times have bad habits or undesirable characteristics and villains may not be villainous to their friends. Small, unique details or quirks can lend a sense of reality to a character. The ancient Chinese writer, Han Yu (768–824) said 'The seven constituents of emotional make-up are: joy, anger, sorrow, fear, love, hatred and desire. A man of superior emotional make-up will display these emotions in a balanced manner'. Writers, though, do not always write of characters with 'superior emotional make-up' because those with unbalanced emotions can be far more interesting; the obsessive, for instance, or the hate-racked, the lovelorn.

It is worth noting some wise almost paradoxical words on charac-ter by the novelist Henry James. 'What is character but the determin-ation of incident? What is incident but the illustration of character?'

See also ANTAGONIST; BACKSTORY; DIALOGUE; HERO; HEROINE; INTERIOR MONOLOGUE; PROTAGONIST; SHOWING AND TELLING; STOCK CHARACTERS; STREAM OF CONSCIOUSNESS

CHICK LIT

Chick lit became a recognized literary genre in the 1990s. It is almost exclusively written by women about single women in their late twen-ties and thirties. It is almost always humorous and sometimes witty but at the same time it deals with issues that are of concern for the age and kind of women for which it is written. Basically it is a branch of light romantic fiction and the central figure is invariably looking for a settled relationship or marriage. However, it bears little relationship to the kind of romantic novel represented by the older Mills and Boon fiction or the novels of writers like Barbara Cartland.

There is a considerable element of social realism in chick lit, albeit of a limited variety. The central character is usually educated and works in the city, in an office, in publishing, in a financial institution or something similar. She may hope to find a handsome prince but will settle for a senior figure in her place of work. She is not a princess and may be struggling with obesity, bad habits, mild neurosis and almost always has relationship problems. The settings are never exotic but are more likely to be urban and the heroine probably lives in a flat, perhaps sharing with one or more others who give her the opportu-nity to air her anxieties and share her occasional joys. The flatmates may have problems of their own.

The novels characteristically have pastel-coloured covers with titles in flamboyant, erratic print and they are likely to show elements of a fashionable lifestyle such as cocktail glasses, handbags and trendy clothing.

Chick lit is not in the feminist tradition and many would not even call it post-feminist. It has been criticized by some feminists. After all, feminists in the past, and today, would balk at being called 'chicks'. The criticism is often misplaced because the authors would claim their books to be nothing more than entertaining escapism with perhaps a soupçon of seriousness. One would not criticize soap operas because their authors lack the literary finesse of Shakespeare.

Bridget Jones' Diary by Helen Fielding published in 1997 is generally regarded as the first and archetypal chick lit novel and it brought the genre to the attention of the public. The appeal of these novels is that the heroine is not little princess-perfect but, like most of the readers, fraught with imperfections and anxieties. Sex also plays an important part in the novels as presumably in the lives of their readers. When sex isn't available, shopping may be a reasonably desirable substitute.

Undoubtedly one of the sources of the popularity of chick lit is that the central theme of many of the novels is women dissatisfied with their lives (jobs, men or lifestyle) and who seek to improve their lot. Clearly it is a predicament women (and men) experience in real life: hence the appeal. It is a theme which has been popular in many different kinds of novel since Dickens and before. H. G. Wells, in *The History of Mr Polly*, had his hero realize 'If you don't like your life, change it'. The chick lit heroine has similar thoughts, although she might not express it in that way, and the story concerns her bringing about the change. Many readers, no doubt, would like to do the same. Earlier novels referred to would treat the theme seriously for the most part; chick lit deals with it light-heartedly.

One less prolific spin-off from chick lit but which has produced some best-sellers is what has been referred to as 'mommy lit'. These novels have essentially the same kind of heroine as chick lit but she has moved on, married and had children. The theme is coping with married life and juggling with the problems of motherhood and possibly a job. Generally recognized as the first and seminal example of 'mommy lit' is a novel by Alison Pearson called *I Don't Know How She Does It*. The title says it all.

Some of the novelists writing chick lit include Helen Fielding, Katie Fforde, Kathy Lette, Sophie Kinsella, Wendy Holden and Emily Barr.

See also LAD LIT

CLICHÉ

A cliché is an overused or hackneyed phrase or expression which, because of overuse, has lost its effectiveness. When we read the cliché 'as black as coal' we know that it means very black but because we've heard the expression so often it is quite likely that we will just skirt over the description. Had a more original expression been used it would have been more effective. Sometimes, of course, the more original expression itself becomes a cliché. Thus, when the poet and dramatist Dylan Thomas wanted to describe darkness in his play *Under Milk Wood* he used the expression 'Bible black'. This made listeners to the radio play pause and think but since the early productions of the play the phrase has been overused and become something of a cliché itself. Careful revision should be used with the aim of eliminating all kinds of cliché.

The lesson of this is that we should always try to make descriptions telling and original but without being so bizarre that the expression becomes an end in itself and detracts from the thing being described. Poetry is admired for its originality of expression and the author of *Thoughts in a Dry Season*, Gerald Brenan, once said: 'The cliché is dead poetry'. The cliché can lead to dead prose as well.

Not all clichés are purely descriptive. The following are expressions using cliché:

His bark is worse than his bite.
Taken for a ride.
Don't tempt fate.
You can take a horse to water.
It's raining cats and dogs.
Because it's there.

There are literally hundreds of such expressions. You will know them because the cliché is always over familiar. The temptation to write one should be resisted – straightforward writing and original descriptive expression is best.

In 2004 the Plain English Campaign conducted a survey to identify the most irritating clichés. The following were the first five: 'At the end of the day'; 'At this moment in time'; 'Like' (as a form of punctuation); 'With all due respect'; and 'To be honest'.

The term cliché refers not only to expressions but also sometimes to characters, ideas, notions and situations (clichéd characters are usually referred to as 'stock' characters. An example of the cliché of idea is the way in which the crime or detective story often explains a character's propensity for crime as the result of an unhappy or abusive childhood. The fact that this has been an accurate analysis of some criminal's behaviour does not prevent it from being a cliché. Someone once said 'All the great clichés are true'. It is merely that it is a familiar explanation – and an easy one for the writer. In the romantic story an equally familiar cliché revolves around the fact that two characters who dislike, almost hate each other at the beginning of the story, have invariably fallen into each other's arms by the end. The horror story is usually replete with creaking doors, lights which fail to go on, ghostly presences, inhuman sighs and inclement weather.

See also STOCK CHARACTERS

CLIFFHANGER

A cliffhanger is mostly associated with the serial story and refers to the ending of a serial episode on a moment of suspense. In adventure serials the cliffhanger ending invariably left the hero or heroine in a predicament from which it seemed almost impossible to escape – but they always did at the beginning of the next episode. Slightly less melodramatic cliffhangers were employed by nineteenth-century writers like Dickens and Hardy, who usually first published their novels as serials.

Cliffhanger endings were employed for two reasons: (1) suspense is popular with readers, and (2) it is more likely that readers will buy the next issue of the magazine if they want to find out what happened. So cliffhangers had a commercial purpose as well. The cliffhanger is an exaggeration of a technique which must be used by all writers if they are to be successful. It is essential that the reader must want to know what happens next. It is this curiosity that leads the reader, in the case of a novel, to read on to the end. The work must sustain the reader's interest if it is to be worth that investment of time. It is the job of the writer to arouse that interest and then satisfy it. The cliffhanger is not the only technique for doing this but it is the most dramatic.

The writer of the cliffhanger is quite deliberately creating a sense of tension, anxiety and suspense in the reader. In Charles Dickens' most sentimental novel, *The Old Curiosity Shop* (1840) one of the central characters, Nell Trent, more commonly known as Little Nell, has a largely tragic life. As she is a sympathetic character, readers were genuinely worried what fate Dickens had in store for her. It is said that readers in New York waited at the quayside to get the episode which revealed poor Nell's fate. Tears were shed when it was known.

Cliffhangers, of course, are frequently employed by novelists who have no thought about serial publication. They can be a means of creating suspense and engaging the attention of the reader.

Thomas Hardy has a literal cliffhanger in *A Pair of Blue Eyes* (1873). A character falls part way down a cliff following an accidental slip and is saved, rather daringly for the time, by a girl who tears up some of her garments to make a rope.

Cinema serials (which disappeared in the 1950s) and children's comics employed serials with cliffhangers as part of their staple diet. The silent film serial *The Perils of Pauline* (1914) is noted for the cliffhanger where Pauline is tied by the villain to a railway line as an express train approaches. Will Pauline escape on time? See the next exciting episode!

The writer's skill lies in inventing predicaments for the characters and finding plausible ways of how they might be freed. Major characters usually escape; minor characters might not.

See also MELODRAMA; SERIALS AND SERIES; SUSPENSE

CLIMAX

In the typical story plot, rising action follows the exposition, the rising action culminates in a climax, then follows falling action and a resolution or denouement.

The climax is the high point of interest and drama and often involves emotional intensity. It can take place at the end of the rising action when one of the following occurs:

- A confrontation between the protagonist and antagonist.
- A revelation of something which changes a character or circumstances.
- Something forces a change in the protagonist's outlook.
- The end of an era, a conflict or a war.
- The uniting of the protagonist with another.
- The recognition of a previously denied truth.
- The finding of something.
- The discovery of the truth about someone.
- A reversal of fortune occurs or a reversal in desires or expectations.
- The start of a new phase of life for the protagonist or another character.

A particular story and the author's preference will dictate what sort of climax occurs. A surprise of some sort is a popular choice.

Some critics distinguish between crisis and climax. For those who do, crisis refers to the point of greatest tension in the story and climax refers to the breaking of that tension. Clearly the two go together and are near each other in the story.

See also DENOUEMENT; EXPOSITION; PLOT; RISING AND FALLING ACTION

CLOSURE

Closure has become a fashionable word. It is used to refer to the way in which an extended parliamentary debate may be deliberately ended. It is also used to refer to any matter which is closed. In literature some critics use it of the ending of a story or novel which is brought to a definite conclusion (as opposed to open-ended).

See also DENOUEMENT

COINCIDENCE

Almost everyone experiences coincidences in life and yet authors are derided when they occur in fiction. This is probably because in life coincidences happen arbitrarily and they are often not very important whereas when writers use coincidence in fiction, it is perhaps the only way to solve a problem.

Coincidences are random and haphazard; we expect an author to have planned everything in the story. The reader expects good reasons why things happen. If the story requires two people to meet who would not normally do so, a logical reason must be found. It is not good enough that they just happen to use the same café one day or happen to meet in the street.

The biggest temptation for the writer is to use coincidence at the ending. This should never occur. The storm must not suddenly stop, for the lovers to be brought together. If there has been an eternal triangle, the problem must not be solved by one party being killed in an accident or having a sudden longing to realize a long-standing (but unmentioned) ambition to go to New Zealand. If the protagonists are being threatened by some danger, it must not be eliminated by some more powerful force. Most of all, a final problem must not be solved by some magical or fantastic intrusion which neatly rounds things off. The ancient Greeks in their drama were tolerant of a god intervening at the end to resolve things and bring them to a conclusion. The modern writer should not resort to that.

Some great writers have made use of coincidence, Thomas Hardy, for example. If it is to be used at all, coincidence must be used with caution.

See also DEUS EX MACHINA

COLLABORATION

Writing is usually a solitary activity and most novels and stories are written by individuals working on their own. The very process of writing does not allow two people to work on a manuscript at the same time.

Nonetheless, there have been fiction-writing partnerships. Caryl Brahms and S. J. Simon wrote many detective stories together until Brahms's untimely death. Their most popular book, *A Bullet in the Ballet*, is still in print. Nicci French is the pseudonym of a husband and wife writing partnership who write popular thrillers. In both cases, the pair share or shared the writing. Significantly both these collaborators were or are concerned with crime thrillers and it may be that partnerships can be useful in working out ingenious plots. Another advantage of collaboration is that there is someone to check, correct and edit the other's work. An essential of such a partnership is that both writers devise a similar style of writing so that the reader does not notice changes from one to the other.

Collaboration is more common in film and writing for television.

COLOPHON

A colophon is the term used for a publisher's logo.

COMMISSIONING EDITOR

A commissioning editor is the person who commissions books for a publisher or considers proposals or manuscripts that have been submitted to a publisher. He or she also works with authors on commissioned works. (In the US the term acquiring editor is more commonly used.)

COMMITTED LITERATURE (*LITTÉRATURE ENGAGÉE*)

Committed literature (or 'engaged literature') is literature committed to a cause, usually political. The term became popular after the Second

World War when the French existentialists reacted against the notion of 'art for art's sake', literature judged solely on its aesthetic qualities. Oscar Wilde once said, 'All art is quite useless' and he clearly thought it should have no utilitarian or political purpose. He changed his mind after being sent to prison and his last work, *De Profundis*, was a plea for humanity towards prisoners and prison reform. Clearly one of the reasons for the interest in committed literature in the post-war period was to do with the effect of the war. Committed writers were totally against the Wilde dictum. They believed the writer and the reader have a serious responsibility to society.

There is a problem with commitment in literature which lies in the question 'committed to what?' Some writers are on the left, some the right; some are religious, some are atheistic. In addition, it could be argued that there was nothing new in the idea of commitment in the post-Second World War period. Charles Dickens had been committed to a number of social causes in his novels. Bernard Shaw was committed to a number of social, political and philosophical positions and, later, D. H. Lawrence saw his work as a message about how we should live our lives. To a greater or lesser degree many writers have commitments. With such a general term it is unwise to apply it only to the existentialists. The committed writer must also guard against didacticism; the purpose of fiction is not primarily to preach. However, some of the greatest committed writers such as Dickens, Brecht, Sartre and Grass cannot be accused of didacticism. They raise questions rather than supply cut and dried answers although some critics might accuse Lawrence of being biased.

See also DIDACTICISM; EXISTENTIALISM (EXISTENTIAL NOVEL); NOVEL

CONCEIT

A conceit is a figure of speech which is really an elaborate simile or metaphor. It makes a fanciful comparison. Conceits are used more by poets than prose fiction writers. A danger of the conceit is that it sometimes goes too far and becomes laughably absurd or is misunderstood. The metaphysical poets of the seventeenth century were fond of using the conceit. The French symbolists and later English poets influenced by them, such as T. S. Eliot and Ezra Pound, revived its use.

The following conceit is from the poem *To His Coy Mistress* by Andrew Marvell (1621–78). The conceit conveys the advice to 'make hay while the sun shines', to live for now because soon we might be dead. More specifically the narrator of the poem is trying to get his mistress to succumb to him. Note the use of personification in the last two lines.

> Let us roll our strength and all
> Our sweetness up into one ball,
> And tear our pleasures with rough strife
> Through the iron gates of life:
> Thus, though we cannot make our sun
> Stand still, yet we will make him run.

See also SIMILE AND METAPHOR

CONFLICT

Most people yearn for a peaceful existence but ironically in fiction one of our chief interests is conflict. Fictional plots virtually depend on conflict which means the opposition or struggle between two forces. In most stories it is a struggle between the central character, the protagonist and either another character (the antagonist) or some other agency.

A fundamental element of plot is that the protagonist meets some obstacle to their aim or goal outlined at the beginning of the story. Shakespeare's Macbeth, for instance, wants to be king. The primary obstacle to his ambition is that there is already a king on the throne. Result, conflict.

There are five basic conflicts in fiction. These are:

1   Conflicts between people; what may be called *Relationship* conflicts. These conflicts occur often in fiction as they do in life.
2   *Social* conflicts are also common. In these the protagonist may be pitted against a semi-anonymous organization such as a government department although the department will be represented by one or more individuals.
3   *Environmental* or *Situational* conflicts occur when the protagonist's main opposition is from something like the elements, being lost in the jungle or in space. Stories based on these conflicts will usually be adventure stories.
4   The more thoughtful and sophisticated story may be concerned with *Inner* or *Psychological* conflicts. The protagonist is opposed by dark inner feelings or demons.
5   *Religious* or *Spiritual* conflicts are concerned with belief, morality, the supernatural and ghosts.

Human relationships and human nature are rarely straightforward so many fictions will be concerned with a protagonist who is beset by more than one kind of conflict. Shakespeare's Hamlet has inner conflict because he cannot bring himself to take action against the man who he believes killed his father. He is also opposed by other members of the court. The issue is further complicated by the fact that his mother is in love with his father's murderer. In Thomas Hardy's *Jude the Obscure* (1898), Jude's ambition to go to university and become formally educated is thwarted largely by a social system that did not consider a member of the working class to be suitable material for university education. Jude's obsessive nature and his weakness for women also got in the way of his dreams and ambitions.

The following lists outline some common examples of the five different kinds of conflict:

Relationship conflicts
boyfriend/girlfriend
father/mother/son/daughter
husband/wife
youth/age
boss/employee
adolescent/adult
teacher/pupil
lecturer/student
eternal triangle
foreigners/indigenous
neighbours
gang rivalry
snobbery

Social conflicts
social class clashes
race clashes
impersonality of city life
institutions cause problems:
    prisons
    hospitals
    schools/colleges/universities
    government departments
    places of work
slums/poverty
social services

Environmental/situational conflicts
storm
desert
jungle
sea
mountains
outer space
animals (associated with some of the above)
war
riot
terrorism
urban jungle/crime
race against time

Inner/psychological conflicts
guilt
jealousy
self-doubt
revenge
conflicting duties
love
ambition
secrets
envy
passion
obsession
vengeance
ennui

Religious/spiritual conflicts
belief/lack of belief/loss of belief
haunting
demons
ghosts
exorcism
the unknown
morality
self-sacrifice
good/bad
right/wrong

These lists should be viewed tentatively and it is obvious that some overlap exists. Some of the bases of conflict could be placed in more than one category. Love for instance could be a cause of inner conflict or it could be to do with a relationship. In a novel set during the war, the war is a major situational conflict in the story but there are often relationship conflicts between, say, an officer or a sergeant and members of the other ranks.

Often there is a moral or value judgement element to conflict. For years Western novels and films were one of the most popular genres of fiction and this was probably because the stories were centred around the basic conflict of good and bad: the good cowboy versus the Indians, or rustlers, or crooks, or the railway men (proponents of industrialization against a more natural way of life). There were clear-cut goodies and baddies to create the conflict. One of the reasons for the demise of the Western was that Indians, or Native Americans as they came to be called, could no longer be regarded as villains but rather as victims because of changing attitudes in society. One could say that the loss of a traditional antagonist, the Red Indian, led to the loss of a particular genre of novels and films.

The crime story, too, of course, was a clear case of good against bad. More recently, in both novels and films, morality is less clear-cut. The protagonist is often portrayed as having moral flaws as well as virtues and the antagonist or villain is frequently not all bad.

One of the most interesting fictions to expose the volatility of the good hero pitted against a villain is *The Pledge* by Friedrich Durrenmatt. In this novel, a detective's last case before his retirement concerns the murder of a child. He is distraught that he cannot solve the crime and he makes a pledge to the mother that he will continue on his own to try to find the killer. Another murder occurs and again the victim is a blonde female child who the murderer has lured to her death. All the murders take place in a defined locality. In desperation and after a few years the detective starts a relationship with a woman who has a child who is physically like the earlier victims. They run a roadside petrol station and the ex-detective intends to use the girl as a lure. It transpires that the girl has been approached by a lorry driver who has said he would like to meet her again. A trap is set, the girl is used as bait – and nothing happens, the suspected murderer does not come. The girl's mother is horrified when she discovers how they have been used and the police dismiss the detective as a madman. The detective goes into a mental decline. In the final chapter of the novel the reader, but none of the characters, discovers that the detective had been right about the murderer, it was simply that he had been killed in a car crash on his way to meet the girl.

What Durrenmatt exposes in this novel is the fickle way we make moral judgements. If the murderer had come and been caught, the detective would have been a hero. Because he did not the detective's dubious and immoral use of people, including a child, is exposed. The end would have justified the means as it so often does in life. Durrenmatt suggests the means are often more important than the ends. He also takes a genre story (detective fiction) with its usual range of conflicts, but he turns the genre on its head towards the end.

Dialogue can be used as a device for creating conflict in fiction. People in real life often conduct their conflicts through arguments and arguments form part of many stories. In some cases, especially in drama, argument may be central. For example many of Bernard Shaw's plays centre on characters arguing, sometimes on quite philosophical subjects. At the other extreme, marital breakdown is exposed in sustained and furious arguments between a husband and wife in Edward Albee's *Who's Afraid of Virginia Woolf?* In the novel, of course, more action is required. Conversation would be unlikely to work in a novel that was merely argumentative.

Just as plot depends on conflict so conflict in fiction leads to suspense. The outcome of any conflict is not something that should be obvious or easily anticipated by the reader. The writer's task is to make the conflict situations such that oppositions seem equal and therefore the outcome is always in the balance. Similarly if there is a hero he or she should not always easily win against the antagonist. This creates suspense.

See also PLOT AND STORY, SUSPENSE

CONNOTATION AND DENOTATION

A connotative word is one which has a literal meaning as well as an implied association. For example, the words solitude and 'loneliness' both refer to the state of being alone. But in western society 'solitude' is more likely to suggest a positive state whereas loneliness describes a state of sadness in being alone. The connotations of solitude are positive; those of loneliness are negative. Paul Tillich wrote that 'Language has created the word loneliness to express the pain of being alone, and the word solitude to express the glory of being alone.' Tillich's remark demonstrates how connotative words have a kind of inbuilt emotional content.

The description 'waif-like' in the past referred to 'being like a waif', that is, like an abandoned or thin, possibly undernourished young person. The connotations were negative. Since the late twentieth century waif-like has connotations of a certain kind of fashion model and the state of being waif-like has more positive associations. The connotation of the word has changed.

Denotative words, on the other hand, are words which for the most part have single, literal or basic meanings. On the whole they lack connotations, 'box' for example. There are few absolutes in language, however, and while knife for instance would be usually classed as a denotative word, it might have negative connotations for someone who had been attacked with a knife.

Writers must be aware of connotative meanings and their possibilities and take care in their choice of words. Sometimes context may dictate that they should choose a connotative word, at other times the context may suggest avoiding such a word.

CONSISTENCY

Readers do not like errors and inconsistencies in novels but love to point them out. Errors occur mostly with regard to places, times and characters. The writer should always be certain that there is accuracy with regard to where characters are likely to be once these places have been established. If a canal or forest is going to be essential to the plot, the novel should not be set in a mountainous district or an arid region. If the story occurs over a considerable period of time, it is essential to have worked out the time-line of major occurrences in advance and the age of the characters at these times.

The worst error is inconsistency of character. Soap operas are often accused (correctly) of being plot-driven and in order to make the plot work or be interesting, some characters are made to behave in an uncharacteristic way. This should never occur in fiction. Once the character, their habits and quirks, their likes and dislikes, their weaknesses and strengths have been established, they should not be suddenly changed for the sake of the plot. On the other hand, people do sometimes change, so if small changes are prepared for and good reasons given for them, this may be acceptable.

Errors and inconsistencies with regard to facts can be avoided by thorough research.

See also CHARACTERS

CONTRACT, PUBLISHING
A publishing contract is the agreement drawn up between the publisher and the author stating date for delivery of manuscript, amount of advance, royalties and any other conditions to which both author and publisher must adhere.

COPY EDITOR
A copy editor works on the manuscript of a book to ensure accuracy of fact and correct use of language. He or she ensures a final copy of the manuscript is ready for submission to the printer.

COPYRIGHT
As soon as a person writes something on paper or saves it on disc, they own the copyright. In other words, only he or she can claim ownership, sell the material and make a profit from it. The material may be any writing (novel, short story, article, song lyric, play, work of non-fiction or journalism, leaflet, etc.). Copyright also applies to music, paintings, drawings, sculptures, architecture, maps, etc. The copyright of letters written to you remains with the writer even though they are your property. Photographers retain the copyright of photographs even though they may have been commissioned to take the photograph. There is no copyright in titles. This is largely because there are millions of titles and it would be easy to name a work with a title which has already been used.

The works must be original and have involved skill and labour. Unless they are highly original, there is no copyright in ideas. Thus many writers of works of non-fiction (historical books, for instance) may take ideas from other sources provided they do not simply copy them exactly and they acknowledge them.

It is possible to sell your copyright but it is unwise to do so if you think you may make a profit from it. Even when a work is published, the copyright belongs to the author, not the publisher – unless the author sells the copyright to the publisher. Copyright continues for seventy years after the author's death or seventy years after publication if the work has been published posthumously. An author may leave the copyright of their work to a specified person in their will.

If the authored work is done as part of the writer's employment then copyright belongs to the employer. This would apply to most journalists. The work of freelance journalists for newspapers and magazines, however, remains the copyright of the writer. A university could claim the copyright of an academic work done by an employed academic if the work was closely connected with their paid work. In most cases, though, as these works are done in spare time and rarely lead to huge profits, the university makes no claim to the copyright. Universities are more concerned with the kudos that staff publications bring to the institution.

The symbol © placed usually at the end of an article or at the beginning of a book denotes copyright but it is not necessary to use the symbol.

Breach of copyright is a civil rather than a criminal offence but damages can be awarded in breach of copyright cases, especially if the offender has profited by another's work or prevented the author from making profits which were rightfully theirs. The current law is described in the Copyright, Designs and Patents Act 1988.

See also PLAGIARISM

CROSSOVER NOVELS

Traditionally there has been adult fiction and children's fiction. Obviously children, especially sophisticated readers, read adult fiction when they are still children and some adults continue to read children's books. Publishers, however, until recently have always had a clear demarcation between the two types of fiction.

Crossover fiction refers to those novels that are published, advertised and reviewed and deemed equally suitable for children and adults. The Harry Potter books by J. K. Rowling are cases in point. All the novels have been published with two book jackets; one for children and one, slightly more sober version, for the adult market. The Adrian Mole diaries by Sue Townsend have appealed to teenagers and adults alike. The William books by Richmal Crompton published between 1922 and 1970 (with reprints still published along with audio versions) are an example of earlier children's books that also appeal to adults, especially since many of them have been broadcast by the BBC. Crompton's first William story was in fact published in an adult magazine but the publisher was aware of the potential appeal of these stories for children and when they were published in book form the children's market was targeted.

Some one-off novels (as opposed to the series mentioned above) are also marketed for both teens and adults. A notable example is *The Curious Incident of the Dog in the Night-Time* by Mark Haddon. It is a novel about a boy who suffers from a form of autism. His outlook on life is very individual and this enables the author to give unusual perspectives on a number of issues and things. Another successful crossover book is *How I Live Now* by Meg Rosoff, a story about a fifteen year old American girl sent to rural Britain during the Second World War. It is a nostalgic love story and has appealed widely.

Most writers do not deliberately write crossover fiction; they probably have one audience in mind but the publisher recognizes the crossover potential.

CUT-UP TECHNIQUE

Cut-up is an infrequently used technique most famously demonstrated in beat writer William Burroughs's novel, *The Naked Lunch*. The technique involved cutting up pages of the novel's manuscript, once written, and re-arranging the pieces fairly arbitrarily. Burroughs argued that the technique was basically anarchic (most people felt *he* was) and broke the 'central system' of the power of language that he believed was used to manipulate people.

The technique was actually invented or discovered by a minor writer called Brion Gysin when he was cutting a mount for a drawing with a Stanley knife. He cut through the layers of newspaper the mount was resting on and when he re-arranged the cut up pieces of newspaper he found they produced interesting, rather surrealistic results. Some people dismiss the technique as a gimmick and few writers have taken it up. Needless to say, the resulting incoherence of cut-up literature can make meaning difficult for the reader.

DENOUEMENT

'Denouement' comes from the French word meaning 'unknotting'. In literature a denouement is the unravelling, resolution or explanation of puzzling things which have happened earlier in the plot of a story. The denouement occurs after the climax or final dramatic event.

One of the easiest ways of understanding denouement is to consider the traditional detective story such as an Agatha Christie mystery. A crime or crimes occur and eventually the detective reveals the criminal. This is the climax of the story. But the reader may not fully understand why the detective has come to that conclusion. The denouement provides an explanation, usually in words, from the detective who will explain what has led him to solve the crime, why previous suspects could not in fact have done it, what the motivation was, and an explanation of any other loose ends. It is essential that a denouement is provided otherwise the reader may have a sense that there are loose ends which the author cannot explain. At its worst, the reader may feel cheated by the author.

Denouements, of course, do not just occur in detective stories. In any story which has raised mysteries or puzzling incidents or motivations which have no obvious explanations, these explanations must be provided near the end. Just occasionally an author may deliberately end on a sense of irresolution or mystery, but there must be a good reason for this.

See also PLOT AND STORY

DESCRIPTION *SEE* EXPOSITION; SIMILE AND METAPHOR

DETECTIVE STORIES

The detective story has been a popular genre of fiction for over a century. Its basis is simple: the protagonist, a detective, attempts to solve a crime that is usually a murder. The detective may be one of the following. Examples are given:

- *A policeman or police detective*   Inspector Rebus in novels by Ian Rankin; Dalziel and Pasco novels by Reginald Hill; Jack Frost in novels by R. D. Wingfield; Maigret in novels by Georges Simenon.
- *A private investigator* (more usually found in American fiction than British)   Sherlock Holmes in stories by Arthur Conan Doyle; Philip Marlowe in novels by Raymond Chandler; Mike Hammer created by Mickey Spillane; Precious Ramotswe in stories by Alexander McCall Smith.
- *An amateur detective*   Father Brown by G. K. Chesterton; Miss Marple in novels by Agatha Christie; Nancy Drew in novels by Carolyn Keene, and others.
- *An investigative journalist*   Philip Dryden in novels by Jim Kelly.
- *A lawyer*   Various characters in novels by Scott Turow and John Grisham.
- *A forensic expert*   Dr Kay Scarpetta in novels by Patricia Cornwell; Dr Temperance Brenna in Kathy Reich's novels.
- *A psychological profiler*   Cracker in work by Jimmy McGovern.

In addition there are a few historical detectives such as Brother Cadfael, a twelfth-century monk detective in Ellis Peters' novels.

Lindsey Davis writes crime stories set in the ancient Roman Empire.

With the exception of Agatha Christie's Miss Marple, women police detectives and private investigators were not common until their potentiality was recognized about twenty years ago. Now there are many in written fiction and on TV.

There are subgenres of the detective story, some of which are indicated by the categories of detectives listed above but the main recognized subgenres are as follows:

Police Procedural Novels

In these the detective is a policeman and solving the crime is a team effort rather than an individual one although it is fairly likely that one detective will be the protagonist. The writer of police procedural novels must be well acquainted with how the police operate. The most noted and popular author of this genre is the late Ed McBain (pseudonym of Evan Hunter, under which name he wrote general novels). His police procedurals are set in New York in the 87th precinct and a single detective usually takes centre stage. In order to avoid too large a cast of characters, the protagonist detective is often a maverick who will work alone (and against the bosses wishes) if need be. Jack Frost in R. D. Winfield's novels sometimes takes this role.

The Whodunit

In the previous category, as in most detective stories, the main issue is who did the crime but the Whodunit tends to refer to those novels where the readers are able to pit themselves against the criminal on an equal basis with the detective in the story. All clues will be provided and the criminal will be revealed at the end or the reader will have worked out who it is.

Private Investigator Novels

The nature of the crime, the criminal, the investigation and the solution is the same as in the previous categories, but the detective will be a private investigator, sometimes in conflict with the police who resent their job being taken on by an amateur. Often, of course, a relative of a victim will hire a private investigator because there is some personal reason why they do not wish to go to the police. Sometimes the private investigator will be investigating a missing person rather than a murder – at first.

Legal Detective Stories

In these a lawyer, who has often been hired by a falsely accused person, will act the detective before dramatically exposing the real criminal in court. As with police procedurals, the author must be familiar with court procedure and legal matters.

Historical Detective Fiction

Whether there were any detectives in ancient Rome and thirteenth-century Britain is a moot point but clearly authors and readers interested in both history and crime make these a small but relatively popular subgenre.

Psychological Detective Stories

The criminal in these stories is invariably a psychopath or serial killer and the emphasis is on a criminal psychologist rather than the official police detective, although the latter will act for the psychologist and probably argue with him or her a lot. Experts are rarely respected in detective stories. Potential authors must obviously research the work of criminal psychologists.

The One-Off

This is not a generally recognized subgenre but there are stories where the protagonist is neither policeperson, private investigator, nor lawyer but simply gets involved because a crime has occurred, perhaps involving a friend, and they are drawn into the events, sometimes reluctantly, sometimes because the police have given up on the case or do not believe a crime has been committed. In some such stories, the police are on the case but the protagonist also works on it and succeeds against the odds.

Hard-boiled Detective Stories

These are usually American private investigator stories and they are usually first-person narratives, narrated by the protagonist who is often cynical, hard drinking, a womanizer and willing to cut corners. They are sometimes also characterized by sharp narrative with protagonists who have a ready line in quips.

Conventions of the Detective Story

The detectives referred to previously in various novels are very rarely straightforward characters. Ever since the eccentricities of Conan Doyle's Sherlock Holmes with his opium habit, rudeness and violin playing, writers have been prone to give their detectives problems and oddities of character or habit. Few of them go home at night, play with the children, go to bed and return refreshed to work the next day. The commonest problem is a rocky marriage caused, it is implied, by long hours with consequent neglect of the spouse. In some cases the spouse has already left and loneliness is a problem. Loneliness in fact seems to be an occupational hazard of many detectives. Quarrelling and being irritable with colleagues for no good reason is also common; sidekicks are unmercifully pilloried. Many detectives take to drink or worse. A fair proportion at some time are thrown off the case by their superior because of their behaviour, but they are usually reinstated because of their expertise.

Another convention which has largely died out (but not in TV stories) is the fact that murder seems to occur in country houses more than in any other kind of property. There is room for more detective stories with a working-class background. Locked rooms are also fairly common and when a private investigator is the detective, bungling policemen are de rigueur.

Most good contemporary writers of detective fiction avoid these conventions and try to be more original, and the aspiring writer should strive to do the same. If the story has a contemporary setting, things in the contemporary world must be acknowledged to exist. In the past a common situation was for a potential victim to be trapped somewhere in isolation without any means of communicating with the outside world. This is unlikely to be believable in an age of mobile phones. The relatively recent means of identification through DNA should be acknowledged and used.

Some conventions perhaps have to be followed if the genre is going to work. The writer cannot avoid having a protagonist who individually solves the crime even though we know that in real life most crimes are solved by teamwork and no individual is ever celebrated as the sole solver of the crime. More than in any other genre, there are series of novels about a single detective (Rebus, Maigret, Wexford, Frost, Morse, etc.). How many detectives, police or private, are involved in murder after murder? As someone remarked, if the Morse stories were true, Oxford would be the murder capital of the world. Another convention is that for obvious reasons, the psychopathic serial killer who for a time murders anyone he fancies, never gets near to killing the detective, except perhaps in a final showdown.

Publishers of detective fiction will probably welcome a good novel that manages to avoid most of the conventions mentioned. On the other hand, readers do not seem to mind them and even accept them as part of the nature of detective fiction. Perhaps familiarity breeds popularity. One of the attractions of detective fiction is its 'neatness'. A more detailed analysis of the detective story plot follows.

The Plot

The plot of most genre detective stories follow this pattern:

Exposition   The inciting incident is a murder which is described or a body has been found and is being examined by forensics or policemen. Next the detective is brought in.

Problem   Who is the victim? Why were they killed? Who killed them?

Complications   Clues are sparse. Identification may be a problem. Background of character is investigated. There are false trails. A number of possible suspects emerges. Some have alibis. Are they lying?

Struggle   Some suspects eliminated. More clues found.

Setback   It proves to have been a false trail with red herrings.

Added complications   Another murder occurs. This may help to establish the guilty party because of common links.

Climax   Detective makes breakthrough.

Denouement   Criminal caught. Loose ends explained. Maybe a shootout or trial and conviction.

Variations on this plot structure are possible and characterization of participants may cause other complications. If the narrative is in the third person, scenes can be described from the point of view of the criminal as well as the protagonist or the crimes may simply be described. The crime which is the inciting incident is often vividly described without revealing anything about the criminal except his or her modus operandi.

Those who aspire to write detective fiction sometimes feel the whole business is just too complicated. What the potential writer should remember is this: the writer knows who the criminal is from the beginning. Because of this it is easy to give them motives but also to give other characters (who become suspects) motives even though they have not committed any crime, thus causing the detective problems. It also makes it easier to lay red herrings. Sherlock Holmes' methods of deduction seem unbelievable and clever but one has to remember that the author worked from the answers to the questions, whereas Holmes (and the reader) have to work out the answer from scratch.

Any aspiring detective story writer should take a favourite novel, summarize it and analyse how the plot has been worked out.

Most of the detective stories referred to are relatively modern. Those readers particularly interested in detective fiction may wish to read some of the earliest examples of the genre, e.g. Edgar Allen Poe's *The Murders in the Rue Morgue* (1841) and other short stories by him; Charles Dickens' *The Mystery of Edwin Drood* (1870) and Wilkie Collins' *The Woman in White* (1860) and *The Moonstone* (1868).

See also INCITING INCIDENT; MYSTERY FICTION; PLOT AND STORY; STORY AND NOVEL CATEGORIES; SUSPENSE; THRILLERS

DEUS EX MACHINA

Deus ex machina is Latin for 'god from a machine'. In certain Greek plays by Sophocles and Euripides (and also in some Roman plays) the plot is resolved in the last act by the lowering onto the stage, from a crane-like device, of a god who resolves all the problems.

No modern writer of fiction would resort to such a device but the term has also been used to refer to any unexpected and sometimes coincidental or rather improbable character or event that resolves the plot. For instance, in some nineteenth-century novels an unexpected bequest or legacy may solve a family's problems. In many Western films, the sudden and fortuitous arrival of the cavalry to save some community or regiment might be regarded as a deus ex machina. In Charles Dickens' *Great Expectations* Pip's fortunes are saved by Magwitch's secret good deeds and eventually by his bequest to Pip but Magwitch's actions have been prepared for by Dickens from the beginning of the novel.

The modern writer of fiction aims for plausible resolutions rather than for the use of a deus ex machina. Coincidences are also eschewed.

DIALECT AND ACCENT

Dialect and accent are features of language, particularly spoken language. There are hundreds of different accents in Britain, everyone has one and there are also many dialects. To what extent should these be acknowledged in writing fiction and in particular in writing dialogue?

Before giving answers to these questions, it might be useful to consider the nature of human language. It is, after all, the main tool for any writer. It may first be useful to look rather at human communication because we communicate some things without language.

Human communication can be described as shown in the box:

Human Communication		
Linguistic elements	Para-linguistic elements	Non-linguistic elements
Vocal and written symbols – words	Vocal quality – tone, e.g. husky resonant whispering laughing sobbing sarcastic, etc.	Signals symbols, e.g. visual proxemic kinesic tactile olfactory

The non-linguistic element is what is more commonly called 'body language'. Most body language is visual (smiles, scowls, nervous tics, bored looks etc.). Others in the list are sometimes used. 'Proxemic' refers to the distance you are from the person you are speaking to, this is important and depends on the relationship. 'Kinesics' refer to movement. Some people gesture and move a great deal; others do not. The 'tactile' is concerned with whether, while talking, a person touches the other. Some people lightly touch an arm, pat a child's head, clap someone's back; others never touch the other person at all. We are more likely to touch a friend than an enemy. The 'olfactory' sense refers to smell and in human communication it is less important now than it used to be. With modern hygiene, soap, deodorants and artificial perfumes natural human smells have been more or less obliterated.

As writers we are concerned mainly with the *linguistic* feature in the diagram, although the writer must sometimes find some way of conveying the other features. *Spoken language* is called by linguists 'primary transmission' for two reasons. Historically human beings spoke before they were able to write. Each individual learns to speak first. Babies learn to speak, but they are not taught formally to do so. On the whole, they pick it up. Written language or secondary transmission came second historically and the individual almost always learns to write later than they learn to speak. The teaching of writing is formal often occurring in school.

While they are obviously related, it is useful to remember that spoken and written forms of language are quite different in many ways. There are three elements to language:

Lexis	(words)
Grammar	(the rules for stringing words together)
Phonology	(sounds)

When we consider these we see that speech and writing have differences as shown below:

Speech	*Writing*
Lexis or words	Lexis or words
Grammar	Grammar
Phonology	Written symbols

One might add that, for the sake of clarity, human beings have added punctuation to writing. There is no punctuation in speech although we use pauses and emphases possibly as a means of gaining clarity in what we say. The features mentioned earlier, para-linguistic and non-linguistic elements, are not strictly language, but they go along with speech and not writing.

The importance of all this for the writer of fiction cannot be over-emphasized. It is clear that in face-to-face, real life conversation the sounds, the body language and the gesture and emphasis all play subtly together in an instant. We do not think about what sort of expression we are going to use or whether we will stand one foot or two feet away from a person while we speak. The hearer also picks up the signals from the speaker without thinking about it consciously – although they may think about the conversation later. So a lot is going on when we converse; much more than can usually be conveyed by the writer of dialogue in fiction. Such dialogue is mainly the 'words that were spoken' and the writer may add in a few comments about mode of expression and body language. But if the writer wants to avoid boring the reader, he or she will not want to include everything that goes on in an everyday conversation. Most writers will point out only features that they consider to be particularly important.

Returning to the matter of accents and dialects, bearing in mind that accent concerns only the differences in sounds made, whereas dialect is about regional variations of sounds, grammar and vocabulary. Grammar and vocabulary differences are much fewer than sound differences. During the course of the last century dialectal vocabulary and grammatical differences have diminished probably because of the influence of broadcasting, education and more frequent travel.

It is highly noticeable that fiction writers for the most part ignore accent and dialectal differences in characters and they present all their dialogue in standard written English. Partly this is because there is no generally accepted way of writing down different accents (other than using the phonetic alphabet which few people are familiar with) and partly because many readers may find it difficult or irritating.

There are exceptions. Irving Welsh in *Trainspotting* writes in a simulated Scottish dialect because it is essential to the story. Mark Twain in *Huckleberry Finn* uses the Mississippi dialect of his hero narrator. He also tries to convey the way Huck's Negro friend, Jim, speaks. In *The Catcher in the Rye*, J. D. Salinger simulates the dialect or argot of his narrator. All these novels are narrated by a character. D. H. Lawrence writes in standard written English but Mellors in *Lady Chatterley's Lover* is given a simulated Nottingham working-class dialect because social class is an important theme in the novel. Social class and dialect often intermix.

The lesson of all this seems to be to stick to Standard English unless there is a good reason not to. It is also worth considering the nature of spoken and written English as described above because it will help in making decisions on how to present dialogue, what to leave out and what to put in.

See also DIALOGUE; SLANG AND SWEARING

DIALOGUE

In daily life people constantly talk to each other and characters in fiction must talk to each other too unless the story concerns someone marooned in isolation. However, characters in fiction do not and must not, talk in the same way that people do in everyday life. Dialogue is the name given to the talk of characters in fiction.

If you listen to conversations on buses, in cafés, at work, at college, you will notice a great deal of inconsequential talk as well as occasional coherent and meaningful conversation. This depends on the situation. Conversations about work at work will be more coherent in most cases than idle chatter in a bar. In the latter there will almost certainly be repetitions, opening statements that are left unfinished, interruptions, laughter, hesitation and even meaningless noises. Many conversations will be ungrammatical. You will not find many of these in fictional dialogue. It would be both difficult to read and very boring and it would slow down the story. On the page it would probably not even seem natural.

The most common opening gambits of real conversations are to do with the weather and asking after people's health or well-being. Again, it might be natural, but it would be tedious if characters in stories did this every time they met.

What then is the nature and purpose of dialogue in fiction?

Nature of Dialogue

(1) First and foremost fictional dialogue must *seem* natural even if it isn't exactly the way people really talk.

(2) It must simulate conversation insofar as it is dialogue by having relatively short utterances from those involved passing from one speaker to the other. It is not often that one person is given the opportunity to speak at length without some interruption or comment from the other. An exception to this may be if one character has asked another to relate a complicated story. Even then there would probably be interruptions and questions.

(3) Attempts should be made to find slightly (or extremely) different styles of writing for the speech or voices of different characters. People have different styles of speaking; so should characters in fiction. For example, a teenager will speak in a different way to a businessman. Beware of using current slang expressions for a character; many of them date very quickly. Take a look at the novel *The Catcher in the Rye* (1951) by J. D. Salinger for an interesting example of teenage speech conveyed in writing. Probably no one ever spoke exactly the way Holden Caulfield speaks but even now years after the book was written, it somehow rings true. Notice also how Salinger uses his character's way of speaking to

convey a lot about his personality. A similar example from an earlier time is Mark Twain's *Huckleberry Finn* (1884). Here Huck, a 14-year-old, is conversing with Jim, a young adult slave in Missouri 1840. Jim is uneducated and in the following extract shows that he is unaware that people in other countries speak other languages. Huck narrates the story but note the difference between the speech of Huck and Jim:

> I told (Jim) about Louis Sixteenth that got his head cut off in France a long time ago; and about his little boy the dolphin, that would a been a king, but they took and shut him up in jail, and some say he died there.
> 'Po' little chap.'
> 'But some says he got out and got away, and come to America.'
> 'Dat's good! But he'll be pooty lonesome – dey ain' no kings here, is dey, Huck?'
> 'No.'
> 'Den he cain't git no situation. What he gwyne to do?'
> 'Well, I don't know. Some of them get on the police, and some of them learns people how to talk French.'
> 'Why, Huck, doan' de French people talk de same way we does?'
> '*No*, Jim; you couldn't understand a word they said – not a single word.'
> 'Well, now, I be ding-busted! How do dat come?'
> '*I* don't know; but it's so. I got some of their jabber out of a book. S'pose a man was to come to you and say *Polly-voo franzy* – what would you think?'
> 'I wouldn't think nuff'n; I'd take and bust him over de head. Dat is, if he warn't white . . .'

Obviously we cannot know exactly how people spoke in America at that time, but the passage is worth studying to note how we can assume it is really a simulation rather than a phonetic rendering of how both white and black people spoke at that time. The actual accents cannot be conveyed. It is worth remembering that unless we are one of those people (and they are very few) who can speak all the many accents spoken in the English-speaking world we cannot pick up from a written version exactly the way people speak.

(4) For the most part, dialogue is written grammatically and in sentences, unlike much real talk. There can be exceptions to this. Characters may sometimes utter single words or short phrases, especially when replying to a question.

Purpose of Dialogue

Rarely is the purpose of dialogue simply small talk. The following are the main things writers try to do with dialogue:

(1) Dialogue can be used to reveal the personality and characteristics of a character (see (3) in Nature of Dialogue). Characters, like people in real life, reveal themselves by what they say and by what they do. For instance, a sarcastic person may make sarcastic remarks rather than the narrator telling the reader he or she was sarcastic. The hypocrite and boaster may blow his or her own trumpet and make claims but do nothing or do the opposite.

(2) The nature and personality of characters can also be revealed by other characters talking about them. Different characters within a story frequently have a different view of another particular character.

(3) Dialogue can contribute to the development of plot by providing information to the reader through one character telling another about something that has happened. Care must be taken that this technique is used logically. It is not advisable to have a character tell another something that they would obviously know in order to convey it to the reader.

(4) Dialect or written simulated accent can convey a type of character and where they come from. Many of D. H. Lawrence's novels use dialect. Lawrence's working-class characters often speak a dialect whereas his middle-class characters speak Standard English. A more recent example is *Trainspotting* (1993) by Irvine Welsh. Here is the opening of *Trainspotting*: 'The sweat wis lashing oafay Sick Boy. Ah wis jist sitting thair, focusing oan the telly, tryin no tae notice the cunt. He wis bringin me doon. Ah tried tae keep ma attention oan the Jean-Claude Van Damme video'. Virtually the whole novel uses language of this type. Some people find it awkward to read but one becomes accustomed to it and it has a definite rhythmic quality.

(5) Conflict is central to plot and story creation. Conflict may be physical but effective conflict can simply involve disputes and arguments between characters, these will be best conveyed through dialogue. Such disputes will almost inevitably contribute to character development. Who gives way first; who wins the argument; who gives up without a fight.

(6) The background to a new character can be revealed to the reader by other characters talking about the person rather than the author/narrator simply providing the information. Similarly a past event can be described by one character to another.

(7) Different points of view on a subject or situation or another character can be provided by characters talking rather than by the narrator

describing them. The reader may then judge the validity of the views presented. What may have been taken for granted can be presented in a new perspective by the use of a character. The point of view must, of course, fit in with the established views of the character who gives it. What has apparently been presented as taken for granted may be undermined when another character presents another perspective.

(8)   Very dramatic situations can often be conveyed best through dialogue. For instance, one character may be confronted with a revelation by another character that changes their life or at least their attitudes. A common example of this is shown in the traditional detective story where the sleuth reveals who the culprit is to the said culprit and often in front of many others.

(9)   Lying can be used to create interest in some situations. For example, a character may tell another character something which the reader knows is a lie.

Some Hints on Dialogue Writing

- Think about the characters – their lifestyle, their jobs, their friends, their family and their place in it, their sex, age, desires, ambitions, their personality. How would they speak? Try to make their mode of speech appropriate to their personality.
- Think of people you like, loathe, love, find interesting, want to meet again and again. How much has this to do with what they say and how they say it?
- Remember a great deal can be learned from what people *do not* say.
- When writing dialogue, say it to yourself in your head. Does it sound real and authentic?
- For an alternative to the use of inverted commas as a way of distinguishing speech in fiction, you could examine James Joyce's autobiographical novel *A Portrait of the Artist as a Young Man*. Joyce uses dashes to introduce pieces of speech, nothing else. The technique works but few other writers or publishers have used Joyce's method. The method is used frequently in continental fiction.
- Don't let your characters indulge in small talk. It is boring and dialogue should advance the story and reveal something new about the characters, situation or plot. There may be exceptions to this. Note how in the film *Pulp Fiction* we learn about the two protagonists early in the film when they are talking about burgers and French fries during a car ride.

- Beware of slang. Current slang expressions may be forgotten next year. However, the use of slang is a way of placing a story in a particular period and with characters of a particular type, e.g. 1960s dance clubs, politicos in 2005.
- Use swear words carefully in dialogue and only when they are appropriate to the character and the situation. Some people in reality swear a great deal. This is unlikely to work in a story.
- Do not overuse 'John said . . .', 'Jane said . . .' i.e. the names of speakers in dialogue. Once the sequence of speech is under way it is not usually necessary to name the speaker at the beginning or end of each and every one of his or her utterances. But check when you are revising that it *is* clear who is speaking. Better still, have someone else check for you.
- Listen to people conversing and if possible make notes of their conversation. Could you use it in story dialogue? Compare it with a piece of dialogue in a novel or a TV play.
- Don't waste words. Keep dialogue brief and succinct. A writer of sparse dialogue is the American novelist James M. Cain. In one of his novels a man and a woman are lusting after each other at the beginning of their affair. The scene continues ' "Bite me," she said. So he bit her.' You cannot get sparer than that!

Writing Dialogue

For readers who may have forgotten or are not sure of the actual technique of writing dialogue the following may be useful.

Most writers and publishers follow a convention in presenting dialogue in fiction. You can discover this convention by examining a few novels and short stories. Some people question the need for the rather cumbersome business of actually writing or word processing dialogue with its considerable use of punctuation marks. It is true that a few novels (and the Bible) manage without the use of speech punctuation and this does not seem to cause confusion but most publishers require dialogue to be written or punctuated in the accepted way so it is best to follow the conventions.

The following passage illustrates most of the techniques (the numbering refers to the notes that follow).

1   He greeted his sister distantly as was his custom and said, 'We need to discuss the reading of the will as soon as possible'.
2   'Trust you to be concerned about that! They're hardly cold in their graves,' said Alice.

3   'You know I've got to get back to London by tonight.' Eric tried to placate her. 'Fiona's working and I've got to look after the kids,' he said.

4   'Oh, of course, it wouldn't do to inconvenience Fiona,' Alice said bitterly, 'even though there's been a death in the family.'
'Life goes on,' he said.

5   'Everything has to be done at your convenience. It's always been like that, ever since you were a child. And you're not much more mature now. What time are you going?'
Eric restrained himself from an outburst against his sister.

Here are some comments on the points above:

1   The spoken words are placed between inverted commas and they begin with a capital letter even though the beginning of the sentence is 'He greeted . . .' The spoken words are a sentence within a sentence.

A change of speaker should be indicated by a new paragraph. This is seen throughout the passage. It helps the reader to note the change of speaker even when his/her name is not mentioned.

2   When the instruction of who is speaking follows the spoken words, it is divided from the spoken words by a comma as well as the inverted comma. The comma would be replaced by a question mark or an exclamation mark if it was appropriate. The comma, question mark or exclamation mark comes before the inverted comma.

Note that although Alice's utterance here is two sentences, only one set of inverted commas is necessary.

3   Note how 'Eric tried to placate her' divides two sentences of dialogue. As the spoken sentences are separated, the inverted commas must be closed and opened again so that they only surround the spoken utterances.

4   Notice how 'Alice said bitterly' is placed between the two parts of a single sentence of dialogue, so the first word of the second part (the word 'even') does not take a capital letter.

5   Here Alice utters a few sentences all at once so only one set of inverted commas is necessary at the beginning and end of her speech. Also we are not told it is Alice speaking, simply because at the end of the sequence it is obvious that it must be her. Names are best not mentioned more than is necessary for clarity.

In the above passages, single inverted commas are used. Double inverted commas may be used by some publishers, especially American publishers. Be consistent and use the convention used by most publishers.

See also HE/SHE SAID; INTERIOR MONOLOGUE; PHATIC (PHATIC COM-MUNION); SLANG AND SWEARING

DICTION

Diction is a term used in two ways. It means:

- the choice of words to effectively express the meaning which the writer or speaker wishes to convey;
- the pronunciation or enunciation of spoken language. A clear speaker is said to have 'good diction'.

The writer is obviously concerned with the first meaning of diction. The concept reminds us that whatever meaning is to be conveyed, there is always more than one way to do it and usually a choice of words may be used. For instance, if a 'thin' character is to be referred to or described, we may use the adjective 'thin', but we might choose one of the following: slim, skinny, waif-like, slender, slight, lean, svelte, willowy or sylph-like. The word chosen will convey something of the attitude of the writer to the person, or if the word is part of a character's speech, it will reveal something of the attitude of one character to the other. Some words have more positive connotations than others.

Note these two sentences. Both may be about the same people and situation but the choice of words conveys to the reader quite different viewpoints on them depending on which is used:

She asked him to be quiet while she considered the matter.
She demanded that he shut his mouth while she concentrated.

The writer should be aware of the alternative possibilities of language and diction and choose according to the context and the attitude of the narrator or the character who is speaking.

See also CONNOTATION AND DENOTATION

DIDACTICISM

Didactic literature moralizes, instructs and teaches as well as enter-tains. At its worst, it preaches. It is exemplified by an early example from 1765, a version of which is still in print today. This is *Goody Two-Shoes* published by John Newbury (the author is unknown). It is the story of Marjorie Two-Shoes (nicknamed Goody) who with her brother was orphaned as a child. They have many ups and downs in their lives, mostly downs but Goody ends up happy, in a good marriage and with considerable property and assets. In the course of the story the virtues of learning to read are extolled, kindness to animals is encouraged, patience in adversity is recommended, the controlling of bad temper is advocated, public service praised and Goody even pontificates on the folly of believing in ghosts. Goody is on the whole virtuous and it is hinted that her prosperity stems from this. *Goody Two-Shoes* was a best-seller in Britain and America for about fifty years. It was not aimed only at children but also 'children six feet tall'.

Children's literature has often been didactic but so has adult fiction. Modern novels for children on social themes such as race or drugs could be considered to be didactic but they rarely preach directly. The fiction writer should not preach, children as well as adults dislike this. Moral tales (of which *Goody Two-Shoes* is an example) were overtly didactic but no less popular for that up until the end of the nineteenth century.

The danger of didactic fiction is that both story and characters become subservient to the lesson which the author wishes to get across and they become lesser works for that. The modern reader, critic and author should realize that didacticism still thrives, even though in a less obvious way than in the past. Most satiric novels, for instance, could be regarded as didactic. George Orwell and Aldous Huxley, among others, warned of the danger of accepting specific political and scientific developments uncritically.

Anti-war novels indirectly and sometimes directly condemn war as a means of resolving problems. Is this a kind of didacticism? Perhaps the difference in the didacticism of later works in comparison with books like *Goody Two-Shoes* is that the author of the latter moralizes on personal and individual matters whereas the later writers are concerned with more general political issues.

Inevitably fiction writers often take the moral issues which affect their characters as central themes in their fiction and the author will have a view on these issues and may be sorely tempted to show his own view in the best light. The temptation should be resisted and attempts made to be even-handed.

DIEGESIS

Diegesis is a story's space-time continuum, the story's individual universe which may not be exactly that of real life even in an apparently naturalistic story. A soap opera like *EastEnders* has a patina of realism about it but does it really represent a naturalistic community with truly believable people and events? Any one event may seem plausible but the series as a whole and what happens stretches belief. The series has created a fictional world of its own.

The notion of diegesis can most easily be appreciated with an example which is further from everyday reality. If one considers the series of six *Star Wars* films, they all contain a common 'world' which is quite different from our real world. The diegesis of *Star Wars* is an alien universe even though it includes recognizable human emotions and characteristics in some of its inhabitants.

The Western novel and film has a different diegesis and while the space-time continuum of Westerns is recognizable over a large number of films, it is disputable whether such a world as is represented ever really existed. Similarly, the world of the detective story, while having a patina of reality about it, creates its own world, a world where frequently a single detective solves a crime.

The diegesis of Kenneth Grahame's *The Wind in the Willows* is distinctive. Most readers suspend disbelief while reading the novel and appreciate the humour and the simulation of human emotions which exist within the created animal world which is of course a complete fantasy.

DYSTOPIAN NOVEL

Whereas the utopian novel is about a good or ideal society or world, the dystopian novel describes an imaginary society which is undesirable or even horrifying but which is feasible in the light of the way in which human nature and people's use of science is progressing. Writers who write dystopian novels usually intend to warn the reader of some danger.

The twentieth century began with a belief that science would lead to a better world but misuse of science, and the First World War (1914–1918) in particular, caused disillusionment, especially among writers, and so dystopian rather than utopian novels became a recognized genre. H. G. Wells continued to write utopian novels for some time but even he succumbed to pessimism and disillusionment in his final years, largely because of the invention and use of the atomic bomb in the Second World War. His last book, *Mind at the End of its Tether* (1945) is like a cry of despair by a man who had been almost congenitally optimistic about the possibilities of scientific progress. This book is not a novel.

One of the outstanding dystopias of the twentieth century is *Brave New World* (1932) by Aldous Huxley. Huxley is particularly interesting because he partially overcame his disillusionment and thirty years later in 1962 he wrote a utopian novel called *Island*. Writing about the use he himself had made of modern psychology and science, he tried to show how human beings could live in harmony. The title of the novel, however, suggests that only some human beings could do this, and they have to create their utopia on an island while the rest of humankind continues in its misguided ways.

Brave New World is interesting also because the dystopia is actually a happy place for the inhabitants; it is just that their happiness is artificially created and at the expense of their true humanity. They are born in test tubes, conditioned to be what is necessary to their society and also conditioned to be happy with their lot whether it be a scientist or a dustman. Huxley appears to conclude that we need unhappiness to appreciate happiness. We need some suffering in our lives in order to enjoy better times. In other words, even if Utopia were possible, it would be undesirable because we would no longer be human.

The other very well known dystopia in the twentieth century is George Orwell's *Nineteen Eighty-Four* (1949). This is a much more political novel than Huxley's and Orwell envisages the world becoming more totalitarian and repressive. Although 1984 is now some time in the past, the future state which Orwell conjured up in the novel still provides a healthy warning to us even though things have not yet panned out as badly as he thought. One of the interests to the reader of any utopian or dystopian novel is to judge what the author got right and wrong when imagining the future. Both Orwell and Huxley have been proved prescient in much of what they wrote.

There have been many dystopian novels written over the last 100 years, some with broad canvases like those of Orwell and Huxley, whereas other writers pinpoint a particular undesirable feature of our society. For instance *A Clockwork Orange* (1962) by Anthony Burgess concentrates on the possibility of conditioning people using psychological methods and concludes that even if we could make criminals better people, it would be undesirable because it would reduce the human being to a trained animal or zombie.

Catch-22 (1961) by Joseph Heller focuses on the absurd way in which human beings think that they can solve problems by making war. *The Handmaid's Tale* (1985) by Margaret Atwood explores how women are subjugated in a theocratic, totalitarian state and stripped of any independence.

The dystopian novel is probably more popular than its utopian counterpart for two reasons. Rather perversely, we as readers are often more interested in negative things than positive ones and just writing about people being happy in their lives and work (as in the utopian novel) is not very engrossing. Second, most people genuinely do not see much possibility now of life and its problems improving, except in minor ways. As soon as diseases are conquered, new ones appear. War and disharmony between nations continues now as it always did. Religion and race seem to raise insuperable problems. Needless to say, to write a convincing utopian or dystopian novel, the writer must be possessed of considerable scientific knowledge and possibly political knowledge as well as a fertile imagination. Writing the dystopian novel will also involve research.

See also SCIENCE FICTION; UTOPIA (UTOPIAN NOVEL)

EDITION

An edition is a complete single printing run of a book or a single version of a book. Some books go into many editions, some may not go beyond the first. The actual number of copies of an edition is decided by the publisher. Book collectors usually collect only first editions.

EDITORIAL DEPARTMENT

The editorial department of a publisher consists of the employees involved in commissioning books, editing, copyediting, and sometimes acquiring permissions (for the use of quotations, pictures, etc.).

ELLIPSES

Ellipses are most commonly used to indicate the omission of a letter from a word (such as 'o'er' for 'over') or the omission of one or more words from a sentence or quotation (such as the use of leader dots as in '. . . the root of all evil' for 'The love of money is the root of all evil'). This is more often called elision.

In fiction or narrative, *ellipses* refers to the omission of events and details which are unimportant to the plot and would in fact detract from its development. So a day in the life of a character in a novel would consist of exposition of events important to the plot and omit the character's eating of meals, slipping out to the supermarket, bathing, answering the door to a salesman and so on. Life consists of many routine and boring necessities, fiction omits these for the most part and thus provides a somewhat heightened version of the reality of its characters. Absolute realism would include everything; but would readers want it?

Ellipses are essential for the writer of fiction. On the whole, what should be included and what omitted should not present any problems.

See also PLOT AND STORY

EMPATHY

Empathy is a term derived from the German word *einfuhlung* meaning 'feeling into'. Empathy is an identification with things or people. Someone watching a boxing match may show on their face similar expressions to one of the boxers and even punch their fists, they are getting so involved. With regard to the novel and theatre; we may identify with or empathize with a character – feel as they feel, even feel as if we are doing what they are doing. The degree to which different people empathize with a character is contentious and immeasurable, but most people have experienced empathy in connection with characters or situations in literature. It seems to be a matter of putting oneself in the other's place and understanding their feelings in a very vivid way.

The writer, however, can never guarantee that empathy will occur for the reader even when the writer hopes it might. Writing the character or incident as well as possible is all a writer can do.

See also PATHOS AND BATHOS; SYMPATHY

EPIGRAM

An epigram is a short, witty saying or remark, either written or spoken. It can be simply funny, satiric, pointed or critical. Some authors are good at composing epigrams and they place them appropriately in their fiction. It may be that the writer creates a character who is noted for being epigrammatic. The word is also used to describe a short, witty poem, usually with a point being made at the end of it.

The dramatist, Oscar Wilde (1854–1900), is renowned for the use of epigrams in his plays. Many of his characters, rather unnaturally, seem able to utter them spontaneously. Here are just a few of Wilde's epigrams:

> I can resist everything except temptation.

> Work is the curse of the drinking classes.

> Education is an admirable thing, but it is well to remember from time to time that nothing that is worth knowing can be taught.

> A thing is not necessarily true because a man dies for it.

See also APHORISM; EPIGRAPH

EPIGRAPH

An epigraph is a quotation which is placed at the beginning of a novel and which relates to the main theme of the novel. Sometimes additional epigraphs precede each chapter or section of the book and they will relate specifically to a theme in that chapter or section.

An example is the epigraph given in E. M. Forster's novel *Howards End* (1910). The epigraph is 'Only connect!' and, rather unusually, it is part of something one of the characters in the novel says. (Usually an epigraph is a quotation from a famous writer or person.) Forster's epigraph alerts the reader to the importance of this statement when it is made: 'Only connect! That was the whole of her sermon. Only connect the prose and the passion, and both will be exalted, and human love will be seen at its height.' The same epigraph also refers to a related theme in the novel: the fact that different social classes find difficulty in making connections.

See also APHORISM; EPIGRAM

EPIPHANY

Epiphany refers to the manifestation of a god. In the Christian calendar 6 January is the Feast of the Epiphany, the manifestation of Christ to the Magi.

James Joyce used the word and gave it a literary meaning. He suggested that ordinary objects or sometimes people, apparently out of the blue, might take on a radiance and provide a sudden positive revelation to the observer. The experience was intuitive, a sudden experience of great understanding. In real life some people have said that it came to them suddenly and without thought what they should do with the rest of their lives. This would be the equivalent of a Joycean epiphany. Perhaps Joyce called it an epiphany because it is akin to a religious experience in that there is no rational explanation for the feeling.

The most famous of a number of such epiphanies is in Joyce's *A Portrait of the Artist as a Young Man* (1916) when the protagonist, Stephen, sees a girl paddling in the sea and is overwhelmed by the sight. There is clearly a sexual element in Stephen's response, but this is not always the case with epiphanies. A cynical critic has observed that Stephen is not alone in getting an overwhelming feeling at the sight of a pretty girl and would not call it an epiphany. In Joyce's collection of stories the *Dubliners* (1914) each of the fifteen stories is said to contain an epiphany. The best-known of these is in the last story *The Dead* when a husband attending a party sees a look on his wife's face when she is standing at the top of some stairs and is overwhelmed with loving feelings for her. Ironically she later confesses to him that the look was caused by the memory of her first lover many years ago.

Most people will have had an experience where an ordinary object has taken on some inexplicable significance. Critics, however, are uncertain whether these experiences need be given a special name, and in literature significant things and experiences can be described without resort to suggesting they have mystical connotations. Such incidents appeared in literature before Joyce and will continue to do so.

EPISTOLARY NOVEL

The epistolary novel is one that is told entirely in the form of letters. It is a technique used by one of the earliest English novelists, Samuel Richardson (1689–1761) in his novels *Pamela, or Virtue Rewarded* and *Clarissa*. It is a technique which has gone out of fashion probably because it is limiting and gives an impression of artificiality. Recently it has been modified so emails or telephone calls have been used, but usually only in the short story form. Occasionally novels have been written which are simply single letters giving only one point of view on an event. A recent example is *Incendiary* (2005) by Chris Cleave. This novel gained some publicity because it was about a wife's supposed letter to a terrorist after a terrorist attack in London which killed her husband and nearly a thousand other people. Coincidentally, it was published on the same day that a terrorist attack occurred in London on the 7 July, 2005.

See also POINT OF VIEW

ERRATUM SLIP

The author, copy editor and proofreader are responsible for ensuring the accuracy of everything in a book but if an error slips through an erratum slip may be inserted into the printed copy pointing out the error or errors.

ESCAPIST FICTION

Literature is often divided by critics into the more serious kind and escapist work. Escapist fiction is, as the name implies, a means of escaping from the rigours of everyday life and its problems. It is regarded as a way of relaxing rather than overworking the brain. Escapist literature is hard to define but it consists of novels, stories and plays with some or all of the following characteristics:

- It is easy to read with a straightforward linear storyline.
- Language is undemanding.
- Characterization is basic with clear-cut good and bad characters who are judged by their actions rather than some inner motivation.
- The characters serve the plot rather than the plot arising from the characters.
- The ending is clear-cut, probably happy or at least with the protagonist achieving what he or she set out to.
- Action is important.
- A moral, if there is one, will be spelt out. Readers will not be invited to contemplate moral dilemmas.

Popular best-sellers usually come into the category of escapist fiction although sometimes a more serious work becomes popular. Popular romance, detective stories, science fiction and adventure stories are usually categorized as escapist, but there are always exceptions. Ruth Rendell's Inspector Wexford series of detective stories are regarded as escapist, but Rendell writes more serious psychological crime stories under the pseudonym of Barbara Vine.

See also CHARACTERS; FICTION; PLOT AND STORY; SUSPENSE

EUPHEMISM

The term euphemism comes from the Greek *euphemos* meaning 'to speak well' or 'fair of speech'. Euphemistic words or phrases are mild words and expressions used in place of harsh, blunt, crude or vulgar ones. Linguists might argue that words are neutral but everyone realizes that some words with the same or similar meanings are more acceptable than their alternatives, some are considered to be downright offensive. Context must dictate, and the speaker or writer of the word must decide which is the most appropriate for the purpose. We would expect a doctor to request a sample of 'urine', not 'piss'.

The following subjects are the main ones that contain words for which euphemisms are often used. The main word or phrase is given on the left and some euphemisms are shown on the right:

Death; dead, died	went the way of all flesh
	passed on
	slipped away
	went west
	gone to his/her rest
	kicked the bucket

Sometimes the euphemistic word itself requires a euphemism. We may use the term 'kicked the bucket' in some contexts to detract from the seriousness of death, but it would be insensitive to use this phrase in front of the recently bereaved.

Parts of the body

nudity, nakedness	au naturel, in one's birthday suit
breasts	boobs, bust, cleavage
posterior, arse	bottom, butt, backside
genitals, penis/vagina	privates, ha'penny, jewels, muff, pills

Bodily functions

fart	break wind, raspberry, let off
defecation/urination	call of nature, number one/two, pee,
pissing/shitting	piddle, the trots
vomiting	chunder, heave, upchuck
sweat	perspire, in a lather

Clothes

| knickers, brassieres, | underwear, lingerie, smalls, |
| | unmentionables |

Sexual relations

| sexual intercourse | making love, Ugandan affairs, having it |
| | off, shagging |

Other subjects which contain words for which there are euphemisms include:

bathrooms/lavatory menstruation religion race homosexuality war, disability, old age, drugs, job titles

The subjects of euphemism change over time. Euphemisms are less used now about sexual matters, parts of the body and prostitution than they were in the nineteenth century. Today we are more sensitive (or at least our governments are) on the subjects of war, weaponry, and military conflict. Their effects are softened by the use of euphemisms such as 'collateral damage' and 'friendly fire' to hide something more violent and deadly. Euphemisms tend to arise in connection with subjects which society at a particular time is sensitive about.

Religious euphemism has also declined and people are more open about the use of religious words. In Old Testament times the word for God, Yahweh, could not be written in full. When writing about God only initials were used. We have no such compunctions now but respect for other people's religion often involves being careful about the language used.

There are thousands of euphemistic words as can be seen by consulting a dictionary of euphemism (see Further Reading and Useful Websites).

See also CONNOTATION AND DENOTATION; SLANG AND SWEARING

EUPHUISM

Euphuism is a very ornate and elaborate style of writing which uses a range of figures of speech. The word comes from the Greek meaning 'well-endowed'; it is prose well-endowed with fanciful flourishes. In 1578 and 1580 John Lily wrote two narratives, *Euphues, the anatomy of wyt* and *Euphues and his England,* both of which demonstrate this with its use of antithesis, similes, metaphors, allusions and mythology.

Few prose writers admire or use euphuism today. Most are more concerned with plainness of language with an emphasis on communication and limited and careful use of figures of speech. Writers who indulge in euphuism would be accused of being 'high flown' or 'pretentious'. Occasional passages in a novel may stray towards the euphuistic in order to highlight some important incident or idea. Probably one of the most euphuistic novels is Oscar Wilde's *The Portrait of Dorian Gray* (1891).

See also PURPLE PASSAGE

EXISTENTIALISM (EXISTENTIAL NOVEL)

Existentialism is a philosophy (some would say a pseudo-philosophy) that is difficult to define because it embraces different thinkers and writers with divergent ideas and beliefs or non-beliefs. Because of the complexity of the subject, this entry will confine itself to identifying some of existentialism's main themes and mentioning some of its important exponents who wrote fiction.

It is important in the history of nineteenth- and twentieth-century literature if for no other reason than that existentialism produced some significant novelists and dramatists. Unlike traditional philosophers who frequently indulge in abstract thought at the expense of more practical, human matters, existentialists try to work everything out in terms of individual human beings and their problems. Many of them are attracted to the novel or drama as a way of conveying and working out their ideas.

The following example demonstrates the difference. A writer attended a lecture given by a linguistic philosopher who spent an hour considering the difference between two statements: 'The box is on the table' and 'The table is under the box'. Few members of the audience felt that it was a problem which had practical application for their everyday lives. The existential philosopher, on the other hand, is likely to take bigger issues such as the extent to which life is worth living in the light of the possibility of suicide.

Many exponents of philosophy and religion since ancient Greek times have contended that good and ethical systems are, or should be, the same for everyone. Existentialists, since the work of the Danish Søren Kierkegaard, reject this idea and claim that good and truth are subjective. Just as beauty is in the eye of the beholder, so is truth. 'I must find a truth that is true for me', Kierkegaard said. This *freedom* and *choice* become the key concepts of the existentialists, although Jean-Paul Sartre later modified what may have become a purely selfish philosophy by arguing that the existentialist's freedom of choice must not interfere with the freedom and choice of others. Thus a high degree of individual responsibility is important in modern existentialism.

Sartre also coined a phrase which has become almost a mantra of existentialism '*existence precedes essence*' (we exist first and determine our existence by choice). Most religions and political systems have an idea of what constitutes Christian, Muslim or Sikh behaviour. Codes of conduct are laid down; the law and religions uphold them. Existentialism acknowledges no essence or essential human being, each existence is individual and that individual must work out his or her own salvation. Again *freedom* and *choice* are the key words.

Of course most people find existentialism problematic because it leads to an uncomfortable state of existence compared with one where everything is laid down for all individuals in a moral code or set of rules. The existentialists must work out all possibilities for themselves and then make their choices. For this reason, existentialists suggest that they are often in a state of angst, anguish or anxiety, as they confront the many possibilities of what they must do with their lives and how they should behave. There is no simple book of rules for them. At its extreme, Sartre shows how angst can lead to a state of nausea where even everyday objects appear to be alien to the sufferer.

All this leads to another important feature of existentialism: that the human world is not ordered and rational but absurd. The feelings of an individual living in an absurd world are probably best conveyed in Albert Camus' novel *The Outsider*. The existential novel will frequently portray the central character as isolated or alienated from his social milieu and other people – a person living in an absurd world.

The following authors deal with various existential themes although not all of them would have accepted the label 'existentialist'. Indeed, the term was not used much until the twentieth century but exponents of existential ideas date back many centuries.

Henri Barbusse (1873–1935)
Samuel Beckett (1906–1989)
Albert Camus (1913–1960)
Fyodor Dostoevsky (1821–1881)
Eugène Ionesco (1909–1994)
John Fowles (1926–2005)
Franz Kafka (1883–1924)
Jean Genet (1910–1986)
Ernest Hemingway (1899–1961)
Jean-Paul Sartre (1905–1980)

See also ABSURD LITERATURE

EXPOSITION

Exposition is a general term which refers to detailed description of an event, person, theory, problem, situation or a combination of these. With regard to fiction, exposition usually refers to the opening of the story or drama that sets the scene and introduces the main character or characters. It frequently also suggests the nature of the story and the problem of the protagonist. It supplies background information which is necessary for the reader to understand what happens later and why. There may be further exposition when completely new characters or situations enter the story but the initial exposition is the most important. Some writers, however, may write an opening sequence to a novel which is a kind of hook to entice the reader and then follow this with the exposition.

It may seem straightforward enough to introduce the characters, setting and situation but a simple description which merely provides the facts is uninteresting and authors often write an exposition which is indirect and attractive but also gets over the essential information.

The opening of Charles Dickens' *Our Mutual Friend* (1865) illustrates an exposition which seems straightforward but in fact the symbolism later reveals the River Thames as a source of life and death.

> In these times of ours, though concerning the exact date there is no need to be precise, a boat of dirty and disreputable appearance, with two figures in it, floated on the Thames, between Southwark Bridge, which is of iron, and London Bridge which is of stone, as an autumn evening was drawing in.
>
> The figures in this boat were those of a strong man with ragged, grizzled hair and a sun-browned face, and a dark girl of nineteen or twenty, sufficiently like him to be recognisable as his daughter. The girl rowed, pulling a pair of sculls very easily; the man, with the rudder-lines slack in his hands, and his hands loose in his waistband, kept an eager look-out. He had no net, hook, or line, and he could not be a fisherman; his boat had no cushion for a sitter, no paint, no inscription, no appliance beyond a rusty boat-hook and a coil of rope, and he could not be a waterman; his boat was too crazy and too small to take in cargo for delivery, and he could not be a lighterman or river carrier [. . .] he directed his daughter by a movement of his head. She watched his face earnestly as he watched the river. But in the intensity of her look there was a touch of dread or horror.

In this exposition, Dickens gives some essential details of the pair and what they are doing but he deliberately holds some things back to create suspense and mystery. The reader is told what the man isn't rather than what he is, and the last line of the paragraph suggests it is not something pleasant; but for the moment, the reader can only guess. The writer here vividly conveys the setting of the dark, dirty river. His reference at the beginning that there is no need to be precise about the year is not vagueness but rather the fact that what happens in the novel has happened before and is likely to go on happening. In a huge novel like this with many important characters other expository sequences occur as they are introduced.

The following opening from Sussana Moore's *In the Cut* (1995) uses a much more indirect form of exposition:

> I don't usually go to a bar with one of my students. It is almost always a mistake.
> But Cornelius was having trouble with irony.

Without telling the reader directly, in just a few lines, we have learnt that the narrator is a college lecturer who is fairly formal and perhaps not entirely successful at what she teaches. At this stage the reader does not know that the narrator is female but a few lines further on she again indirectly informs the reader 'I am beginning to sound like one of the spinster ladies who used to take an interest in me in boarding school . . .'

In addition there is an implied reason why she may be rather formal and that she went to boarding school also reveals something of her background. In a few lines the character and setting are introduced. These are expended and the protagonist's main problem is established in the rest of the first chapter.

Exposition can be conveyed by dialogue; one character telling another something can be a useful means of conveying information to the reader. Care must be taken with this method. Note the following conversation between a husband and wife:

> 'We've not taken the kids anywhere together for ages. Why don't we take them to the bug house at the zoo? You know you're interested in entomology'. Jane tried to interest her husband in a trip out.
> 'Well, I'll think about it', Jack said.

Assuming the writer wished to convey Jack's interest in entomology this is a clumsy and unnatural way of doing it. They both must have known it so why would she say this?

Exposition is an interesting example of how fiction demonstrates the art, rather than just the practice of writing. The introduction of character, setting and the character's problems could be stated very simply but this would invariably lead to a very dull introduction. The three methods mentioned (direct but withholding detail, indirect and dialogue) together with the examples demonstrate how something can be rendered evocatively rather than mundanely. Consider alternatives to Dickens' exposition. There are many ways in which he could have introduced the Thames, his two characters and what they were doing. His choice adds mystery, suspense and atmosphere.

There are other methods which can be used. A newspaper or police report could be quoted, the author could plunge straight into an action scene; a first person report by a subsidiary character might provide the exposition; a letter could do the same. There are numerous possibilities.

Sometimes a simple word or phrase might establish something for the reader. A mention of Tate Modern indicates a London scene – and possibly a character's interest in art. Arthur's Seat or Princes Street would conjure up Edinburgh; the Angel of the North, the environs of Newcastle upon Tyne. The mention of handbag or lipstick suggests a female character. Character might be indicated by 'said with a choked off giggle' (nervousness), 'avoiding her eyes' (lack of confidence), 'made no attempt to come forward' (reticence), 'jumped around like a banshee' (excitement).

Clearly whether the novel is a first or third person narrative will have a bearing on the exposition. The first-person narrator is likely to reveal things about him or herself even if they appear to be telling the reader about other characters or events. Often the first person narrator will be the central character as in George Orwell's *Coming Up for Air* (1939). It is a novel about a man who, at the age of forty-five, decides to leave his wife, children and job to find fulfilment in his life. Notice how in this opening, there is the beginning of character exposition even though the character is describing his home and morning routine:

> The idea really came to me the day I got my new false teeth. I remem-
> ber the morning well. At about a quarter-to-eight I'd nipped out of bed
> and got into the bathroom just in time to shut the kids out. It was a
> beastly January morning, with a dirty, yellowish-grey sky. Down below,
> out of the little square of bathroom window, I could see the ten yards
> by five of grass, with a privet hedge round it and a bare patch in the
> middle, that we call the back garden. There's the same back garden,
> same privets, and same grass, behind every house in Ellesmere Road.
> Only difference – where there are no kids there's no bare patch in the
> middle.

It is all there at the beginning: the routine, the boredom, the dullness and sameness. Who would not want to escape from this? And notice that marvellous first sentence.

See also DIALOGUE; OPENINGS; PLOT AND STORY

FABLE

A fable is a very short story in which the characters are usually animals or inanimate objects with human traits. Fables are a very old form of story, the earliest known being attributed to Aesop in the sixth century BC. Some are satirical or critical of human foibles. There is invariably a moral, meaning or observation on human behaviour in the fable. Often the moral is spelt out at the end of the fable. An example is 'Slow and steady wins the race' at the end of *The Hare and the Tortoise*. This is a curious fable because slow and steady never won the hundred yards dash!

Fables were not devised specifically for children but their brevity and cast of animal characters have earned them popularity with younger readers. The moral element probably endorsed their suitability for children. William Caxton, Britain's first printer, published a collection of fables in 1484.

Apart from Aesop, the French writer, Jean de la Fontaine in the seventeenth century wrote many fables. Fables are found in a number of cultures and countries including Russia and Negro America (the Brer Rabbit stories of 1880).

Few fables are written today but the old ones continue to be republished and short stories for children about animals are, of course, still popular.

See also DIDACTICISM; FAIRY TALES; PLOT AND STORY

FABULA AND SJUŽHET

These terms are part of Russian Formalist or Structuralist theory of story or narrative. *Fabula* refers to the chronological series of events in the narrative, the story or content of the narrative. If a person summarized the story of a whole novel in, say, 2000 words, they would end up with an account of the main events of the *fabula*. *Sjužhet* refers to the way the story is told; that is, whether it is told chronologically or by means of occasional flashbacks and flash forwards, and whatever other literary devices or figures of speech the author may choose. It also includes whether the story was told in first- or third- person narrative, whether the first person was a character in the novel or whether multiple narrators were used.

The *fabula* is more or less constant once the story has been decided upon; but that story can usually be told in a number of different ways. In other words, the *sjužhet* can vary. One critic described the *fabula* as the skeleton of the story. Graham Swift's *Last Orders* is a novel about the lives of half a dozen characters and their relationships. The story is about the death of one of the men and how the other men take his ashes to be scattered in the sea. The story could have been told chronologically by a third-person narrator. Instead Swift begins with the journey after the funeral of the men to the seaside and different characters, in flashback, tell their stories. The *fabula* (the chronological series of events of the overall story) in Swift's *sjužhet* is given a non-chronological treatment and varied points of view on the events of the past and present.

Whatever story an author thinks up, that is only half the task. Equally important is deciding the best way to tell it, for many writers the latter causes more problems than the first. The *sjužhet* is something every writer of fiction should consider very seriously. Too many beginning writers just start writing and get locked into a form for their story that may not be the ideal one. There are always many ways of telling a story and clearly the writer should spend some time deciding which one will be best for the task in hand.

FAIRY TALES

Fairy tales are stories set in an indefinite past and they concern fantastical and magical events with an abundance of giants, ogres, wizards, dwarfs, witches, dragons and other strange creatures. Frequently human characters are part of the stories as well. In *Hansel and Gretel* the main characters are human but a witch also plays an important part in the story.

Fairly tales were originally part of an oral tradition of storytelling in many countries from Ireland to Australia and they were modified as they were handed down. In Britain fairy tales were published in book form in the seventeenth century. Some of them were taken from French and Italian publications.

Although fantastical in content, many of the stories are rooted in the aspirations, concerns and fears of ordinary people and those of children in particular. In times when life expectancy was not very long, many children were orphaned and hence a number of stories portray wicked stepmothers. Violence was a part of many people's lives and this too is reflected in some stories. Death as a subject is not avoided. In modern versions of the tales, the violence is often toned down or omitted. In an early version of *Rumplestiltskin* the little man stamps his foot in anger so hard that it goes through the floorboards and in retrieving it he severs his leg and goes off on the bleeding stump. *Snow White* originally was a much more violent and bloody tale than the one found in most books for children today.

Psychologists have suggested that the tales reflect human fears and desires and hearing them or reading them helps children come to terms with some of the darker aspects of growing up and of the adult world. Other psychologists completely reject this view.

The authors of many of the oldest fairy tales are unknown. These include most of the tales collected by Jacob and Wilhelm Grimm from Frankfurt (1785–1863, 1786–1859) who spent a good part of their lives tracing and collecting folk songs and fairy tales. Some of their most famous discoveries were *Hansel and Gretel, Snow White and the Seven Dwarfs, Rumplestiltskin, The Golden Goose* and *The Twelve Dancing Princesses.*

The other name most associated with fairy tales is the Danish writer, Hans Christian Anderson (1805–1875). Whereas the Grimms simply collected stories, Anderson wrote over 150 himself although some were based on folk tales. He was also influenced by the *Arabian Nights* which had been read to him as a child. Some of his tales are optimistic but many reflect social concerns and his own deep pessimism, said to be a character trait caused by a poverty-stricken childhood (he was brought up in a slum) and his lack of success in love. Some of his most famous stories are *The Little Match Girl* (one of the most tragic fairy tales), *The Princess and the Pea, The Tinder Box, Big Claus and Little Claus* and *The Little Mermaid* (a love story verging on the sadistic).

Some modern authors pen new fairy stories but the traditional tales have retained their popularity and are likely to do so for some time. Oscar Wilde, possibly influenced by Hans Anderson, published a collection of fairy tales, *The Happy Prince*, in 1888. Like Anderson's, the stories portray a rather bitter view of life but children like them and they have never been out of print. Wilde is said to have written them for his own children. The best-known is probably *The Selfish Giant*. Wilde published a second collection in 1891. These were written as much for adults as for children. Many fairy tales appeal to adults as well as children which is fortunate since most parents have to read them to their offspring. Writers with an interest in children and fantasy may wish to try writing new fairy tales. Writers such as Angela Carter in *The Bloody Chamber* have adapted traditional fairy tales for an adult readership.

See also FRAME STORY

FAMILY SAGAS AND AGA SAGAS

A family saga is a novel that recounts the story of a family or sometimes interrelated families usually over a considerable period of time and involving a few generations of the families concerned. It frequently involves the family in major historical events (like a war, or the General Strike) and is always grounded in a particular geographical setting. The background and setting is well researched. There are likely to be relationships formed, relationships in difficulties and relationships broken. Similarly fortunes are often made, lost, and occasionally retrieved. Thus the rich life can be compared with relative hardship. Sometimes the family is ruled over by a matriarch or patriarch. The novels can be historical or concern the recent past.

The family saga is a genre that is both a staple part of popular fiction (they are often best-sellers) and also serious literary fiction. Among literary examples of family sagas in the twentieth century are:

The Forsyte Saga by John Galsworthy (1922) followed by sequels.
All That Swagger by Miles Franklin (1936). Franklin was the pseudonym of the acclaimed writer of the coming of age story, *My Brilliant Career* (1901).
Roots by Alex Haley (1976).
The House of Spirits by Isabel Allende (1982).

While all of these novels have been very popular (helped by TV and film versions), the best-selling authors of family sagas today are Susan Howitch and Philippa Carr.

The Aga saga is a spin-off from the family saga. It tends to cover a shorter period in the life of its characters and rather than being about distinctive families, the Aga saga may concern itself with a cross section of a community, usually a rural community. The name Aga saga refers to the fact that the characters are usually middle class, reasonably affluent and may well have an Aga cooker.

As in the family saga, the social and geographical settings of these novels are accurate and perceptive. This is certainly the case with Joanna Trollope, often thought of as the seminal writer of Aga sagas, although her literary scope is much wider. Her novels *The Choir* (1988), *A Village Affair* (1989) and *The Rector's Wife* (1991) are examples of Aga sagas and their subjects cover birth, death, romance, love, loss, fear of change and the whole gamut of human emotion.

Although there are other important elements in them, Emily Brontë's *Wuthering Heights* and Jane Austen's novels could be described as family sagas. One of the best-selling novelists of all time, Catherine Cookson, frequently wrote family sagas.

See also STORY AND NOVEL CATEGORIES

FANTASY FICTION

Whereas science fiction usually speculates on possible developments on present science and technology and the effects of these on humanity, fantasy fiction is concerned with a world, people and artefacts that may bear only a passing relationship with ours. It is largely imaginary, with fantastic people, animals and objects that do not behave like those in our world. Fantasy fiction, in effect, is magical and there is no pretence that things are realistic or natural.

An example known to almost everyone is *Alice's Adventures in Wonderland*, the 1865 novel by Lewis Carroll (1832–98). In the story, Alice falls down a well into a strange land where she can become gigantic or tiny by eating a magic mushroom. She meets odd, talking animals and the Queen of Hearts and she has strange adventures. Another well-known children's fantasy is Frank L. Baum's *The Wonderful Wizard of Oz* (1900). This is the story of a child being swept away into a strange land of weird creatures and unusual adventures. Both are scary, funny and full of adventure.

The previous two books were written for children but like much fantasy they also appealed to many adults. The eighteenth- and nineteenth- century Gothic stories are an early kind of fantasy that was principally for adults.

The Hobbit and *The Lord of the Rings* by J. R. R. Tolkein are fantasy novels more for adults although the former was written with children in mind. Some serious themes are tackled by Tolkein but the landscape and figures in his world are as imaginary as those of Carroll or Baum.

In the twentieth century there are two strands of fantasy written for adults. First, there are novels and stories by authors such as Angela Carter, Gabriel Garcia Marquez, Milan Kundera and Fay Weldon that mix fantasy and realism and where the overall aim is to comment seriously on the modern world. Some of these novels are usually termed magic realism.

A more obviously escapist form of fantasy is called 'Sword and Sorcery'. Robert E. Howard's *Conan the Barbarian* (1930) is an example which had many sequels, and Howard had many imitators. Battles and hand-to-hand combat are mixed with magic landscapes, wizards, witches, evil and good queens and princesses. Another example of the sword and sorcery genre is Richard Corben's *Neverwhere* (1968).

Possibly one of the most popular fantasies of recent years is Joss Whedon's *Buffy the Vampire Slayer*. This began as a 1992 film, then in 1997 it was made into a TV series (which ran for some years) and there have been spin-off novels as well as books about Buffy and her art. Fantasy fans, like science fiction fans, frequently take their characters very seriously. In the case of Buffy, the fan base is teenagers and adults as it is with most fantasy. The most successful literary fantasies of the last decade have been the Harry Potter books by J. K. Rowling beginning with *Harry Potter and the Philosopher's Stone* (1997).

Anything goes in the fantasy novel and there is no necessity for anything to be explained rationally. For those who embrace fantasy, magic is sufficient explanation.

See also GOTHIC FICTION; HORROR AND VAMPIRE STORIES; MAGIC REALISM; SCIENCE FICTION; STORY AND NOVEL CATEGORIES

FICTION

In a book concerned with the elements of fiction, a general definition of the term may seem superfluous. Nonetheless, there may be some merit in considering the difficulty of finding a concise, satisfactory definition.

One suggests that fiction is about made up characters and events which are not true. Another suggests that works of fiction are works of the human imagination, describing untrue and imaginary people and events. Most definitions emphasize these points – the use of the imagination in creating fiction, and the fact that fiction is concerned with events and characters that are made up rather than true.

If we take any single novel as an example of fiction, these definitions seem to be accurate but they beg a number of questions. (Non-fiction novels are the exception.)

It is beyond the scope of this book to go into what is meant by *imagination* but it is quite clear that characters, for instance, do not usually come entirely from an author's mind or imagination but are usually a composite of personalities that the author has known, read about or heard about. By putting the character with others into situations which the original people never experienced, the author has created a character that appears made up, original and not a simple representation of a real person. Occasionally, of course, a novelist may base a character very closely on a friend or acquaintance. D. H. Lawrence and Aldous Huxley did this and lost friends in the process.

If this is accepted as a likely process which most authors undertake, the idea of making up characters is not necessarily a complete act of the author's mind and imagination; rather it is a careful construction from aspects of characters which were, indeed, known and true.

Even clearer is the fact that settings and events in novels are usually based on real places and occurrences, although the author's task is often to put the events, along with the characters into unusual combinations. Even fantasies and science fiction stories, although superficially untrue and not set in recognizable places, may reveal truths about human behaviour.

If these observations are generally accepted, it explains a remark made by the artist Pablo Picasso who observed that the lies of art tell us great truths. It is this as much as anything which has afforded literature the high status it enjoys in most societies. It can convey emotional truth and understanding of the human condition in a way which so-called factual writing often cannot convey – even though the actual events and characters in the fiction are not true. The contemporary novelist Julian Barnes remarked in an interview broadcast on the BBC in May 2005 that 'Fiction is a pack of lies that is true'.

It is also useful to consider fiction from the reader's point of view. Why are millions and millions of hours spent annually on reading things which aren't true? There is nothing mysterious about the answer to this. Students, when asked why they read fiction almost invariably say they do so for pleasure. A second reason frequently given is that it enlarges their knowledge and understanding of other people and the situations they get into. It enlarges, in a sense, their understanding of the human world.

The second point above suggests a commonly accepted notion of the nature of fiction – that there are two types: what is sometimes called literary fiction on the one hand and, on the other hand, popular fiction. It is the former which is probably better suited to enlarging our understanding of human behaviour, but that does not mean that it should not entertain as well. Popular fiction, too, may help us to learn about people, but it tends to concentrate on the entertaining element and in some cases it may be unrealistic both in characterization and plot. Popular fiction tends to be categorized into genres such as thriller, detective, adventure, light romance and science fiction. The distinctions, however, are not hard and fast. Many novels straddle the dividing line between literary and popular fiction and some critics would dismiss this categorization altogether.

Fiction writers display great skill, art and imagination in the way they construct their stories. We have probably all had the experience of saying after reading an impressive novel or story, I've never read anything like that before or how did the author think of that?

See also THE CANON; FANTASY FICTION; GENRE; INTERTEXTUALITY; NON-FICTION NOVEL; NOVEL

FIGURES OF SPEECH

Figures of speech are literary devices that take use of language beyond the ordinary in order to achieve some special effect or meaning. They are used mainly in poetry but also in prose and in everyday discourse. The most common figures of speech are similes and metaphors.

See also HYPERBOLE; IRONY; METONYMY AND SYNECDOCHE; PERSONIFICATION

FLASH FICTION

Flash fiction is an American term given to fiction variously defined by some as being up to 500 words long and by others as up to 1,000 words long – certainly no more. Flash fiction often contains only one character but they are not always first-person narratives. A large cast is inadvisable. Fiction of this brevity is said to have been encouraged by the demands of the internet for short pieces that are easily read on-screen. Certainly examples can be found on the internet but some magazines over the years have published very short fiction and competitions for very short stories have been held.

Writing very short fiction can be a useful exercise in story writing. To make a complete story with a rudimentary plot and characters is not easy, beginners are frequently tempted to write more than is necessary and not to prune or edit.

There are certain guidelines to be kept in mind in order to write successful flash fiction. Obviously there is no point in trying to cover, for instance, the life of a character over a period of time; so whereas the novel may trace the love, marriage and divorce of a couple as its basic material, the short fiction might take a single incident in a marriage and the ending might simply imply some closure. A story concerned with childhood might take but one incident of jealousy, a fight, winning or losing, discomfort or embarrassment.

In this kind of fiction this brief there is no time or space for preamble or scene setting. The scene must be identifiable from a short exposition which will probably simply remind the reader of a setting they already know something about – a shopping mall, a First World War battlefield, a classroom. All can be concisely conjured up. The action of the story should start straight away. Often in these stories the incident or characters are written so that there is some mystery about them but a revelation occurs at the end which explains everything. The surprise ending provides satisfaction in a story which cannot delineate character or incident in depth.

Flash fiction is sometimes referred to as sudden fiction.
See also MINI-SAGAS; TWIST ENDING STORIES

FLASHBACK

A flashback is a sequence in a novel or story that recounts an incident that occurred earlier than the point in time reached in the main narrative. It can be days, weeks or years earlier. The incident to which the reader is taken back must have some important significance for what is occurring in the novel's present time. It may help to explain a character's behaviour or state of mind or it may provide motivation for present actions; it may explain why the character has behaved in a particular way.

A possible scenario for the use of flashback would be a story showing at the beginning the protagonist in some dramatic situation, for example, in dire peril, lost in the desert, about to be killed by a madman. The reader would be left in suspense while a flashback explained how they had got into this situation.

A flashback is usually a sequence narrated in the same way as the rest of the novel; it is not merely a character remembering something and recounting it to another character (although clearly that is an alternative technique which could be used). A memory, of course, could spark off the flashback although, interestingly, it is possible that the flashback sequence is not remembered consciously by the character that it concerns.

Some argue that flashbacks should be used only if really necessary and as infrequently as possible because they can be confusing for the reader and they do not progress the main action of the story. To avoid reader confusion, the flashback should be clearly signalled in some way such as providing a few sentences at the beginning of the flashback to indicate the story has gone back in time. Similarly the end of the flashback or the return to the main narrative should be signalled. The whole sequence could also be placed between line gaps in the text which could begin and end with a series of stars (******).

Flashbacks are much easier to signal in a film: characters can be made to look younger; costumes can be dated; old-fashioned objects and vehicles may be used. The flashback sequence sometimes begins with a shadowy or framed screen.

A modern novel which uses extensive flashback is *Last Orders* by Graham Swift.

The term analepsis is also used for flashback.
See also FORESHADOWING (FLASH FORWARD)

FOCALIZATION

The term focalization is used more in film criticism than as a literary term. In the former, it means one of two things: (a) the action or scene is seen apparently through the eyes of a character and the audience sees just what this character can see; (b) an object can be focused on in order to highlight it because of its importance in the unfolding plot. For example, a character may be shown to have possession of a knife even though it is not used until much later. The first technique is used rather notoriously in the 1960 film *Peeping Tom* directed by Michael Powell in which a murderer photographs his victim at the moment of their death because a spike emerges from the camera. The audience sees what the murderer is looking at through the viewfinder. Having the camera apparently where the character's eyes are, or looking over the character's shoulder can also achieve this kind of focalization.

The most obvious focalization effect in literature is by the use of a first-person narrator or in novels where there is multiple first-person narration. In William Faulkner's novel *As I Lay Dying* (1930) a family takes their dead mother, by horse and cart, to the place where she chose to be buried. The novel, which is set in Missouri, is in sixty chapters or short sections, with the various members of the family narrating these sections. Each has different priorities and thus focuses on different things in spite of the overall purpose of taking their mother to be buried. For example, the father, Anse, is really more obsessed with getting a new set of false teeth in Jefferson; a naive daughter, Dewey Dell, is concerned about finding a cure for her unwanted pregnancy; an idiot son, Darl, is fixated on a dead fish because it is the only other thing he associates with death.

The type of focalization described in (b) above also plays a part in fiction, particularly thrillers or mystery stories. The art is to mention some object that is crucial to the solving of the mystery but without making it too obvious that it is later to play an important role in the story.

See also FOREGROUNDING; RED HERRING

FOLK TALES

Folk tales are short stories that have been passed on by oral tradition. Many have been collected and published. Folk tales are part of folklore and usually therefore reflect aspects of a culture or a country's beliefs and values. They are found in most countries. They are not now written. They always begin as 'told' stories, passed on by word of mouth. Some appear to have been written specially, such as *The Three Bears* (1837). (This has been attributed to the poet Robert Southey although some critics dispute this.) Some may regard *The Three Bears* as a fairy tale and there is a similarity between some folk tales and fairy tales. Fairy tales, fables, legends, tall stories, even shaggy dog stories sometimes came under the label folk tales.

See also FABLE; FAIRY TALES; LEGENDS

FOREGROUNDING

The school of literary critics of the 1920s and 30s known as the Russian Formalists noted that literary language differs from everyday language because of the use of particular techniques which draw attention to the language itself and in turn the subject matter is highlighted or foregrounded. This is mainly achieved by the use of literary devices or figures of speech such as similes, metaphors, onomatopoeia, repetition, alliteration, etc. In poetry the most common foregrounding techniques are rhythm and rhyme. Foregrounding is part of stylistics which is concerned with the study of literary language.

Foregrounding in prose fiction is achieved through the use of many of the same literary devices used in poetry but there are also some that are largely peculiar to fiction. *Fabula* and *sjužhet*, for instance, which are concerned with the content of a story and the different possibilities for presenting it: the use of flashback, for instance. Think also of the differences in the way a novelist might describe a street or a building in comparison with the way the same place would be described by an architect or a layperson. The fiction writer will tend to use foregrounding most at particularly important episodes in the story. *Highlighting* is a term sometimes used with the same meaning as foregrounding.

See also *FABULA* AND *SJUŽHET*; FIGURES OF SPEECH; FOCALIZATION; PURPLE PASSAGE

FORESHADOWING (FLASH FORWARD)

Foreshadowing is the revelation, early on in a story or novel, of something significant which actually happens much later in the chronological sequence of events. The foreshadowing may be a plain statement or may just be hinted at.

A good example is in Vladimir Nabokov's novel *Lolita* (1959). The novel is narrated by Humbert Humbert and on the very first page he writes: 'You can always count on a murderer for a fancy prose style'. So although the murder does not occur until near the end of the novel the reader knows from the beginning that the central character is going to murder someone. Clearly an author would not make such a revelation if the story was a simple murder mystery.

The important question is why does an author reveal an important event before it happens rather than follow the usual method of letting such events come as a surprise to the reader? In the case of *Lolita*, there is more than one possibility. Nabokov may wish to let the reader know that this is not the usual kind of suspense or crime novel where a murder might come as a surprise and the revelation of who did it is something to be worked out by the reader. He does, however, create another kind of suspense. The reader who keeps the early statement in mind may well be asking: who is the narrator going to kill and why? It is quite possible also that an early guess will be wrong. Another possibility is that the rather throwaway remark at the beginning demeans the importance of murder and, as the reader discovers, possibly worse things happen in this novel.

Whenever a story is read where foreshadowing occurs, it is worth asking why the author used it. Writers, if they are tempted to foreshadow, should make sure they have good reasons for doing so.

Foreshadowing is sometimes referred to as flash forward and prolepsis.

See also FLASHBACK

FRAME STORY

A frame story is a story which contains other, shorter stories within the main narrative or frame. Probably the most famous frame story is Chaucer's *Canterbury Tales* written in the fourteenth century, albeit a story in verse. It tells of a group of pilgrims travelling to Canterbury who entertain the group by each relating a tale. The stories are unconnected in content. The Italian writer Boccaccio's *The Decameron* also written in the fourteenth century concerns a group of ten people hiding away from the plague. Each tells the other stories to pass the one hundred days they spend in hiding.

The Arabian Nights or *The Thousand and One Nights* is a collection of stories made in about 1450 of older stories. The frame is that the stories are supposedly told by Scheherazade who after being a favourite was condemned to death by King Schahriah. She preserved her life by telling him tales every night, and not revealing the ending until the next night. After managing to engage his attention for one thousand and one nights, he was so taken with her stories that that the death sentence was lifted. Such is the power of story!

Framed stories are not very popular now but the anthology of stories by a single author is the nearest equivalent. The most acclaimed example from the twentieth century is James Joyce's *Dubliners* (1915). Joyce's book contains fifteen stories that are self-contained but reveal more to the reader if they are read together. The stories concern childhood, adolescence, maturity and public life and in each case show how the religious and social ambience of Dublin in the early twentieth century had a paralyzing effect on the emotional life of Dubliners. Dublin itself is the framing device.

Short story writers who publish anthologies of their stories do not nowadays usually erect a frame but sometimes they rather wish to show their diversity and range. Nonetheless, a frame of sorts is sometimes apparent to the reader because most authors tend to have subjects and themes which they repeat with variations. For instance Angela Carter in her anthology of stories *The Bloody Chamber* (1979) bases all her stories on fairy tales, giving them themes which are more relevant to her own time. Ian McEwan's first published fiction was an anthology of stories called *First Love, Last Rites* (1975) and the stories centre round the themes of childhood and sexuality. In the one or two stories where the characters are not children, the protagonist is childish or child-like. In a recent anthology by the Booker Prize short-listed author, Mick Jones, called *Ten Sorry Tales* (2005) all the stories are grim and concern obsessions or eccentrics.

Another kind of framing occurs in some novels; for instance, Emily Brontë's *Wuthering Heights* and Joseph Conrad's *The Heart of Darkness*. In *Wuthering Heights* the main story of Cathy and Heathcliff is distanced from the reader at four levels by the use of different narrators. Lockwood is the outer frame narrator (after Emily Brontë, of course) and he hears the story of Cathy and Heathcliff from Nelly Dean who in turn hears part of it from other characters. In *The Heart of Darkness* an anonymous narrator relates Marlow's story about Kurtz which he has got from someone else. The method ensures that the reader can never assume everything is true or objective; whereas that would be expected with an omniscient narrator.

The beginning writer might well experiment with some of the ideas raised by the framed stories. For instance, when a story has been written, the writer might consider writing it from the point of view of another character or simply from the point of view of a character if an omniscient narrator told the first version.

Frankfurt Book Fair

The Frankfurt Book Fair is an international annual event for publishers and people connected with the book trade. Books are displayed; rights to books are bought and sold by publishers and film producers.

Genre

The French word *'genre'* means kind, sort, type or category and in English it is a word used to classify types of literature, art, music, film, etc. The ancient Greeks referred to the genres of literature as poetic or lyric, epic or narrative, and drama. There was no novel then.

The word is often used loosely and in slightly different ways. For instance, the genres of literature are usually regarded as fiction, poetry and drama but some would refer to the genres of fiction as novel, short story and play. Similarly the novel is a type of fiction with many genres or subgenres within it such as: romance, *Bildungsroman*, picaresque, Gothic, Western, mystery, thriller, detective, social realist, science fiction, pulp, chick lit, lad lit, war, horror, humorous, coming of age, etc. Poetry too has its genres, for example lyric, epic, narrative, haiku, sonnet.

With regard to the genres of the novel and short story, both readers and publishers, and also writers, find the concept useful. Many readers, for instance, often prefer and in some cases only read one type or genre of novel. Some readers prefer only romance, some thrillers, some read just science fiction. Thus, if publishers identify their fiction as belonging to a particular type or genre, they will make it easier for the reader to choose the sort of book they want. Publishers also find it easier to market their published novels and some specialize in a particular genre. Novelists also frequently write a certain kind of novel. We all know what kind of novel to expect from, say, Stephen King, Ruth Rendell or Barbara Cartland although occasionally it can be dangerous to make such assumptions. Stephen King, for instance, writes more than merely horror novels even though they are his specialism.

Literary novels are often regarded as more serious works of fiction and they tend not to fit so easily into a known genre.

Genre fiction tends to have certain conventions. At its simplest, in the detective novel, a crime will occur early on, a detective (private or police) will endeavour to solve the crime, during which time more crimes will probably occur, and almost always the said crimes will be solved and the criminal brought to book. Needless to say, there can be many variations on this convention.

There are fashions in fictional genres. For example, chick lit is a relatively recent and very popular version of the romantic genre. With regard to detective stories; in the past the criminal was always the 'bad guy' and the detective the 'good guy' who saw justice was done. In recent times there is sometimes a moral ambivalence about the detective and sometimes the criminal is not all bad. This may reflect a more realistic view of both human nature and the police.

Writers frequently find a genre of fiction a useful crutch in their writing endeavours. If you decide to write a romance or a detective story, you know in advance some of the ingredients you will have to give your readers and you have plenty of models to provide you with suggestions. This is not to say such novels are, or have to be, formulaic. There are always interesting variations to be found even for the genre novel and the novelist who finds the original variation is likely to be the one who succeeds.

See also INTERTEXTUALITY; STORY AND NOVEL CATEGORIES

GHOST-WRITER

A ghost-writer is someone who writes a book, article or paper on behalf of someone else who takes the credit.

They are usually contracted by an agent or publisher to write a book for someone who has a commercial story to tell but hasn't the writing skills to tell their own story or deal with the subject. The most commonly ghost-written books are the autobiographies of celebrities, actors and sportspeople.

Ghost-writers are mostly the unacknowledged and anonymous people of the writing world. Neither the person whose name appears on the book, or the publisher, wishes to admit the book is ghost-written although in recent times occasionally the ghost-writer may be acknowledged and a name appear in very small print in the credits for the book. Ghost-writers are usually paid a fee for their work and possibly a royalty depending on sales. They will never receive as much as the person they are writing for. They are writers who have expertise in some field. For instance, the autobiographies of sports men and women are often written by sports journalists. In the case of autobiographies, the ghost-writer will usually interview the person extensively to obtain the appropriate material. Occasionally a celebrity may have written their own book, but so badly that a ghost-writer is employed to restructure and rewrite it.

Ghost-written books are usually non-fiction, although there have been some cases of ghost-written novels. These are usually by a celebrity who may have an idea for a story but cannot execute it well. The model Naomi Campbell published a novel called *Swan* which she admitted had been ghost-written.

The ghost-writer is not to be confused with the book editor. The ghost-writer writes the whole book. Book editors read books intended for publication and may suggest changes or point out sections which need correction.

The ghost-writer is not someone who takes up such work as a career. Usually people with an established writing career will be invited to ghost-write. Publishers, of course, often use the same people for ghost-writing, so it *can* become a career for a writer. Many see it as a rather thankless task because of the anonymity of the ghost-writer.

Gossip and Literature

Very few people would equate gossip with literature but, oddly enough, D. H. Lawrence did. In *Lady Chatterley's Lover* he recounts how the female protagonist, Connie Chatterley, feels guilty when she overhears Mrs Bolton, their servant, gossiping to her husband. Her guilt is slightly relieved by the fact that Mrs Bolton's stories are never malicious. Lawrence comments thus on Mrs Bolton's gossip:

> She had unloosed to him the stream of gossip about Tevershall village. It was more than gossip. It was Mrs Gaskell and George Eliot and Miss Mitford all rolled in one, with a great deal more that those women left out. Mrs Bolton was better than any book, about the lives of people.

Note how Lawrence compares Mrs Bolton's gossip with the work of three distinguished novelists.

Before hearing more gossip, Connie muses (and it clearly reflects Lawrence's view):

> After all, one may hear the most private affairs of other people, but only in a spirit of respect for the struggling, battered thing which any human soul is, and in a spirit of fine discriminative sympathy. . . . It is the way our sympathy flows and recoils that really determines our lives. And here lies the importance of the novel, properly handled. It can inform

and lead into new places the flow of our sympathetic consciousness, and it can lead our sympathy away in recoil from things gone dead.

Lawrence's general point is a useful one. It alerts the writer to the fact that some of the best stories may be provoked by ordinary human behaviour (the subject of gossiping) and that the writer would do well to have a keen ear for what is going on among his or her friends and acquaintances – and what they are gossiping about. Whether we deal with these in fiction sympathetically or only with what Lawrence calls 'spurious sympathies' is a matter for the individual writer. Lawrence was as aware as anyone that much gossip is malicious.

See also FICTION; PLOT AND STORY

GOTHIC FICTION, HORROR AND VAMPIRE STORIES

There is an overlap between Gothic fiction and horror fiction, and vampire fiction is sometimes seen as a separate but related category. The overlap is caused by the fact that they are all intended to horrify or frighten the reader. The temperament and beliefs of the reader will decide if they do. Some readers avoid the genre completely being totally unconvinced by it; for others it is a favourite genre.

Gothic (sometimes spelt Gothick) is the original term for what many would now call horror fiction. The word originally referred to Goth or Germanic and it denoted a style of architecture of supposedly medieval origin in which castles were notable for their towers, pointed arches and vaults. The word became associated with fiction after the publication of Horace Walpole's *The Castle of Otranto* in 1764.

Other Gothic novels followed, most proving more popular than Walpole's seminal work: *Vathek* (1786) by William Beckford (another medieval story), Ann Radcliffe's *The Mysteries of Udolpho* (1794) and Matthew Lewis's *The Monk* (1797). All contained horrific events and elements of the supernatural. In the nineteenth century many such novels were published and two of them have retained their popularity and influenced modern Gothic and vampire stories. These were Mary Shelley's *Frankenstein* (1818) and later, Bram Stoker's *Dracula* (1897). Both have never been out of print, have had many imitators and have spawned literally dozens if not hundreds of films and TV thrillers, many of which bear only a passing resemblance to the originals.

The appeal of *Frankenstein*, and the horrific element of the novel, is undoubtedly the monster created with the aid of science. Clearly science itself and its dangerous possibilities may be a fear for some people. *Dracula*, of course, popularized the idea of the vampire whose victims became vampires on their death. Dracula, in spite of being horrifying, also had a certain sexual attraction. Like Mary Shelley, Bram Stoker utilizes what for some is a real fear, the possibility of some kind of alien survival after death.

Although popular, monsters and vampires are far from the only subjects or objects of horror stories. A common thread is that the horror bears some relationship to the underlying or deep-seated fears of human beings. This is the appeal; there is both fascination and repulsion.

The American writer Edgar Allan Poe (1809–1849) in his short stories dealt with burial alive (this has been the subject of at least two recent films) and the horror of the expectancy of a ghastly and slow death in *The Pit and the Pendulum*. He invented many other ingenious horror scenarios.

The characteristics or ingredients of the horror novel are these:

blood	misuse of science
burial alive	monsters
darkness	revenge
disfigurement	screams
doubles or doppelgängers	seduction and sexual attraction
drugs	storms
eerie atmosphere	supernatural
fear	superstition
ghosts	torture
guilty secrets	unidentifiable sounds
haunted houses	vampires
madness	vaults and cellars

While the original horror ingredients still enjoy some popularity in both fiction and film there is a tendency for modern horror writers to set more realistic horrific events within a naturalistic and sometimes mundane setting. An example of this is Ira Levin's novel, *Rosemary's Baby* (1967), up until the end this appears to be a naturalistic story of a young married couple expecting their first child.

The most prolific and probably the most popular contemporary horror writer is the American, Stephen King. His first novel, *Carrie* (1976) concerns a school student with telekinetic powers. Apart from this, the setting and most of the characters, mainly high school students, are realistic. *The Shining* (1977) set in an isolated, closed-down hotel contains supernatural events or appears to; they may, in fact, all be in the mind of the protagonist who appears to be going mad. *Misery* (1987) takes horror to an even greater realistic level with no supernatural element at all. The story concerns a novelist who is in effect kidnapped by his greatest fan who proceeds to torture him unmercifully when he will not accede to her wishes. The claustrophobic, menacing atmosphere is well realized and one gets the impression that this was a situation that King himself in some way feared might happen, or it may be an allegory on how a public figure feels when intimidated by admirers. These novels and many other King stories have been filmed with varying degrees of success. He continues to come up with original and imaginative modern takes on horror.

From the beginning vampire stories, and Bram Stoker's *Dracula* is a case in point, frequently had a sexual element and the vampire had both a repulsion and attraction for women. The vampire's embrace, deadly 'kiss', and penetration of the victim are all part of this myth.

Most writers who turn to horror must decide whether to follow some of the traditional Gothic elements concerned with the supernatural or follow the alternative path of dealing with some aspect of the very real horror that certainly exists in the world today. One way of devising a horror story would be to think of what are people's major fears (the unusual and individual ones as well as the more obvious ones) and to weave an unusual, possibly allegorical story around that fear.

See also PSYCHOLOGICAL NOVELS; STORY AND NOVEL CATEGORIES

GRAPHIC NOVELS

A graphic novel is a novel in comic strip form. Unlike most comics they are full length, that is about the length of a text novel, but the story is told in pictures with dialogue and a small amount of narrative usually at the top or bottom of the frame (a single picture within a comic). They are usually in A4 format although some are smaller. Many graphic novels today are published with adults in mind, although some are for children. While comics are often associated with children, it should be borne in mind that when they started in the latter part of the nineteenth century they were designed for adults as well as younger readers. They were a reaction on the part of a moralistic publisher to the violent and salacious so called 'penny dreadfuls', cheaply produced and cheap to buy tales of crime and misdemeanours. The idea was successful. Penny dreadfuls disappeared and comics became extremely successful. They soon became aimed more directly at children.

In the 1940s and 1950s American comic book publishers published many classic novels in strip form in an effort, supposedly, to encourage children to read the classics. These were A4 size colourful publications usually of sixty-four pages.

In the 1980s some publishers in America and Britain attempted to rejuvenate a slowing comic market by introducing novel length comics for adults, called graphic novels, in order to alleviate the stigma that comics were just for children. Although they have never become very popular, they continue to be published and some have achieved acclaim for their seriousness as well as what is often imaginative artwork. 1987 saw the publication of *Maus* by Art Spiegelman, a story about the experiences of the author's father and his escape from a German concentration camp. *Watchmen* (1987) by the writer Allan Moore and the artist Dave Gibbons is about ageing superheroes who come out of retirement to find justice for one of their number who has been murdered. Although harking back to superhero figures like Superman, the novel has serious intent as has most of Moore's work. *The Dark Knight Returns* by Frank Miller also turns a traditional superhero on his head. He uses the figure of Batman who has turned fifty, is brooding on the death of his parents, and is a psychopath to boot.

Some graphic novels are written, drawn and painted by one person – as in the case of Art Spiegelman. Very often the stories and dialogue are written by one person, the artwork by another, and the lettering by another graphic artist. In America particularly, many of the writers and artists are employed by the publishers or commissioned by them for a work which has been discussed. The publishers frequently own the rights in the traditional comic characters. It would probably be foolhardy for a novice writer/artist to embark on the considerable effort that goes into a graphic novel without first finding out from a publisher if they might be interested in the project.

HALF-TITLE

The half-title is the short title of a book printed on the recto (right hand page) before the full title.

HE/SHE SAID

Dialogue in fiction is usually followed by an indication as to who said the spoken words for example, 'John said'. Sometimes this is put before the spoken words. In a long two-way conversation the names may be dropped after the first few exchanges because the reader has got the rhythm of the conversation and does not need to be reminded of who is speaking each time. If what is said is a reply to a question, then 'Mary replied' may be used instead of said.

There are many alternatives to said and replied and the writer must choose the most appropriate. Some alternatives include retorted, barked, smiled, laughed, cajoled, snarled, pestered, whispered and shouted. There are many more. Another construction the writer can use is to add an adverb to the verb said, for example *he said rudely, smilingly* and *bashfully*. Again, there are many others. Another possible construction is he said with passion, she said with annoyance.

There are dozens of alternatives to the basic he/she said or what are sometimes called saying verbs. Some writers use the whole gamut; others stick to the simple he/she said. On the whole using one of the alternatives every time may show an inadequacy in the dialogue. The words themselves ideally should indicate the emotion behind their use although occasionally the manner of speaking will have to be indicated by the writer.

The American novelist Elmore Leonard has written advice to writers in ten points. 'Never use a verb other than "said" to carry dialogue' and 'Never use an adverb to modify the verb "said" . . .' are two of them. The writer must decide, having an absolute 'rule' is perhaps too prescriptive.

See also DIALOGUE

HERO

From a literary point of view, the hero is the central character in a novel, play, story or poem. The term is now used for both male and female characters, although prior to the latter half of the twentieth century the word would have been assumed to be referring to a male. The word heroine is still sometimes used for female central characters.

The literary definition of hero does not usually suggest any single, particular characteristic of the main character but the word hero has more meanings than the literary one so the characteristics associated with heroism in the popular imagination are often associated with the literary hero. These characteristics include bravery, enterprise, courage, fighting for a cause and strength, although not necessarily just physical strength. The hero is usually a person of action, but this action may not be physical; it could be standing up for a belief, defending the weak, or someone who does a good deed in a malevolent world. Triumph is not necessarily the reward of the hero. Sometimes the character's heroism is only fully recognized after their death.

The action hero is very popular, especially in films and adventure stories. Very few central characters in fact fit the popular conception of the hero for the simple reason that a very good character that always succeeds would be rather boring. Characters must be human and that means having good and bad characteristics as most people do. The literary hero will nonetheless finally achieve positive results in spite of weaknesses. Think of some of the central characters created by Dickens.

The hero then can take many forms but probably the one constant is that the reader will admire and possibly identify with the character. The hero's main qualities are positive; hence the popularity of the hero in children's fiction. Good triumphs over evil through the agency of a hero. Reader identification with a main character could also be said to be a key ingredient of the most popular stories.In myths, legends and some fairy stories, the hero is descended from the gods and has magical powers to right wrongs or destroy evil (the dragon, for instance).

The term protagonist is used by many critics instead of hero simply because it does not suggest preconceived ideas of the nature of the central character.

See also ANTI-HERO; HEROINE; PROTAGONIST; VILLAIN

HEROINE
A heroine is the main female character in a novel, play, story, film or poem. The term is not much used now and the term hero is used for heroic female characters along with their male counterparts.

See also ANTI-HERO; HERO; PROTAGONIST; VILLAIN

HISTORICAL FICTION
Historical fiction is set in the past and concerns past events and people, how far in the past is open to question. Anything in the past could be regarded as historical but in practice the genre called historical fiction is usually concerned with a time at least a century ago.

There are three basic types of historical fiction: (a) that which concerns and tells the story of famous historical figures (*Julian* written by Gore Vidal in 1964 is an example); (b) stories of ordinary or imaginatively realized characters placed by the author within a particular historical setting (Robert Louis Stevenson's *Kidnapped* is an example);

and (c) stories of made up characters with known historical figures and events in the background (the novels of Georgette Heyer are examples). For instance, the story of a soldier in Napoleon's army would almost certainly make mention of Napoleon, although he may not be an active character in the story. It has been suggested that the first type of story (a) is the lazy writer's way out because the basic story is laid out ready-made by historical events and the characters have existed. For example, a novel about Joan of Arc or Queen Elizabeth I would have to keep largely to the known facts. There would be no point in telling such a story if the writer was to make up elements of their lives. On the other hand a story of someone connected with Elizabeth's court would involve creating an original plot while also keeping to the known background facts.

Whichever kind of story is written, considerable research is necessary to achieve authenticity of background and characters. The enthusiasts for historical fiction are not tolerant of basic mistakes.

Academic historians divide into two camps about the legitimacy and value of historical fiction. Some accept that it stimulates interest in history and they excuse its inadequacies as history. Some purists despise all novels that claim to know what on the whole cannot really be known unless there is definite historical source material: thus, a novelist who suggests what famous people actually said or thought is anathema. We just do not know these things.

Historical fiction writers should certainly attempt to find out the different mind-sets of people in the past and not describe historical events from a contemporary perspective. To do this, the writer must become steeped in what people believed at the time and how they experienced events.

It is clear that people spoke differently in the past, even if we go back a hundred years, but most writers will opt for a fairly neutral form of dialogue, avoiding contemporary idioms and expressions which would jar with the reader. Anthony Burgess was an exception and his novel about Shakespeare *Nothing Like the Sun* attempts to simulate the speech of the Elizabethans.

One thing the historical author can do which historians of some periods ignore is to give the perspective of ordinary people on significant events of the past. But again, the problem arises: to what extent can we know this perspective.

The good historical novelist can also bring historical figures to life in a way the historian cannot. There is no reason why an author should not speculate from the known facts about how someone may have reacted to the turbulent events of their time or analyse motives for the actions they take. Readers of historical fiction, and they are many, know they are not reading pure history and they presumably read fiction because it offers something which a study of history does not.

It must be assumed that any writer who decides to write historical fiction must be interested in history in general and, perhaps, a particular period. Research in the form of reading a great deal on the period is essential, together with visits to museums, old buildings and examination of artefacts of the period.

The field is open to a number of approaches, from the historical romances of Georgette Heyer and the escapist novels about Harry Flashman by George MacDonald Fraser to the meticulously researched novels set in Greece and Rome by Mary Renault and Robert Graves for example, (Renault's *The King Must Die* 1958 and Graves's *I Claudius* 1934). As well as his superb *Julian*, Gore Vidal's other historical novels are recommended as models, especially *Burr* (1974) which is the story of Aaron Burr whose life has all the ingredients of a pulp novel and which Vidal raises to a higher plain. Burr became Vice President of the US, failed to become President, killed one of his rivals in a duel, and his estranged wife was finally granted a divorce on the day he died. A recent meticulously researched novel of Victorian times is Julie Myerson's *Laura Blundy* (2000).

See also STORY AND NOVEL CATEGORIES; WAR NOVELS

HOOK

Writers use hooks to draw readers into the story as a fishermen uses a hook to catch a fish. The hook is an exciting, mysterious, engrossing or humorous beginning in order to get the reader engaged and willing to read on.

Not every hook works for everyone, of course. Most viewers will have had the experience of switching on a TV play and being so put off by the opening that they have switched off or, after reading the first page of a novel, abandoned it.

Beginning with a brutal and dramatic murder, even one written superbly, will not attract those who are squeamish about violence. There is no point in devising a startling and exciting hook if the rest of the story does not live up to it. A boring opening passage will lose the reader.

The writers of literary novels are less likely to use hooks. They do not want to engage the reader by what may be regarded as melodramatic effects. Nonetheless some serious literary novelists are not averse to using the hook. In the nineteenth century, Charles Dickens in the opening of *Great Expectations* used a startling hook concerning a small boy threatened by a vicious criminal. More recently Ian McEwan in *Enduring Love* used a dramatic hot air balloon accident for the same purpose.

Depending on the type of story being written, devise a hook to suit the subject. A study of some novel openings will pay dividends.

See also OPENINGS

HUBRIS

Hubris is overweening pride or arrogance and traditionally it was seen as a major cause of the downfall of heroes in Greek and Roman tragic drama. The nature of the pride took many forms but the worst was considered to be that pride which led someone to believe they could compete with a god.

Adam in the Biblical story of the expulsion from Eden exhibits hubris. Pride and arrogance in connexion with politics, the military, religion, business, and even the family are still fairly common themes in fiction as in real life. Politicians are sometimes accused of hubris when they become arrogant through becoming accustomed to power.

See also TRAGIC FLAW (*HAMARTIA*)

HYPERBOLE

Hyperbole is a figure of speech which involves exaggeration or over-statement with the use of extravagant language for serious emphasis, comic effect, or occasionally ironic effect. It is from the word hyperbole that we get the word 'hype'. The exaggeration is such that no one will take hyperbolic statements literally. If someone is described as being 'as thin as a rake', we do not expect to see someone with a two-inch waist. If someone says: 'I'm yours for a cream bun', recognize it as hyperbole and not an invitation to go down to the confectioner's. Notice that 'as thin as a rake' is a simile and hyperbole is often mediated through similes and metaphors: e.g. 'he drinks like a fish', 'he's built like a house'.

Hyperbole is as common in everyday speech as it is in literature and many examples of hyperbole, including some given above, are also clichés. Other examples include 'as old as the hills', 'died laughing', 'could eat a horse', and 'this shopping weighs a ton'.

Hyperbole is the mainstay of some comic writers. It is one of the commonest sources of humour in Richard Curtis' and Ben Elton's popular TV series *Blackadder* and in Elton's novels, for example *Popcorn*. It is exploited by Louise Rennison in her series of comic novels for teenagers and Adrian Mole in the novels by Sue Townsend is known to exaggerate humorously. Roald Dahl often indulges in hyperbole. Most children, of course, are masters of hyperbole which may be why they enjoy it.

IMPRINT

The imprint is the name of the publisher printed in the book, usually on the title page.

INCITING INCIDENT

Inciting incident is a term fairly rarely used because the concept is usually encapsulated into the *exposition* of a fiction (the introductory part of a story which outlines the setting, main characters and situation). The inciting incident is that part of the exposition which concerns an incident which incites or sparks off the action. In a romance, it might be the meeting of two people who become lovers. In a detective story, it would probably be a crime. In an adventure story there are many possibilities. In Robert Louis Stevenson's *Treasure Island*, for instance, it is the discovery of a map showing the location of treasure. In Shakespeare's *The Merchant of Venice*, it is the reluctant accepting of a loan of money from an enemy. In William Golding's *The Lord of the Flies* it is the fact that a group of schoolboys are involved in an air crash which lands them on an uninhabited desert island. The American novelist, Joyce Carol Oates' novel *The Falls* (2004) has a quite startling inciting incident. The protagonist, a young woman called Ariah Erskine has just married and she and her new husband are honeymooning at Niagara. On the morning after their wedding, the husband gets up early, goes out, and throws himself into Niagara Falls. The event leads to a dissection of family life constantly marred by the tragedy.

It is useful for the storywriter to ask whether there should be an inciting incident to get the story going.

See also EXPOSITION; PLOT AND STORY; SUSPENSE

INSPIRATION

Inspiration is something which many people think is the gift of the writer or creative person and they view it as something rather magical –

or rather people believe that the artist latches onto something from thin air or their imagination and this enables them to create a story, poem or picture. Some student writers who haven't been able to write something excuse themselves on the grounds that they were not inspired.

This kind of inspiration is a myth. Writers are unlikely to pluck a story from thin air. The genesis of the writing will have been a person, an incident, an experience, relationships, another story drastically modified, a piece of music, a work of art, an object or a memory. We may not always remember in detail the spark which led to our creative urge but there will have been one.

Sometimes during a writing project a problem might occur. For instance, the writer may be hard pressed to think of a plausible way to get a character out of some predicament or they may not be able to think of how to resolve a problem to do with the plot. Some writers have found that if they leave the task and take some time off, when they return to writing, a solution to the problem comes to them seemingly instantaneously. This could be called an act of inspiration but it is more likely that it is just part of the psychology of the human mind that allows it to work on a problem and come up with a solution unconsciously. Probably the best piece of advice about inspiration was given by the American novelist, John Updike, when he was asked about it in an interview. He said 'I only work when I'm inspired, and I see to it that I'm inspired every morning at nine-o-clock.'

A more realistic view of inspiration relates to the way in which the writer should be alert to things which may become the starting point or part of a story, novel or poem. The writer must be a keen observer and listener. Unusual or interesting things should be noted and written down if there is any possibility that they could be useful ingredients. He or she should study and make profiles of all kinds of characters, and catalogue instances of human behaviour from the ordinary to the criminal or heroic either from real life or from newspaper articles. One of these 'ideas' may be the starting point for a complete novel or part of a story.

Inspiration is sometimes referred to when the writer cannot start writing. The blank sheet of paper seems alien. Inspiration won't come. This is when it is worth remembering John Updike's remark: just get down and write something. If you haven't got a subject which demands that you start writing, perhaps it is time to leave off until you do. When you have a subject that fires the interest and imagination, it will be difficult not to want to write it down. It is worth remembering that most fiction writing is prefaced by a careful exercise in planning and construction of plot, characters and other features of the story. When these have been worked out, it should be easier to get writing.

See also NOTEBOOKS, CUTTINGS AND JOURNALS; WRITER'S BLOCK

INTERIOR MONOLOGUE

In most fiction there is a mixture of narrative describing action or events, dialogue between characters, description of people and things and the thoughts of characters. In many respects the least straightforward to represent fictionally are the thoughts of characters.

Throughout the day we constantly think. These thoughts are not always coherent; we flit from one subject to another and back; some thoughts seem to pass instantaneously; others we put into words and they pass more slowly. Often more than one thing is on our mind at the same time or it seems that way. Occasionally we appear to think visually with no words involved and large numbers of ideas pass through our minds in a second.

The following is typical of the way thoughts are represented in mainstream fiction:

> Jake thought about what he would say to his wife. He knew he should tell her the truth, confess his infidelity with Ruth, but he was not ready to tell her and he felt she may not be in a fit state after her illness to accept that their marriage was over in everything but name. Then there was the matter of the kids; they would have to be told that he had betrayed their mother. Altogether, he decided, it would be better to live the lie for a while longer.

Unlike the way thought is described in the paragraph before the extract; these thoughts are logical, ordered and uninterrupted by matters extraneous to the main subject of Jake's guilt at his infidelity.

Representing the way thoughts really occur, the same passage might begin more like this:

> Never like that with Ruth. Sheer sensation. Hard thinking about it. But . . . Ruth will need to know. May suspect. And Nicky and Ray. God, this tooth really hurts. Would they understand? Would they hell! And why should they . . .

The second passage attempts to represent Jake's rambling thoughts more as they might occur. Note that they are not complete sentences as in the first passage. We don't usually think in sentences.

Whether any writer of fiction can really represent thought processes accurately is a moot point. Some critics would also ask if we want to. Fiction is a distillation of what happens in reality. It would be boring to include every thought of a character just as it would be boring if every action in their lives was described or noted. Do we want to be told of every visit to the supermarket or the lavatory?

Nevertheless the attempt by some novelists to represent inner thoughts more accurately (if more fragmentarily) has been undertaken and the technique is called interior monologue (sometimes internal monologue). The first person to use it was the minor French novelist, Édouard Dujardin in his 1888 novel *Les Lauriers sont coupés*. It was perfected by Dorothy Richardson in *Pilgrimage* written in twelve volumes over the period 1915–1958; James Joyce in *Ulysses* (1922) and various novels by Virginia Woolf in the 1920s. The American novelist William Faulkner also used the technique, particularly in *The Sound and the Fury* and *As I Lay Dying*.

Critics have pointed out that isolated passages of thought using something akin to the interior monologue technique can be found in earlier novelists such as Laurence Sterne and Charles Dickens. For instance, Leon Edel in his book *The Psychological Novel* quotes this passage from Dickens' *The Pickwick Papers*. They are random thoughts of the character Alfred Jingle but expressed to another character:

> Terrible place – dangerous work – other day – five children – mother – tall lady, eating sandwiches – forgot the arch – crash – knock – children look round – mother's head off – sandwich in her hand – no mouth to put it in – head of a family off – shocking, shocking. Looking at Whitehall, Sir – fine place – little window – somebody else's head off there, eh, sir? – he didn't keep a sharp look-out enough either – eh, Sir, eh?

It is probably no accident that Dorothy Richardson, James Joyce, Virginia Woolf and William Faulkner began using the interior monologue technique at about the same time as Sigmund Freud's ideas concerning the unconscious were becoming influential. The inner life below the surface of everyday events was at this time regarded as of paramount importance and the motivation for our everyday actions.

These novels enjoy great prestige in the history of twentieth-century literature but the fact remains that the older, possibly less accurate, way of portraying thoughts is the technique still used by most writers of fiction. It also seems to be the method preferred by readers who sometimes find interior monologue confusing and slightly tedious.

It is worth noting that the soliloquies found in many plays (especially of the Elizabethan period) are a version of interior monologue.

They are certainly monologues and they express the thoughts of characters. They are not, however, internal monologue in the strict sense that has been described because they are coherent and never rambling. Think of Hamlet's 'To be, or not to be . . .' soliloquy when he questions whether or not he should end his life. One might think a potential suicide to be rambling in his thoughts. Shakespeare makes Hamlet anything but. He logically pursues the arguments for and against ending his life.

Interior monologue is seen by some critics as a form of the stream-of-consciousness technique used by Joyce, Woolf, Faulkner and Richardson among others. Other critics suggest there is no basic difference between them and they are simply two terms to describe the same thing.

See also STREAM OF CONSCIOUSNESS

INTERTEXTUALITY

In the first *Pink Panther* film Inspector Clouseau, played by Peter Sellers, is talking to his boss and idly spinning a large globe of the world. Without thinking he leans on the spinning globe and is thrown violently across the room. The contrast between the serious conversation, Sellers' expression and this absurd event is very comic. In the next *Pink Panther* film, Clouseau spins the same globe. Instead of being thrown across the room he gets his hand jammed in the revolving globe and cannot retrieve it. The absurdity is again comic. The pleasure the audience experiences from the second scene will depend to some extent on whether they have seen the first film. If they have, their initial response may be 'Not again!' but they will be pleasantly surprised and relieved when a new comic moment transpires rather than just the repetition of an old gag.

To fully appreciate the second text (film scene) we need to know the first text. The second indirectly refers to the first film. This is an example of intertextuality. The term was first used by the French literary theorist Julia Kristeva to indicate how one literary (or film) text is linked to or echoes texts which have gone before it.

Those familiar with the spoof horror film *Scream*, will realize that a full appreciation of it depends on a knowledge of the many references to other horror films that came before it.

T. S. Eliot's long poem *The Waste Land* contains many quotations and references to other literary works. A full understanding of the poem is enhanced if the reader knows what the references signify.

Eliot, however, would have said that the poem could be appreciated without this recognition.

Whenever writers set out to write they draw on other texts even if they do not consciously realize it. The writer of a poem, will almost certainly utilize some of the techniques used by other poets. Even an innovator like the American poet e. e. cummings would not have written his highly original poems had he not been reacting against traditional poetic techniques.

The modern novelist, too, would not write his or her novel without having read and absorbed some of the methods of earlier writers. James Joyce in his innovative 1922 novel *Ulysses* used as a model the Greek classic, *The Odyssey*. The title *Ulysses* provides a clue to this and the novel is about a journey as important to the protagonists as that of Odysseus in the original Greek story. An understanding and appreciation of Joyce's novel is only fully possible if one is familiar with some Irish legends, European history, the Roman Catholic Church and the history of heresy.

Few works indulge in intertextuality to the extent of *The Waste Land* and *Ulysses*, but equally few, if any, contain no elements of intertextuality. If a modern story begins 'Once upon a time . . .' we would immediately start thinking about fairy stories. George Orwell's novella *Animal Farm* would probably appear rather banal if the reader were not familiar with fairy tales and talking animals. Readers expect *Animal Farm* to be more than just a simple animal story and thus will think about what it may mean.

Clearly if intertextuality is used too self-consciously, it can be irritating and puzzling. The author may be accused of being pretentious. However, if any of the common conventions of story telling are used, the writer will almost inevitably be consciously or covertly using intertextuality.

Another type of intertextuality comes close to adaptation. William Golding's novel, *Lord of the Flies* (1954) is a literary version of another novel. Golding had in mind the children's novel *Coral Island* (1858) by R. M. Ballantyne as a model for his modern version of boys cast away on a desert island but their behaviour is very different from the exploits of the boys on the coral island. The themes of the two authors are quite different. Ballantyne is concerned with how boys embrace the challenge of being cast away. Golding shows most of his characters reverting to a kind of savagery with the loss of the veneer of civilization that he believes prevents us from being akin to the animals. The question arises and it is an impossible one to answer: would

Golding have written his novel had he not been familiar with *Coral Island*? Whereas Golding takes a general plot and scene from another book, the novelist Jean Rhys takes a character from a classic novel as the central figure in her novel, *Wide Sargasso Sea* (1966). The character she makes central in her novel is the first Mrs Rochester from Charlotte Brontë's *Jane Eyre*. This character appears briefly as she has in *Jane Eyre* gone mad and is kept secretly in an attic prior to her tragic death. Rhys's novel concerns the first Mrs Rochester's life before Jane Eyre comes on the scene. Her novel is quite different from Brontë's. She is concerned with how women are misunderstood by men.

When we hear a story referred to as a modern *Cinderella* or a character as a modern Heathcliff some element of intertextuality is at work. Past literature can be an inspiration for new works and in no sense is intertextuality a matter of copying or plagiarism.

The above account of intertextuality is largely a practical one. Intertextuality is part of the discipline of semiotics (the science of signs) and of certain branches of literary criticism which inaugurated a revolutionary view of literature and the author. Indeed, some would argue that it is fundamental to a whole view of the human world which differs from that traditionally held.

It was mentioned above that the French theorist and semiotician, Julia Kristeva, introduced the notion and the term in the late 1960s. Another important French writer who extended the ideas was Roland Barthes. It was he who pronounced 'the death of the author'. He meant that traditionally an author is regarded as an originator and a creator, he or she has created something new and original which is unique to him. Barthes suggests this is not really the case. The examples given in section (1) show that Eliot, Golding, Joyce and the authors of the films were dependent on other texts to make their own. Can they legitimately be called creators? I chose to discuss obvious examples of one text using or depending on another. Kristeva and Barthes would argue that this is the case with *every* text or work of art. Some of the influences on these works are not easy to recognize or are so far removed that the reader may be quite unaware of their exact nature. Even an author may sometimes be unaware of their influences. Barthes said, more or less, that it is intertextuality that permits a new text to come into being. He also argues that the reader plays a more important part than has been traditionally allowed. We all read a text differently depending on what we bring to it: our own background and experiences, our knowledge and previous reading. The reader with a very wide knowledge of worldwide literature will read *The Waste Land* and get from it something quite different from the reader who has little knowledge at all of literature. Which reading is correct and is either of them what Eliot wrote or intended?

Needless to say the arguments are more complex than this suggests. Works on modern literary theory and the work of Kristeva and Barthes are extremely interesting and offer challenging ideas on literature and its creation. Some critics, however, reject these notions and still think the author is the most important person connected with an individual text. They would argue that only Shakespeare, the individual writer, could have written *Hamlet* and the other plays – despite the fact that we know he used recognized sources for his plays.

If you are a writer, you will almost certainly use intertextuality but don't rely on it too heavily.

INVECTIVE

Invective is using strong, abusive or vituperative language to attack or castigate a person or institution, an idea, a political system, etc. It is closely associated with satire but invective is more likely to be a passage of writing about a particular person or thing within a book rather than a whole book or article. It would be difficult to sustain invective in a long work and equally it would be difficult to read.

The use of invective suggests little less than hatred for what is being attacked and its purpose seems to be as much to relieve the feelings of the author as to bring about positive change that may be the ultimate aim of satire. Invective frequently uses abusive words, whereas good satire does not need to.

Invective can occur in novels, stories, poems and plays. Jimmy Porter's attacks on bourgeois values and people in John Osborne's play *Look Back in Anger* (1956) are good examples of invective. Shakespeare occasionally uses it, for example in the attacks by and on Caliban in *The Tempest*.

The great satirists are often drawn towards invective when it comes to things they particularly dislike. There are powerful passages by Jonathan Swift, and Aldous Huxley's description of St Francis of Assisi in his novel *Point Counter Point* (1928) is one of the most vicious attacks on an historical person (usually considered a good person) in modern literature. The words are, albeit, from the mouth of a character but one gets the impression that Huxley shared the strong feelings expressed.

'Your little stink-pot of a St Francis, for example . . . Just a little stink-pot
. . . A silly vain little man trying to blow himself up into a Jesus and only
succeeding in killing whatever sense of decency there was in him, only
succeeding in turning himself into the nasty smelly fragments of a real
human being, Going about getting thrills of excitement out of licking
lepers! Ugh!'

Invective in novels is invariably spoken by characters and it reveals
something about them as well as the person being spoken to.

See also LAMPOON, SATIRE

IRONY

Irony comes in a number of forms: for example verbal irony, dramatic
irony and structural irony. They all have in common the fact that what
is said literally is not necessarily the case. In verbal irony the literal
words convey a sense other than what is meant or what the author
intends to point out. For example:

What a piece of work is man! How noble in reason! how infinite in faculties! in form and moving, how express and admirable! in action, how
like an angel! in apprehension, how like a god! the beauty of the world!
the paragon of animals!

We know from the context of the play and the behaviour of several of
the characters, not least of all Hamlet himself, that this is not exactly
true and that he is being ironic.

A similar view of human nature is expressed in *The Tempest* by
Shakespeare. Miranda has been isolated from human beings on an
island with her father and a servant for company. When she first
observes some shipwrecked sailors, she utters the words:

How beauteous mankind is! O brave new world
That has such people in't!

The audience knows that Miranda is naive and will discover that her
view of human beings is rosy rather than true.

The words 'I *do* apologize' can be said sincerely. Depending on how
they are said and according to the circumstances, they may mean the
exact opposite. We would than regard it as *sarcasm*, which is the
crudest form of irony.

Jane Austen is often and justifiably regarded as a great ironist and
her famous opening to *Pride and Prejudice* begins 'It is a truth universally acknowledged that a single man in possession of a good fortune

must be in want of a wife.' While there may be some truth in this the main point of the novel is to show the opposite. Most of Jane Austen's women are in want of a rich husband. If the reader does not appreciate the irony of the opening straight away they will by the end of the book.

Thomas Hardy is another supreme ironist and often the structure of the events in his novels creates the irony. In *Tess of the D'Urbervilles* (1891), Tess is an innocent young girl and because of this she loses her virginity (good leads to bad in her and society's terms). She later loses any happiness she had managed to find by her honesty (again a virtue ironically leads to unhappiness). Hardy's subtitle for the novel was *A Pure Woman Faithfully Presented* and it was itself ironic because what Tess does would be regarded as anything but 'pure' by the standards of her society. Hardy, of course, is questioning society's values more than he questions those of his character.

Dramatic irony in plays often centres on the fact that the audience knows something which the central characters do not. The audience can therefore have the frisson of anticipating tragedy or farce which the characters cannot – unless, of course, there is some authorial twist or reversal.

Dramatic irony is not confined to plays. The film of Graham Greene's novel *Brighton Rock* has one of the most tragically ironic endings of any film. The central character, Pinkie, a petty gangster, has married a teenager, Rose who is desperately in love with him. She thinks he loves her, but in fact he has married her solely so that she cannot give evidence against him if he is charged with a crime. She persuades him against his will to make a recording at a fairground of an expression of love for her. In the recording booth he begins his recording with the words 'I love you . . .' but immediately goes on to say how he really hates her and regards her as a slut who he hopes will die soon. Shortly after this, Pinkie dies while trying to escape from the law. Rose is devastated and goes home to play the record. By chance, the recording sticks after the words 'I love you . . .' The audience knows the ironic truth. Rose does not. It makes an interesting ending although in the novel Rose goes home to 'the worst horror of all' – finding out the truth of what her husband really thought of her.

Irony can, of course, be used for comic or humorous effects although the humour is frequently sardonic. The following authors employ irony in humorous ways: Jonathan Swift, Charles Dickens, Mark Twain, G. B. Shaw, James Joyce, George Orwell, Evelyn Waugh, Iris Murdoch.

ISBN

ISBN stands for International Standard Book Number. This is a ten-digit number unique to a particular book which identifies the title and the publisher and also the language in which it is published. It is a useful tool for all aspects of book publishing and selling. It is often represented as a bar code on the back of the book as well as inside the book.

JOKES

Humour is subjective and a joke which is hilarious for one person may leave another person cold. While many anecdotes are based on real people and experiences, the joke is more likely to be made up.

Anyone who has the facility for making up jokes is probably best employed in radio or working for comedians rather than writing fiction although the appropriately placed joke in a story can enhance it.

It would be unfair to leave a piece on jokes without a joke. The following is an old joke, in fact it has been claimed that it is one of the oldest extant.

> Cicero was visiting a slave market in Rome one day when he saw a slave who was almost identical to him in appearance. Cicero looked again carefully and then asked the slave: 'Was your mother ever in Rome before?' 'No', replied the slave, 'but my father was'.

This joke has the characteristics of all jokes. The humour must occur at the end or in the so-called punch line. Another common characteristic is that it 'puts down' an authority figure.

See also ANECDOTE

JUXTAPOSITION

Juxtaposition is about putting two or more contrasting things side by side in order to bring out the qualities of one or both. Youth and age, religious and irreligious, wild and tame, love and hatred, passionate and cold, innocent and guilty are all contrasts which have been highlighted in fiction by bringing opposites together in one work.

A notable example from nineteenth-century literature is Emily Brontë's *Wuthering Heights* (1847). It is in good part a study in contrasts through juxtaposition. Cathy and Heathcliff, the wild passionate couple, are contrasted with Edgar Linton and Isabella, the steady, conventional married couple. The houses of Wuthering Heights and Thrushcross

Grange and the way of life in each, are contrasted in the novel. Passion and domesticity are highlighted by placing them side by side.

The twentieth-century novelist Aldous Huxley frequently made points by juxtaposing disparate people, incidents and characteristics in his novels, most notably in the significantly titled *Point Counter Point* (1928) and *Eyeless in Gaza* (1936). In the latter, incidents do not take place in chronological sequence but are juxtaposed in order to make points for example about character. An incident in the childhood of a character may be placed next to something which happens to the character in middle age so that the influence of the former can be seen.

Some critics have argued that Huxley's use of juxtaposition is too obvious. This can be a danger in using the technique, but clearly it has many possibilities.

In D. H. Lawrence juxtaposition and contrast are fundamental to his themes concerning the natural way of life in contrast to those imposed by industrial society. In *Women in Love* (1920) the most startling contrast is between Rupert Birkin (based on the author himself) and Gerald Crich, an industrialist. The two sisters, Ursula and Gudrun, are contrasted along with the natural landscape, the mining village and the salons in London. All of Lawrence's novels contain similar juxtapositions.

More recently, David Lodge's *Small World* juxtaposes the world of academe and the world of business. A number of surprising similarities as well as differences are shown.

KÜNSTLERROMAN SEE BILDUNGSROMAN

LAD LIT

Lad lit is not quite the male equivalent of chick lit, as the name would suggest. It is more disparate in content and characterization. This may reflect the fact that book publishers and marketers saw an opportunity after the success of chick lit to identify some novels written by men which did not really fit into the traditional male novel categories of thriller, adventure, spy and crime.

Some of the novels branded lad lit have sensitive, caring, anxious heroes looking as hard for love and stability as the average chick lit heroine. Others focus on male characters that are selfish, anti-commitment, insensitive. Many of the novels are concerned with male pastimes such as sport or pop music.

Nick Hornby is usually regarded as the originator of lad lit although he would reject the label. Certainly his novels *Fever Pitch, High Fidelity* and *About a Boy* contain the characteristic themes and character types. His novels have been best-sellers (and successful films), as have those of Tony Parsons who wrote the successful *Man and Boy*, but Parsons' subsequent novels have been regarded by most critics as simply cashing in on an early successful formula. *Man and Boy* concerns the life of a single father. The novel was said to be more successful with female readers than with men.

The comparative success of chick lit and the relative failure of lad lit as a genre may be due to the fact that women are more willing to admit their faults and weaknesses and read about them than men.

Other novelists who have been categorized as writers of lad lit are Mike Gayle, John O'Farrell, Matt Beaumont and Mark Barrowcliffe.

See also CHICK LIT

LAMPOON

A lampoon is bitter satire in prose or verse. A lampoon in fiction is more likely to appear as a passage possibly uttered by one of the characters. A complete novel could not be a lampoon because it is unlikely that the author would hold up all the characters and events to sustained criticism; the sheer length would dilute the effect. Lampoons mostly satirize or ridicule famous people or institutions. A lampoon is very often the same as a piece of invective and the two passages, by Dickens and Aldous Huxley, in the entry on Invective may also be regarded as examples of lampoons.

See also INVECTIVE; SATIRE

LEGAL DEPOSIT

Legal deposit refers to the requirement of publishers to send a copy of every published book in the UK to the British Library, the University Library in Cambridge, the Bodleian Library in Oxford and the national libraries of Scotland, Wales and Ireland.

LEGENDS

Originally legends were stories of saints; now the term refers to stories coming down from the past but not verifiable by historical record, a myth or fable. One of the most famous legends or series of legends is to do with King Arthur. Such a king is believed to have existed but many of the tales about him (including those of the famous Round Table) are of dubious authenticity. Robin Hood is a similar shadowy figure historically. The story of Beowulf too may have its roots in history but the story handed down has an element of fantasy. Doctor Faustus, like other legendary figures, has been used by a number of known authors as the subject for drama or novels. The most notable are Christopher Marlowe's play (1588), Goethe's remarkable German drama (1808/1833) and Thomas Mann's novel (1947). There are many other plays, operas and novels concerning Faust as a character. In general, legends are stories about events that could have happened unlike most fairy tales. Urban legends are legends that grow up mysteriously. Many people disbelieve them but they are usually about events that could have happened. They are apocryphal, often taking the form of a cautionary tale which varies in the telling but is always told as true.

Even relatively modern popular figures or folk heroes can gain legendary status and sometimes it is difficult to divide the historical truth from legendary additions. Cases in point would be General Custer, Buffalo Bill, Lawrence of Arabia, Howard Hughes and Che Guevara.

See also MYTHS

LIBEL

To libel someone is to write and publish false statements about them that harms their reputation or demeans them in the eyes of others. People cannot be libelled by the truth. Libel comes under the legal category of defamation.

Slander is to defame someone orally. Slander is much more difficult to prove because the slanderous spoken words must have reliable witnesses other than the slandered person. Slander on radio or TV broadcasts (or other recorded speech) is now counted as libel because a public recording is similar to the written word in that it is preserved in a way the everyday spoken word is not.

It is possible for writers of fiction to be the subject of libel actions even though they may have disguised and fictionalized a real person. If a character in fiction is given another name but is based on a real person and that person is clearly recognizable in the portrayal then if libellous remarks are made, a libel has been committed, If a libel is proved, damages are usually awarded and these can be considerable if the libel is considered serious.

Libel does not apply to criticism of work in reviews and the author can do little about it when it is honest opinion. Even in reviews, however, care should be taken.

LIMITATIONS AND SPECIALISM

Shakespeare largely used existing sources and stories as the subjects of his plays. No one criticizes him for not making up his own stories; his greatness obviously lies elsewhere, as a poet and a penetrating observer of the human condition. Whether Shakespeare used other sources for his work because it was customary in the sixteenth century or because he could not devise original stories we cannot know.

Most authors have limitations. Jane Austen is better at portraying women characters than men. She rarely attempts to convey the inner thoughts of men. She knew her limitations. Joseph Conrad, on the other hand, was not very good at portraying women, there are far fewer women than men in his novels. Usually they seem rather romanticized versions of the female. Aldous Huxley has often been accused of being poor at character creation despite the fact he based many of his characters on real people. Huxley was more interested in ideas and his characters often seem just mouthpieces for them. As a novelist of ideas, however, he is supreme. All writers have limitations, most recognize them and play up their strengths.

Another aspect of limitation concerns settings. Charles Dickens, a native of London, was much better at portraying London scenes and characters than the northern ones he attempts in *Hard Times* (1854). Elizabeth Gaskell, however, who was brought up and lived mostly in the north portrays the industrial north much more vividly and accurately in her novels *Mary Barton* (1848) and *North and South* (1854–5).

At a different level, genre novelists usually confine themselves to writing the kind of novel they can cope with and do so for most of their writing careers. Romantic novelists confine themselves to romance and crime novelists to crime stories. Occasionally novelists are more eclectic but writers should probably recognize that they have some limitations and should write what they know they are good at.

LIMITED EDITION

A limited edition is an edition that is restricted to a certain number of copies. Sometimes a published book may be published in a limited edition with leather binding. Books in limited editions may be sought by collectors.

Literary Agent

A literary agent represents writers and their written work to publishers and assists in the sale of the same. An author may, instead of approaching a publisher with a book, put it in the hands of an agent who will try to place the book with a publisher on their behalf. The advantage of this system is that the agent tends to know what is likely to interest a particular publisher. The publisher will know that an agent will not bother them with an unpublishable book or one of a type they do not usually publish. The literary agent will take a percentage of all earnings from the book usually 10–20 per cent. Agents also sell books to film and TV companies for adaptation into screenplays.

MacGuffin

A MacGuffin is a plot device that motivates the characters and advances the story. The term is sometimes attributed to the film director Alfred Hitchcock. Others claim it was coined by a friend of Hitchcock's, Angus McPhail. Hitchcock certainly made extensive use of the device in many of his films as have other directors and writers. Although the term MacGuffin is relatively recent, the actual technique had been in existence long before.

If we take Hitchcock's well-known film *Psycho* (and the novel by Robert Bloch on which it is based), the MacGuffin is the secretary's theft of the money given to her boss. Had she not taken the money, she would not have landed up in the motel where she and others meet their grisly fates.

A MacGuffin can be a useful device for the writer. It is sometimes called an inciting incident.

See also INCITING INCIDENT

Magic Realism

Magic realism is a literary genre in which magical elements appear in an otherwise realistic setting. At one level it is realistic fiction but magical or fantasy elements intrude without any attempt by the author to suggest that these elements are not as feasible as the realistic parts. The magical element is treated by the author and by the characters within the story as being quite natural although the reader will inevitably be thinking 'this couldn't happen'. The overall themes of these novels suggest they are serious and have something to say about reality. They are rarely purely escapist novels.

They are also not like the fantasy genre where a purely fictional, fantastic landscape, situation and characters are conveyed as if they are real.

The term magic realism was first used in the 1920s in relation to visual art and became a recognized literary technique when applied to South American novelists from the 1950s onwards. Some western novelists have exploited and slightly modified the technique and the term has been applied retrospectively to the Bohemian, Franz Kafka (1883–1924) and others. In Kafka's novella *Metamorphosis* (1915) the central character, Gregor Samsa, wakes up at the beginning of the story to find himself transformed into a gigantic insect. Apart from this extraordinary happening everything in the story is perfectly realistic and one of Kafka's themes appears to be that if people and society treat you like an insect, you may as well be one. Samsa is downtrodden by most of his family and the people at his place of work even before his transformation.

One reason why magic realistic fiction has grown in Latin America is that there are, or were, sharper divisions between those sections of society who experienced and embraced twentieth-century technological culture, and those who remained rooted in a past of rural life and superstition.

Some South American magical realist novelists include Carlos Fuentes, Mario Vargas Llosa and Gabriel Garcia Marquez. European novelists who have used the technique are Italo Calvino, Milan Kundera, Salman Rushdie, Vladimir Nabokov, Angela Carter, Peter Carey and Fay Weldon.

Fay Weldon's *The Life and Loves of a She-Devil* is an interesting example of the genre. The female protagonist, Ruth, is plain, verging on ugly. She is six feet two, has a jutting jaw, a hooked nose and moles on her chin. Her husband is having an affair with a glamorous, beautiful novelist called Mary Fisher. The protagonist has a life of drudgery and looking after children. She meets a plastic surgeon who over a few years transforms Ruth into a beautiful, svelte woman that even her husband does not recognize. (He has gone to live with the novelist.) The protagonist in her surgically transformed self embarks on a series of exciting affairs and then launches a long campaign of revenge against her husband and the novelist. The reader of the novel becomes quite aware that the protagonist's transformation is such that it would be impossible by even the greatest plastic surgeon in the world. This is the magic or fantasy element in the novel. But at a psychological level, Weldon has interesting things to say about the place of women in society, about relationships, the importance of looks, female rebellion and revenge.

See also REALISM AND NATURALISM

MARKET

The market for a book is the potential readership of the book. Market also refers to the countries where the book may be sold.

MARKETING

If a writer has written a fiction which he or she believes is publishable, a book or magazine publisher must be found. The author wants to submit the work and begin the process of marketing which will be completed by the publisher.

Manuscripts can be sent to the editor of a magazine or to a publisher's editor in the case of a book. If the work to be offered to a publisher is a full-length manuscript a preliminary letter describing the work and including some pages of the opening may be a wiser course than sending the whole manuscript. It will be considered much more quickly.

It is essential that the writer only approaches publishers who take the kind of material the author has written. The writer must undertake market research by reading potential magazine outlets and studying publishers' lists to find out the kind of work they publish. A novel with a suicidal heroine will not appeal to Mills & Boon. Research can be done in bookshops, libraries, published catalogues and book publishers' sites on the internet. Most include advice for potential authors. In addition, the writer should consult one or both of two invaluable reference works, *The Writer's Handbook* (Macmillan) and *The Writers' and Artists' Yearbook* (A&C Black) – both are published annually. These books list all the major magazine and book publishers with their addresses and details of their requirements. There is a wealth of other useful information for writers in these books including lists of literary agents that provide an alternative way of placing a manuscript (although most agents will only consider book length material).

It is essential to know a publisher's or editor's requirements. Sending a brilliant short story to a magazine which does not customarily publish fiction is futile, time wasting and infuriating for both editor and author.

See also LITERARY AGENT; SLUSH PILE

MELODRAMA

Melodrama has a number of meanings when it refers to literature. In its everyday use it is a term that describes someone's behaviour as exaggerated and dramatic. The word itself comes from the French *mélodrame* meaning 'drama with song or music'. Melodrama is said to have begun in ancient Greece but it became popular entertainment in eighteenth- and nineteenth-century Europe and it thrives today in a somewhat different form. At first it applied to musical plays such as John Gay's *The Beggar's Opera*. Melodramas have the following characteristics:

- Stereotyped characters (very heroic heroes, weak and dependent heroines, and villains with no redeeming features).
- Strong emotions expressed by most characters.
- Straightforward moral lessons.
- Dramatic action (stage technology used to simulate elaborate accidents such as shipwrecks, train crashes, fires, etc., horses often brought on stage).
- Dramatic language and sometimes musical accompaniment.
- Intrigue.
- A series of dramatic events or climaxes before the final one.
- The audience know a secret unknown to the characters, this creates suspense.
- Tragic incidents but a happy ending almost obligatory.

Television soap operas are probably the best examples of modern melodrama and they are the most popular form of fiction just as melodramatic stage plays were in the nineteenth century. In soap operas character is often subservient to plot. In order to create a dramatic plot development, characters behave sometimes in uncharacteristic and inconsistent ways.

Some of the most popular novels come under the category of melodrama.

A problem with the term melodrama is that it is sometimes used pejoratively and in the eyes of many literary critics, melodrama is a considerably inferior form to the serious, literary, naturalistic novel, play or film. A work considered serious by some critics may be regarded as melodrama by someone else who does not hold it in such high esteem. An example of this would be Emily Brontë's *Wuthering Heights*. This novel is considered classic literature by some critics and many readers but those who dislike it point to a number of melodramatic elements such as ghosts, sadistic actions, madness, revenge, cruelty to animals and people and the highly charged, almost unbelievable character of Heathcliff. The novel has serious themes and intentions of course, but so do soap operas.

Melodramatic characters and incidents can be identified in the work of many classic authors such as Charles Dickens and Thomas Hardy. Even modern soap opera script writers would probably not go so far as to have a male character sell his wife to another man during a drunken orgy as takes place in Hardy's *The Mayor of Casterbridge*.

Clearly the dividing line between classic literature and melodrama is problematic, it is vague and flexible and to a certain extent subjective. It is equally clear that the most popular writers of fiction, and those who aspire to join them, would do well not to dismiss melodrama.

METAFICTION

Traditionally fiction has been written with the intention of creating an illusory world in which the reader becomes immersed for the duration at least of reading the story. While reading, the reader often forgets that it is a fiction, a made up story. The writer does not pinpoint or highlight the techniques used to create characters, plot and suspense. Writer and reader are conspirators in creating and maintaining the illusion.

Metafiction is not like this. The author of the metafictional novel, as well as telling us a story, writes *about* fiction and may discuss the techniques and devices being used. It involves self-reflection on the part of the author and alerts the reader to compare fiction with reality. The author, in a sense, becomes a character in his or her story, although probably not one who is involved with the plot. Characters themselves, in metafiction, are sometimes aware that they are characters and part of a story.

Two examples will illustrate some of the techniques of metafiction. In 1969 John Fowles published his novel *The French Lieutenant's Woman*. This is a story about a Victorian gentleman scientist Charles who is engaged to a 'suitable' young woman but who becomes involved with Sarah who has been deserted by the French lieutenant of the title. She spends her days gazing towards France from the Cobb in Lyme Bay. The people of Lyme are scandalized by her past and present behaviour but Charles falls in love with her even though she does not encourage him. She is distant towards him for the most part, but she succumbs sexually to him once and conceives a child although Charles does not know this until a few years after she has left Lyme.

The story is one which could have been the subject of a Victorian novel but it would have been conceived very differently. Fowles appears to want the reader to understand Victorian attitudes by comparing them with those of the mid-twentieth century. He also wishes to inform the reader that he is writing fiction and by doing so inviting the reader to compare fiction with the real world of people. The reader cannot get lost in the story. At one point the narrator, or Fowles, writes 'The story I am telling is all imagination. These characters I create never existed outside my own mind'.

Fowles also frequently uses anachrony bringing the reader up with a jolt by using comparisons that would have been impossible in the real nineteenth-century novel. For instance, Charles has mixed emotions after he has had his sexual encounter with Sarah and Fowles writes 'Charles . . . was like a city struck out of a quiet sky by an atom bomb.'

Charles Dickens could not have written that. On one occasion, after narrating what appears to be a crucial part of the plot, Fowles remarks that what he has described in the last two chapters did not happen in quite the way the reader had been led to believe. (Readers may well be asking if they can trust this author, but perhaps that is what Fowles wants them to do.)

The reader is then treated to three possible endings to the story and must choose which seems to be the most appropriate – or which they prefer. Fowles comments that the last one may seem the most likely simply because it is the last one. Finally, in the last chapter, an important new character appears with this comment from Fowles 'It is a time-proven rule of the novelist's craft never to introduce any but very minor new characters at the end of a book.'

It is worth pointing out that these metafictional interludes did not prevent this being one of Fowles's most popular novels, probably because the story element is gripping from beginning to end.

An even more extreme example of metafiction is Vladimir Nabokov's 1962 novel, *Pale Fire*. This novel consists of a 999-line poem in four cantos (the last line, we learn has been lost) which is preceded by a foreword by a literary critic, and followed by extensive notes commenting on the poem, plus a cross-referenced index. The poet, John Shade, who is dead, and the critic, Charles Kinbote, are fictional as is the fascinating story which emerges from these unusual novel ingredients. There is also much discussion of literature in this novel.

Other metafictional writers include John Barth, Robert Coover, William Gass, Julian Barnes and Peter Carey. While metafiction became something of a fashionable technique in the 1960s (and is still practised) critics have pointed out that *Tristram Shandy* (1767) by Laurence Sterne exhibits metafictional techniques. Other novelists of the eighteenth century did not follow Sterne's example. The reason for its popularity in the twentieth century is probably to do with the fact that novelists, influenced by postmodernism and questioning traditional authorities, questioned their art. The authority of the author was as open to scrutiny as any other authority.

See also ANACHRONY; MAGIC REALISM

METONYMY AND SYNECDOCHE

Metonymy and synecdoche are similar and can be confused. Metonymy is the substitution of one word for another which is associated with it. In the following examples, the metonymic word is italicized:

'The army supported the *crown*'. (*crown* = the country from which the army came).

'*England* won the Cup'. (*England* = the sports team representing England).

'The *suits* are arriving for the inspection this afternoon'. (*suits* = officials).

'The *pen* is mightier than the *sword*'. (*pen* = writing or some written documents; *sword* = violence or armed force).

He *drinks*, you know. (*drinks* = drinks too much, or he is a drunkard).

Synecdoche is a figure of speech where a part of something stands for the whole. Synecdoche can be seen as a special case of *metonymy*. Here are some examples:

All *hands* on deck. (*hands* = sailors)

A choir of one hundred *voices* entertained the throng. (*voices* = the singers)

The deckhand shouted, 'A *sail*! A *sail*!' (*sail* = the ship which had been sighted)

At the livestock market he bought thirty *head*. (*head* = cattle)

I was all *ears*. (*ears* = paying attention)

There should be no deliberate attempt to introduce these figures of speech into writing, except perhaps in poetry. They may occur because they seem appropriate at a particular time or said by a particular character.

Mini-sagas

The mini-saga is probably the most rigid form of fiction ever and yet it can be rewarding both to write and to read. It must be exactly fifty words long, not a word more or less. The title is not counted in the fifty words; contractions count as one word but hyphenated words count as two. The story should have a conventional beginning, middle and end and it may reveal something about character, human behaviour or have a more abstract theme, it must not simply be description. Subjects can be humorous, serious, tragic or thoughtful.

There are two ways to approach writing a mini-saga once the writer has decided on a subject that can be tackled briefly. In the first method, the story is written with brevity in mind but not bothering about a word count. The result will almost certainly exceed fifty words. The next task is to cut and prune any words and material which can be omitted but which will leave a coherent story. The second method involves making a first draft as short as possible and under the fifty word limit. The writer is then free to add description and other words to improve the piece. Anyone wishing to write mini-sagas should see which method suits them best.

Here is an example of a mini-saga, 'Partners'.

> Their embrace was passionate. She felt nothing but love for Alan. If anything it was only exceeded by his love and affection for her. Neither had ever felt such fervent happiness before. They would always be together. Always. She dragged herself away to tell her husband she wanted a divorce.

Mini-sagas were devised some years ago as competition subjects in order to encourage discipline in the writer. Anthologies of mini-sagas have been published.

See also FLASH FICTION

Motif

A motif in a work of fiction is a recurring object, word, phrase, image, character, situation, setting or colour which takes on some symbolic significance. For example, the gold coins in George Eliot's novel *Silas Marner* are, constantly connected with the material riches Silas craves.

He learns, though, that human love in the shape of a golden child (a child with blonde hair) is worth far more than the treasure. Motifs are often in the form of contrasts: light and dark, black and white, good and evil, spring for youth and winter for old age or death.

Motifs sometimes evoke similar symbols from well known works of literature. Just as the eating of the fruit by Eve in the Biblical creation story signifies Adam and Eve's entry into the adult world of responsibility, so the eating of the apple in the fairy tale about Snow White indicates a similar departure from innocence. Other motifs which have been used time and time again are flying birds to indicate freedom and the dove, specifically, for peace.

In William Faulkner's novel *As I Lay Dying* (1930) there is a recurring image of a dead fish on a slab. A mentally retarded character cannot really understand the death of his mother and all he can do is relate her death to a dead fish he has seen on a slab. More than once in the story, in coming to terms with the maternal death, he says 'My mother is a fish'.

There is often a relationship between motif and theme but they are not the same thing. A motif usually conjures up a single idea whereas a theme may conjure up a whole series of ideas or concepts. The motif often makes an emotional impact; a theme is more intellectual.

The term 'leitmotif' is sometimes used for motif.

See also THEME

MYSTERY FICTION

The category mystery fiction is used as an alternative to detective story, horror story, Gothic, thriller and sometimes adventure story. All these story categories almost always contain a mystery, that is, something occurs which raises the question 'How and why did this happen and who or what was the cause of it?'

The reader wants to know the answer and the fact that the answer is not obvious creates suspense. The detective or spy tries to find answers. In the Gothic or horror story, the reader wants to know why strange and horrific events occur. The serious literary story often contains mysteries about the motives of characters but mystery will not be as predominant as in detective stories.

The characteristic of genre mystery stories is that the mystery is almost always solved. (The horror story may be an exception.) A detective story left at the end with the detective not having solved the crime would not be satisfying to most readers.

There is, however, a small body of stories that contain mysteries that are not solved. One of Edgar Allan Poe's stories, *The Mystery of Marie Roget* (1842) is a case in point. Another is Josephine Tey's historical mystery, *The Daughter of Time* (1951) which is the story of the death of the princes in the Tower of London in the reign of Richard III.

A very successful mystery novel, which was made into a film in 1975, was *Picnic at Hanging Rock* by Joan Lindsay (1967). It concerns three girls and a teacher who disappear on a school trip to the outback in Australia. So effective was this story in catching the imagination of the public that many readers thought it was an account of a true event. The novel had such an effective atmosphere that readers did not seem to be concerned that the mystery was unsolved. Curiously, the author had written a final chapter that explained the mystery but withdrew it just before publication. After her death the explanatory chapter was published. Readers can thus now compare the two versions.

In the entry on conflict, the detective novel *The Pledge* (1959) by Friedrich Durrenmatt is discussed. It is a novel that defies the usual conventions of the detective story in that the detective does not catch the criminal and subsequently declines mentally, although the reader, but none of the characters, does find out who he was. Although the novel is highly acclaimed, it was not popular with detective story devotees.

Injecting some mystery into a story, and usually solving that mystery, has been a staple of fiction since its earliest days and it will continue to be so.

See also ADVENTURE AND QUEST STORIES; CONFLICT; DETECTIVE STORIES; GOTHIC FICTION, HORROR AND VAMPIRE STORIES; STORY AND NOVEL CATEGORIES; SUSPENSE; THRILLERS

MYTHS

Unlike legends that are usually embellished accounts of historical figures, myths concern supernatural beings and are often associated with religions. Myths frequently attempt to explain how things came to exist in terms of the knowledge available at the time of their creation. Thus people living today will rarely find the explanations plausible, but because of this myths can tell us a lot about ancient peoples, their beliefs and what was important to them.

One of the most common types of myth is the creation myth. Thus the story of Adam and Eve in *Genesis* is an attempt to explain the existence of human beings on earth. Most people today will go back to theories of evolution. Other cultures and religions have alternative creation myths.

Nowadays we look to science for explanations of the things that myths once explained although myths continue to help explain the past and have an interest for psychologists, anthropologists and writers.

See also LEGENDS

NARRATIVE

A narrative is a story and the term is used for both fiction and non-fiction. It can also refer to poems that have a story element.

See also DIALOGUE; EXPOSITION; NARRATIVE METHODS; NARRATOR

NARRATIVE METHODS

Having decided on a story, plot and the characters who are going to inhabit the fiction, the next vital decision concerns the narrative method to be used. This is sometimes also called the point of view. There are numerous ways of telling a story but the main choice is between first-person narrative and third person.

First-Person Narrative

The three most common forms of first-person narrative are as follows:

1   The protagonist narrates (e.g. *Jane Eyre* by Charlotte Brontë).
2   A witness to the events who is involved peripherally narrates (e.g. Marlow in Joseph Conrad's *Heart of Darkness*).
3   A character or a character other than the protagonist narrates (e.g. Nick Carraway in *The Great Gatsby* by F. Scott Fitzgerald).

The following points may be considered if the first-person narrative form is chosen:

• The narrator will reveal his or her own nature indirectly or directly in the process of narrating.
• Only what narrators have seen, been involved with, or had reported to them by another character can be included.
• The narrator cannot reveal the thoughts of other characters except in the unlikely event that they are told them.
• The first-person narrator can address the reader but this is not usually done.

- Opinions, comments and value judgements on the events are more justifiable than in the third-person narrative method because the reader knows they are one person's opinions.
- The first-person narrator can ostensibly be telling the story to another character or some named person and only indirectly to the reader.
- The epistolary novel (that is, a novel in the form of letters) is a way of telling the story to other characters (the recipients of the letters) and also to the reader. The epistolary novel may have letters written by and to more than one person.
- The first-person narrator may be a participant in the story (including being the protagonist, of course), or merely an observer of the events.
- First-person narration is a technique that some critics feel gives immediacy to a story.
- The writer must create the first-person narrator as a character (like any other) and remain consistent to the character with regard to his or her attitudes and values.
- The scenes and settings of a novel with a first-person narrator are likely to be more limited than a novel told by the omniscient third-person narrator who can cross barriers of time and place as and when they will.
- It is possible to have a novel with multiple first-person narrators. An example is *As I Lay Dying* by William Faulkner. Usually in this kind of novel, the different narrators relate different chapters.
- It is probably not a good idea to use a first-person character narrator if the story is to involve their death but it is not impossible. Alan Bell's film *American Beauty* handles this superbly.
- First-person narratives always use the 'I'. Some first-person narratives use an invisible 'I', that is the reader never gets to know exactly who the 'I' who is narrating is, although in some cases there may be clues and the reader may guess.

The Unreliable Narrator

The term unreliable narrator is used of first-person rather than third-person narrators because they are characters/human beings that may have faults, be biased, make mistakes and, indeed, in some cases, may have serious psychological flaws. In Mark Twain's novels about Huck Finn and Tom Sawyer and J. D. Salinger's novel about Holden Caulfield, *The Catcher in the Rye*, the reader is presented with narrators that most readers would regard as immature; they are after all children or adolescents and some of their views and judgements are what we would expect, even though they can be extremely perceptive about the adult world. The protagonist narrator of Brett Easton Ellis's *American Psycho* is, as the title suggests, a psychopath. The first-person narrator may be a liar and they may not admit it.

Some critics claim that no first-person narrator can be relied upon completely. The reader should certainly, as with real people, assess the character and make due allowances. The writer, of course, must decide what they want to achieve with the character/narrator.

Third-Person Narrative

The third-person narrator knows everything about each character including their innermost thoughts and motives, their past, and if need be, their future. There can be some modification to this omniscience in some third-person narratives, as described below. Some novelists confine their omniscience to just some of the characters, but this is mainly because insights into all the minor characters would be a distraction from the plot.

The omniscient narrator can, of course, comment on the action, make value judgements and moral points but this is inadvisable today when readers resent being preached to. It was, though, common in many nineteenth-century novels.

The main advantage of the third-person narrative method is that the author is in complete control and does not have to be constantly considering the limitations caused by using first-person narration. Another advantage is that the scope of the fiction is extended by being able to give thoughts as well as actions and dialogue. Whereas the first-person narrator frequently uses 'I', the third-person narrator never does.

The following are some of the different third-person narrative styles:

Third-person omniscient narrator   The omniscient narrator knows everything about every character and can move from scene to scene, from time to time, from what a character says to what they think – all with impunity. These narrators have been described as god-like in their knowledge.

Third-person limited omniscient narrator   In this, the narrator's omniscient powers are limited to knowledge of the protagonist. It is a method used in the short story more than the novel. In a way it could be regarded as an alternative to first-person narration by the protagonist in that things are often seen from the point of view of the protagonist. Obviously there are limitations involved in the method but it may be the best in order to achieve a kind of unity and focus and it can provide in-depth characterization.

Third-person objective narrator   This method is used less than omniscient third-person narration. In this the narrator provides description of what is seen and done and said but the thoughts of characters are not provided. It is rather the equivalent of what an astute observer in real life sees and hears except that the narrator has access to places real observers would be excluded from. This narrator is usually impartial and it is left to the reader to interpret the significance of events. It is rather similar to a stage play except that the scenes can be more numerous and varied.

Third-person intrusive narrator   This name is sometimes given to the narrator who does not just report and describe but makes a point of commenting on what happens and gives value judgements on both characters and events. Nineteenth-century novelists such as Jane Austen, Dickens, Thackeray and Hardy employ intrusive narrators. Although not fashionable now some notable modern novelists such as Salman Rushdie and Martin Amis use the intrusive narrator. Apart from the moral stance taken by the narrator, this method is the same as the third-person omniscient narrator.

Second-person narrative   This form is rarely used because it is limiting and many readers find it awkward and unnatural. An example demonstrates this: 'You reached to the door, flung it open and you reeled back in surprise when you saw Adam in a state you had never experienced before . . . This method of narration could have some point if the 'you' who is addressed was a younger version of the narrator. The 'you' also seems to refer to the reader, but the narrator is unlikely to mean the reader. These observations suggest that it is a narrative method to be avoided. In spite of the reservations, though, a key novel of the nineteen-eighties, Jay McInerney's *Bright Lights, Big City* (1984) used the second-person narrative method. The novel is about the drug and disco culture of the eighties and it proved to be very popular.

These are the most commonly used narrative methods (for others, see cross references at the bottom of this entry. Others are possible and have been used. In *The Good Soldier* (1915) by Ford Madox Ford for example, the first-person narrator seems not to understand exactly what is going on or the situation he is describing until at the end things become clear to him and the reader (although the latter may have guessed). Presumably Ford was trying to portray events and characters as they sometimes occur in reality, in other words without the participants realizing exactly what is going on and their significance.

Some experiments in narrative forms are one-offs. A novel by Jeff Ryman called *253* is a character-based novel which takes 252 passengers and the driver who are on a seven-minute journey on a Bakerloo tube train. One page consisting of 253 words is devoted to each passenger. The page is divided into three sections on 'Outward Appearance', 'Inside Information', and 'What s/he is doing and thinking'. Some of the lives intertwine; most do not. It is an interesting experiment but not one that is likely to be taken up by other writers. *253* was published first on the internet in 1996.

Julian Mitchell's experiments were even stranger. One of his novels was published as a box containing the chapters as separate booklets. The reader was invited to mix them up and read them in any order.

The word objective has been used a few times about some of the methods described. It is worth considering whether there can ever be objectivity in the novel. Whatever narrative method is used, whatever means that are taken to hide the novelist behind narrators of different kinds, it must be remembered that is always the author who decided on the narrative method and is the driving force behind it.

See also EPISTOLARY NOVEL; FRAME STORY; INTERIOR MONOLOGUE; POINT OF VIEW; STREAM OF CONSCIOUSNESS

NARRATOR
Narrator is the name given to the person who tells a written or oral story. The various kinds of narrator possible in written fiction are discussed in the entry on Narrative methods. The type of narrator (omniscient, god-like or a subsidiary character in the story) will determine how the story is presented. The narrator contributes to the nature of the story.

See also NARRATIVE METHODS; PERSONA

NET BOOK AGREEMENT
Until 1997 there was an agreement that all books should be sold at a price dictated by the publisher and this was displayed on the book.

The Net Book Agreement was made illegal in 1997 by the Restrictive Practices Court and it caused a revolution in book selling. Shops can now sell books for whatever price they wish and discounting has become common together with an increase in the sale of books in supermarkets. Supermarkets frequently sell books more cheaply than any bookshops but the number of titles they stock is very limited. Invariably it is best-sellers or popular books that are discounted. Small bookshops object because they cannot sustain the discounts offered by bigger shops or supermarkets.

NON-FICTION NOVEL

A non-fiction novel, as the name implies, is a narrative based very closely on real people and events but written in novel form. While a non-fiction book on a subject would never contain dialogue between two participants as no one could know exactly what had been said, the non-fiction novelist has no compunction about using this technique to recreate scenes and conversations. Careful research will have been done to get things as accurate as possible.

The first acclaimed non-fiction novel was the American writer Truman Capote's *In Cold Blood* (1966). It concerned the murder by two men of four members of the Cutter family in a small Kansas community. Capote spent about six years researching the novel. He interviewed the murderers and their friends, friends and relatives of the victims, and inhabitants of the places where they lived. It is said that he was asked and attended the execution of the murderers. They were apparently happy with the attention they received. The resulting book became a best-seller. Capote also wrote other successful conventional novels including *Breakfast at Tiffany's* (1958).

Another notable example of the non-fiction novel is by the American crime writer, James Ellroy. Ellroy's mother was murdered when he was ten-years old and this had a deep effect on him. He indulged in petty crime and alcoholism before becoming a writer. Years later he investigated in detail his mother's murder and wrote *My Dark Places* using the technique of novel writing.

Historical novels based on real people and events are not usually classified as non-fiction novels and the term is usually reserved for works based on contemporary people and events and where the author can interview the participants or at least people connected with them.

Capote received a great deal of criticism, as well as acclaim, for *In Cold Blood* and the methods he used in it. Some critics argued that the book was neither a legitimate novel nor legitimate non-fiction. One of his most vituperative critics was the American author Norman Mailer who some time later rather ironically wrote his own non-fiction novel, *The Executioner's Song* (1979). Mailer's book is over a thousand pages long but covers only nine months in the life of the multiple murderer, Gary Gilmore, until his execution by firing squad.

Non-fiction novels frequently seem to be about criminals and usually dead criminals. There is an obvious reason for this apart from the dramatic nature of the material. Anyone embarking on a non-fiction novel which included living people must clearly take account of the libel laws or ensure they have the full cooperation of all participants.

As fiction is, by definition, imaginatively created characters and events, the argument will no doubt continue as to whether the writer of a non-fiction novel is really a novelist or a journalist.

A non-fiction novel is sometimes referred to as a documentary novel. Anyone embarking on a non-fiction novel must consider the following: the possibility of libel, the necessity for considerable research, travelling to conduct interviews, the chance that a project may not be completed because the research and interviewing is inadequate for a comprehensive portrayal of the story.

See also FICTION; LIBEL; NOVEL; *ROMAN-À-CLEF*

NOTEBOOKS, CUTTINGS AND JOURNALS

It is often suggested that writers keep a notebook with them at all times to jot down ideas which come to them or observations which could be useful for some future writing project. Keeping a notebook is a good idea but some writers admit that they don't work in this way.

Anyone who keeps a notebook should work out some classification system which they think might be useful for them, for example:

- Descriptions of interesting characters met or observed (the things that made them memorable).
- Overheard remarks and dialogue of interest, especially quips or witticisms.
- Interesting/bizarre/dramatic occurrences.
- Unusual situations people get into.
- Personal experiences of interest.
- Plot ideas.
- Conflict situations observed/arguments.

It is also worth starting a cuttings file. Keep any newspaper and magazine articles or reports that might be useful. An index system is essential because the number of cuttings is likely to multiply rapidly and a large pile of newspaper cuttings that have to be waded through is time wasting. A pocket voice recorder may also be useful.

NOUVEAU ROMAN

Nouveau roman literally means new novel and the term anti-novel is used for the same kind of fiction. As the term nouveau roman suggests this type of novel began in France. The main novelists using the technique (introduced in the 1950s) were Alain Robbe-Grillet, Michel Butor, Robert Pinget and Claude Simon. Nathalie Sarraute was said to have been an influence on the movement.

The characteristics of the nouveau roman are objectivity in description (the novelist tries simply to describe the appearance of things, sometimes at considerable length) and with a lack of any value judgements from the novelist. The world just exists and the novelist's task is to convey this. Plot is minimal or even non-existent and characters are ill-defined and sometimes nameless.

Many readers and critics questioned what these novels were about. Their authors may well have simply said that, like the world, they are not about anything, they just are.

NOVEL

A novel is a prose narrative of some length which tells a story of a fictional nature. It may be based on real people and events but it is largely made up. There is no fixed length for a novel but it is usually considered to be about 50,000 to 200,000 words, with occasional works exceeding that length. Shorter works of fiction are referred to as novellas, novelettes, or short stories. One of the paradoxes of the novel is that although it is concerned with made up or untrue characters and events, it often conveys truths about human behaviour and motivation.

The elements or characteristics of the novel are that it contains characters, an exposition, a plot, a setting, a theme, conflict, suspense and usually dialogue. Novels are often categorized according to genre such as romance, historical, thriller, science fiction, Western, etc. They can also be comic or tragic, tragi-comic or something which is not quite any of these.

The length of the novel makes it extremely versatile and flexible and provides authors with scope to develop characters, plots and themes although most popular novels are usually fast moving. The time span of a novel can range from a single day, or even less, to a considerable number of years.

While realism and works about ordinary people (sometimes in extraordinary situations) are popular in the novel, novels are not by any means at all realistic. Fantasy, science fiction and magic realism are quite popular. Action is an almost universal attribute of the novel. People or characters do things and often they develop and grow as a consequence of what they do and what happens to them.

The old romances (stories of chivalry and battles) about King Arthur and others were forerunners of the novel but now the term romance is more likely to refer to popular love stories.

Although strictly speaking an allegory, John Bunyan's *A Pilgrim's Progress* (1678) may be regarded as one of the earliest novels as we know them today in that it is a long story with a number of characters involved in action. In the eighteenth century five writers set patterns and techniques for the novel which have been utilized by later novelists, some of which are still used today. The novelists are listed below. One typical work is given for each.

Daniel Defoe (1660–1731) *The Life and Adventures of Robinson Crusoe* (1719).
Samuel Richardson (1689–1761) *Pamela, or Virtue Rewarded* (1740).
Henry Fielding (1707–1754) *The History of Tom Jones, a Foundling* (1749).
Tobias Smollet (1721–1771) *The Expedition of Humphrey Clinker* (1771).
Laurence Sterne (1713–1768) *The Life and Opinions of Tristram Shandy, Gentleman* (1759–67).

Soon after these early novels were published, the popularity of the form increased and genres started to appear to satisfy a public who liked a particular kind of novel.

See also FICTION; NOVELLA AND NOVELETTE; SHORT STORY; STORY AND NOVEL CATEGORIES

NOVEL OF MANNERS
Comedy of manners is a term usually associated with the drama and plays by dramatists such as William Congreve, Oliver Goldsmith,

Richard Sheridan, Oscar Wilde and Noel Coward. The novel of manners has a similar purpose to these plays. Fundamentally the novel of manners is concerned with the social behaviour, manners, gestures, language use, affectations and often snobbery of a particular social class or smaller social group. The novels are frequently humorous and often satiric. They may focus on the absurdity of social climbing, career climbing, pretentiousness, insincerity, and over-concern for fashion. The social codes of particular groups are often dissected. Frequently a character's impeccable social behaviour and respectability within his circle may conceal unsavoury self-interest. Marriage and infidelity loom large in some of these novels.

Novels of manners do not tend to be psychological; they concentrate mostly on surface behaviour. This does not mean that the novels are superficial and profound insights into how social groups work emerge as the faults and merits of the group are exposed through the interplay of characters.

Jane Austen (1775–1817) is a well-known classic example of an early novelist of manners and her dissection of upper middle-class society may be limited in one respect but it is penetrating of that restricted section of society and particularly of its rituals relating to courtship and marriage.

Evelyn Waugh's novels are mostly novels of manners. His early works expose and satirize the wasteful lives of the upper class bright young things of the 1920s and 30s. His novels are biting and sometimes savage. In his *Sword of Honour* trilogy (1952, 1955, 1962), Waugh analyses army society. A visit to a burial ground in Los Angeles led to one of his most humorous novels of manners, *The Loved One* (1948), a satire on the burial business in California as it relates to human beings and pets.

Many of Kingsley Amis's (1922–95) novels are novels of manners. From his exposure of the academic and social pretensions of university staff in his debut novel *Lucky Jim* (1954) to the late *Jake's Thing* (1979), a pot-pourri of social criticism and bile.

Novels of manners are stronger on character, witty dialogue and narrative than plot and they often concern courtship, marriage and love affairs.

See also STORY AND NOVEL CATEGORIES

NOVELIZATION

A novelization is a novel that has been converted from a film, play or television series. Novelizations are always commissioned works; there is no point in a writer undertaking one from a favourite film. The commissions arise from a deal between the film-maker or TV company and a publisher. BBC drama novelizations are usually published by the BBC which has its own publishing arm. The *Dr Who* TV series has spawned many novels and books about the series.

The term novelization is also used to refer to the conversion of facts into fiction. A true story is written as a novel probably with some additional material and made up dialogue.

See also NON-FICTION NOVEL

NOVELLA AND NOVELETTE

The name *novella* is given to those short novels of about 25,000 to 40,000 words which are too long to be called short stories. The word is of Italian origin (literally meaning 'a new little thing') and it was given in the fourteenth century to longish short stories published in collections.

The novella is not very popular with publishers probably because it must be sold more cheaply than a novel but still has high production costs. It also does not appear to be very popular with readers. Consequently few novellas are published in Britain although they are more popular in the United States.

A novelette is a name sometimes used for an even shorter fiction than a novella, which is from about 7,000 to 25,000 words. The short story is usually considered to have a maximum length of about 7,000 words. The word count of the three forms mentioned is flexible and some critics suggest other lengths. For practical purposes, the new writer should probably not consider the novella and novelette as a sensible proposition because the chances of publication are slim. Established writers are more likely to get a novella published. Occasionally these lengths are requested in competitions.

The following are some notable novellas:

Truman Capote, *Breakfast at Tiffany's* (1958).
Joseph Conrad, *The Heart of Darkness* (1902).
Ernest Hemingway, *The Old Man and the Sea* (1952).
Aldous Huxley, *The Genius and the Goddess* (1955).
Franz Kafka, *Metamorphosis* (1915).
George Orwell, *Animal Farm* (1945).
Robert Louis Stevenson, *The Strange Case of Dr Jekyll and Mr Hyde* (1886).
H. G. Wells, *The War of the Worlds* (1898).

See also FICTION; FLASH FICTION; MINI-SAGAS

OBJECTIVE CORRELATIVE

The objective correlative has achieved a remarkable degree of status and discussion almost undoubtedly because it was a literary device named by T. S. Eliot, although the phenomenon was not new. In an essay on *Hamlet* in Eliot's book *The Sacred Wood*, he wrote 'The only way of expressing emotion in the form of art is by finding an "objective correlative"; in other words, a set of objects, a situation, a chain of events which shall be the formula of that *particular emotion*; such that when the external facts . . . are given, the emotion is immediately evoked.' Critics have questioned Eliot's use of the word 'formula' but he clearly did not mean that there was an easy and easily repeated way of expressing, for instance, grief.

The important point that he is making is simply that the writer rather than telling the reader that a character felt grief, love, despair, hatred or joy, should present some situation or series of events which encapsulate the emotion and make it vivid and likely to provoke a sympathetic reaction in the reader.

See also EMPATHY; SHOWING AND TELLING

OBSCENE PUBLICATIONS ACT

1857 saw the first Obscene Publications Act in Britain. It was all embracing. A publication which contained a small amount of material deemed obscene could be prosecuted, whatever its overall intent might be, as well as an outright and obvious work of pornography. Literary merit or serious intent on the part of the author was no defence. Booksellers as well as publishers and authors could be prosecuted and there could be no witnesses, such as literary critics, brought to court to defend a publication.

Constant criticism of the 1857 Act did not lead to a reform of it until 1959. A number of important revisions were introduced. The main ones were if a work was considered to be '. . . in the interests of science, literature, art or learning' this was a defence and the defence could be supported by literary critics, scientists or other expert witnesses; in addition, the work must be considered as a whole and not on the strength of a single passage which may be deemed by some to be obscene. Authors and publishers could also defend their works.

Some further minor revisions were added in 1964, and in 1977 films were brought within the Act.

The problems with the Act have always been how some key words are interpreted. For a start there is no absolute definition of 'obscenity', certainly not one with which everyone agrees. Nonetheless publications are deemed obscene if they 'tend to deprave and corrupt'. The depravity and corruption caused do not have to manifest themselves in any behaviour but may just be in the mind of the reader of the offending work. How this is ascertained has never been explained and the lack of explanation is covered, in a sense, by the equally vague use of the word 'tend'. It is implied, of course, that judges, lawyers and the self-appointed censors who read the 'obscene publications' are themselves beyond corruption and depravity. The excuse made by censors for their work is usually on the grounds of protecting children.

Nonetheless, many works were successfully prosecuted, although D. H. Lawrence's novel *Lady Chatterley's Lover* which had been banned since the early 1930s, was eventually exonerated after a long trial in 1961. This was because expert witnesses persuaded the jury that the novel had literary merit. The jury were not so concerned with the book's literary merit; the case had to an extent been decided for them by their dislike of the snobbish prosecutor. They had been asked by him if they would consider this a novel they would like their servants to read!

Few novels have been prosecuted under the Act since the 1980s. Censors now are more concerned with film, TV, computer games and the internet.

See also PORNOGRAPHY AND EROTICA

ONOMATOPOEIA

Onomatopoeic words imitate the sound they represent. Onomatopoeia is the one case in language where there is a close relationship between the language symbols and the reality which those symbols represent. Most words are arbitrarily symbolic. The relationship is not complete. No word can ever completely imitate the sound it describes. For instance, *baa* may be like the noise a sheep makes but it is not the same.

There are relatively few onomatopoeic words and they are all to do with sound. Some attempt to represent animal noises such as: 'buzz', 'cheep', 'grunt' and 'tweet'. Other words used for sounds include 'bang', 'boom', 'bubble', 'chuff'. Comics and cartoons use many sound effect words, some of which are made up or adapted, e.g. craaaack.

OPENINGS

Consider these opening sentences to some well-known novels:

> Once upon a time and a very good time it was there was a moocow coming down along the road and this moocow that was coming down along the road met a nicens little boy named baby tuckoo . . . (*A Portrait of the Artist as a Young Man*, James Joyce)

> All happy families are alike but an unhappy family is unhappy after its own fashion. (*Anna Karenina*, Leo Tolstoy)

> For a man facing both Monday morning and utter defeat he did not feel too bad. (*Tropic of Ruislip*, Leslie Thomas)

> It was a bright cold day in April, and the clocks were striking thirteen. (*Nineteen Eighty-Four*, George Orwell)

> As Gregor Samsa awoke one morning from uneasy dreams he found himself transformed in his bed into a gigantic insect. (*Metamorphosis*, Franz Kafka)

> The sun shone, having no alternative, on the nothing new. (*Murphy*, Samuel Beckett)

> Lolita, light of my life, fire of my loins. My sin, my soul. (*Lolita*, Vladimir Nabokov)

> She came running through the rains shoeless, neon signs and traffic signals splintering in liquid reflection beneath her flying feet. She fled like misjoined twins on the slick black asphalt, puddles of red and green, orange and blue splashing up tintlessly to stain her legs with the gutter filth of the city . . . She was bleeding. (*Blood Relatives*, Ed McBain)

It is contended that all these openings are intriguing and that they would engage the reader's attention. This is what an opening should do. These quotations are very short, simply the opening few words and most readers will give the writer a longer chance to establish interest – at least a few paragraphs, possibly the first chapter. But if the beginning does not attract the reader then the book will be put down. Of course the cliché should always be avoided. Edward Bulwer-Lyton has the reputation for writing one of the worst openings in the history of the novel. His first sentence to *Paul Clifford* (1830) begins: 'It was a dark and stormy night . . .'

So what exactly should the opening do? It should have some at least of the following features, preferably more than one of them:

- Get the story going.
- Set the tone and indicate the type of story the reader should expect. Is it going to be humorous, serious, tragic or happy?

- Engage the interest, intrigue.
- Make the reader want to know what happens next.

By the end of a few pages the protagonist should have been introduced and the antagonist or protagonist's problem should have been made known.

These suggestions are generalizations, some good novels have ignored them and been successful.

Leslie Thomas is a leading comic novelist. His opening to *Tropic of Ruislip*. 'Facing Monday morning' and 'utter defeat' may seem serious and almost depressing but the two phrases are almost nullified, at least modified by, the addition of '. . . he did not feel too bad'. Thomas's protagonists are rarely heroes, they are often weak but they take life lightly and expect little. This tone is shown in the structure of one sentence. We are also introduced straight away to the protagonist and a little suspense is created. The reader wants to know why he is facing utter defeat.

Nabokov's opening to *Lolita* is very different. Here, in a few words, passion and obsession are indicated. Tolstoy's opening suggests a serious examination of family life and why some families are unhappy. The examples from Kafka and Orwell are strange and intriguing. In both cases the reader is introduced to alien environments or situations where unusual things happen. Kafka's beginning is so odd (and unbelievable), that some readers may be inclined to reject it as too fantastic. You either go along with his strange view of this man or you don't – and he won't be concerned if you don't. Orwell's opening simply suggests that we are in a somewhat different world – and we are.

Obviously not every opening, however well written and effective in itself, will appeal to all. Readers have different tastes and there is no point in attracting a reader with a false opening that does not reflect the nature of the story. Samuel Beckett's opening to *Murphy* is a case in point. Although there are comic elements in the novel, it is about the alienation and boredom of Murphy that the opening aptly demonstrates.

Joyce's opening obviously reminds us of a child's story, possibly a fairy story. It would be difficult to surmise exactly what this fiction is about but it makes sense in the light of what follows. The novel is about the various stages in the life of the protagonist from babyhood to early manhood and the language reflects the stages the character is at.

Ed McBain wrote popular bestselling crime fiction and his opening to *Blood Relatives* is a model for crime writers. It is very visual, fast-moving and the last short sentence has great dramatic impact. Suspense is created. The reader wants to know why she is bleeding.

Openings are not easy. Gore Vidal's novel *Kalki* opens as follows: 'Where to begin? A week has passed since he wrote that first sentence'. Many writers will have a sense of fellow feeling. If an opening doesn't come easily it is best to write later episodes. There is no rule that says the opening cannot be the last thing an author writes. To sum up:

- Make the opening as dramatic and attractive as possible.
- Make it appropriate to the main content. A reader should not be given false expectations.
- If possible, create some suspense.
- Make the language and tone true to the whole.
- Don't necessarily start with the opening and if you do, go back later to see if it can be improved.

The Inverted Opening

The inverted opening is when, at the very beginning of the fiction, some of the main elements of the story are partially given away. For instance, the opening sentence of a short story for children reads 'The night we burnt the television set, it was no coincidence that aunt Emily broke her big toe and Dad was taken away by the police.'

These odd events are the main ones in the story but it does not matter that they are revealed because it is why and how the events happened that is important. The same is true of these opening sentences of Vladimir Nabokov's novel, *Laughter in the Dark* (1932):

> Once upon a time there lived in Berlin, Germany, a man called Albinus. He was rich, respectable, happy; one day he abandoned his wife for the sake of a youthful mistress; he loved; was not loved; and his life ended in disaster.
> That is the whole of the story and we might have left it at that had there not been some profit and pleasure in the telling.

OPTION

An option is a contract usually made between a film or TV company and the author of a novel or play. The contract gives (for a fee) the company the right or first option to make the literary work into a film or TV drama. If and when the go-ahead is given for a film to be made, the option contract may well have stipulated an additional fee. Film companies take out many options on new novels, most of which are never made into films. The purchaser of an option can sell it on to another company. The contract may stipulate certain conditions which, for instance, the original author may request or demand. Most authors though are glad to get an option on their fiction because there is always the possibility of making more money than will be made from book publication.

See also ADAPTATION

PARABLE

A parable is a short fiction based on human situations and which points a moral or religious lesson. While having affinities with allegories, parables do not tend to contain symbols or symbolic situations.

The best-known parables are those of Jesus found in the New Testament. Some of these provide obvious lessons like the parable of the Good Samaritan which teaches religious and racial tolerance and suggests that goodness does not lie with people of only one creed. Some parables by Jesus are more puzzling but it is useful to remember that Jesus made up parables for particular occasions and situations. Examining the context of a New Testament parable can be revealing.

Greek philosophers and public figures used parables before the time of Christ to illustrate spiritual and moral truths. Parables are rarely written today.

See also ALLEGORY; DIDACTICISM; FABLE

PARADOX

A paradox is a contradictory statement or situation that reveals a truth. A paradox which has been popular in a number of contexts in recent years is 'less is more' (sometimes 'more is less') which was actually coined by the nineteenth-century poet Robert Browning. On the surface the statement seems wrong or absurd and thus it catches the attention (which is the purpose of any figure of speech) and can then be seen to contain a truth in certain contexts. For instance, to have less food rather than more at first seems undesirable but having less may lead to more satisfaction, greater health and in the long term an absence of obesity. In other contexts less money may lead to more happiness; less responsibility to more satisfaction. At first glance, more of whatever is concerned would seem to be the more desirable option, but not always.

There can also be paradoxical situations and these are likely to have a place in fiction. For instance, a released prisoner may find he has less companionship than when he was incarcerated. Tragically, a person who desires to get married and finally has found a marital partner may find they are not as happy as when they were single.

See also IRONY

PARODY AND PASTICHE

Both parody and pastiche imitate other literary works by using similar subject matter and copying the original author's style, possibly exaggerating some of their characteristics and idiosyncrasies. The difference between the two is that parody is usually written to mock and ridicule the original author or work by treating the subject, even if it was serious, flippantly or humorously. Pastiche, on the other hand, is often a kind of tribute to the original author. For example, a number of authors have written stories about Sherlock Holmes because they admire Arthur Conan Doyle's detective stories and some readers are eager for new stories even though the original author is dead. The English novelist Kingsley Amis wrote a James Bond novel in the style of Ian Fleming for the same reason.

There is nothing new about these two forms. Samuel Richardson's novel *Pamela* (1740) was parodied by Henry Fielding in *Joseph Andrews* (1742). Fielding replaced the delectable Pamela with the macho Joseph. Modern parodies of J. K. Rowling's Harry Potter books have been written by Michael Gerber, they are called *Barry Trotter* (2001). At the height of the hype concerning *The Lord of the Rings* a parody called *Bored of the Rings* was published and J. R. Tolkein's *The Hobbit* was parodied in 2003 by A. R. R. R. Roberts (actually the novelist Adam Roberts) under the title *The Soddit*. It was openly subtitled *Let's Cash in Again* which explains why some writers write parodies. Another best-seller published in the early twenty-first century was *The Da Vinci Code* by Dan Brown parodied as *The Dundee Code* and set in Australia. The perennial best-seller *Gone With the Wind* (1936) by Margaret Mitchell was parodied in *The Wind Done Gone* (1937) which told the story from the point of view of black slaves. An official sequel to *Gone With the Wind* called *Scarlett* was published in 1991.

As an exercise, attempting to write in the style of an admired author could provide good practice. 'Spoof' is a word currently used of parody particularly films.

See also INTERTEXTUALITY; SEQUELS AND PREQUELS

PATHOS AND BATHOS

Pathos occurs when a feeling of pity, compassion or tenderness towards a character or situation is evoked in the reader. Pathos will be usually felt towards a hero, an admired character or a victim. The group victims of a disaster will also frequently engender pathos. The undeserved or early death of a character is a subject for pathos. If we have cried over some incident in a book we have experienced pathos. Think of the death of Ophelia in *Hamlet* and notice how it is Gertrude's speech about a young girl's death which is the means by which Shakespeare induces pathos. The speech about the death of so many young men after the Battle of Agincourt in *Henry V* produces pathos in many audiences. At the end of the film *Titanic* the hero's death is further saddened for the audience by the sight of hundreds of silent bodies bobbing about in the icy water as a small boat weaves among them looking forlornly for survivors.

The writer must always strike a careful balance with such scenes if pathos is to be achieved. Even good writers can sometimes go over the top into 'bathos', when an incident or character that should have aroused compassion veers towards the absurd or ludicrous. Dickens in *The Old Curiosity Shop* clearly meant the death of Little Nell to arouse pathos and for the most part it did with his contemporary readers. Many modern readers though find the overblown description almost laughable.

The Scottish narrative poet William McGonagall (1832–1902) has often been cited as the master of bathos although it was far from his intention. He was inspired in his work by a variety of tragedies but his use of language was such that the greater the tragedy, the more absurd and laughable his lines became. Here is his verse on the Tay Bridge railway disaster:

> Beautiful Railway Bridge of the Silvr'y Tay!
> Alas, I am very sorry to say
> That ninety lives have been taken away
> On the last Sabbath day of 1879,
> Which will be remembered for a very long time.

McGonagall never let consistency of poetic technique or feeling for language get in the way of what he wanted to say.

Death is probably what arouses pathos more than anything, especially the death of a child or a young person. People involved in wars and other disasters arouse pity and those suffering from some dreaded disease. Human tragedies also evoke it. To create the desired effect in the reader the author should describe incidents which aim to engender sympathy and pathos fairly straightforwardly. If the reader has already identified or sympathized with the character(s), pathos will come automatically. Bathos often results from an author trying too hard.

See also EMPATHY; SYMPATHY

PERIPHRASIS

Periphrasis is an indirect way of describing or naming something, using more words than are strictly necessary. It is similar to 'circum-locution' and can sometimes be used in the same way as 'euphemism'. In the entry on *pornography* John Cleland's periphrasis is referred to, he never uses either anatomical or crude words for the sex act or sexual organs. He uses flowery, imaginative and euphemistic lan-guage, in other words he is periphrastic.

Usually periphrasis is to be avoided as it is usually a long-winded way of saying something. For instance: 'In the light of the fact that he is just thirteen, he can be forgiven' would be better expressed 'Because he is just thirteen, he can be forgiven.'

A character in fiction may use periphrasis but if an omniscient nar-rator is used in a story periphrasis would be best avoided. There are no rules, of course, where figures of speech are concerned. A first-person narrator who is a character in the story may use it and it can be used for humorous effect as Winston Churchill proved when he retorted to what he regarded as a frivolous question: 'The answer to your question, Sir, is in the plural, and they bounce!' Here Churchill uses periphrasis, circumlocution and euphemism with humour. Politicians are probably the greatest users of periphrasis but to the public it is usually more irritating than amusing.

See also EUPHEMISM; NARRATIVE METHODS; PORNOGRAPHY AND EROTICA

PERMISSIONS

If an author wishes to quote a passage from another published book still in copyright, permission must be sought and usually a fee will have to be paid to the original publisher. Very short quotes often require neither permission nor payment of a fee. Quoting songs or poems or parts of them usually require permission and payment of a fee.

PERSONA

The persona is the voice in a poem or novel that the writer adopts to tell the story. It conveys a point of view. The word comes from the Latin meaning 'mask'. It might be a character but it is usually an unidentifiable and omniscient narrator. It should never be assumed that this voice or persona is the author or that it is the author's opinions and views which are being expressed. The persona, however, very often expresses individual attitudes that may, but not necessarily, reflect those of the author. Authors often adopt a persona in order to distance themselves from events in the novel or poem. It could be argued that the persona is just a character like every other character in the story.

Some critics confine the use of the term persona to the voice in a poem but it is now frequently used with regard to novels. The persona is not at all the same as the protagonist.

In everyday speech the word persona is sometimes used as an alternative to personality, for example 'She has a cynical persona although she's usually positive'. Thus it is used about someone who adopts a personality somewhat different from his or her usual one.

See also PROTAGONIST

PERSONIFICATION

Personification is the endowing of non-human objects, ideas or animals with human characteristics, for example 'The storm gathered its strength, held out its arms and took us in its fierce grip'. A common personification describes the sun 'smiling' on people, or 'looking down' on them. Weather seems to be a popular subject of personification: 'the thunder muttered then broke into an almighty roar'; 'the hail stabbed his cheeks'.

Abstractions can be personified for instance: 'death took hold of her and led her away'; 'we walked through the forest accompanied all the way by fear just a pace behind us'; 'justice was the hero of the hour when the jury delivered their verdict'.

In George Orwell's novel *Animal Farm* (1945) animal characters are personified. Orwell uses the technique common in books for very young children but for different purposes. The personification of the animals in *Animal Farm* has a very serious purpose because it highlights some of the human traits that Orwell is satirizing. Had he dealt in human characters the effect would not have been nearly as effective. Terry Pratchett in his Discworld series of novels has characters that are personifications of abstractions such as death.

Phatic (Phatic Communion)

Phatic or Phatic Communion is a term which was coined by the anthropologist, Bronislaw Malinowski (1884–1942). It refers to speech events which do not communicate essential information but are rather remarks made for the sake of politeness and to acknowledge social solidarity with someone else in circumstances that do not necessarily demand or invite sustained conversation. Phatic is used to put people at their ease and to alleviate possible embarrassment.

Phatic can be understood by considering these examples and thinking of the occasions when we use them:

Hello	Cheers
Good morning	There you go
Pleased to meet you	Bob's your uncle
Nice day	See you later
Lovely weather	How y'doing
Raining again	

When we say 'raining again', we are not regarding the addressee as ignorant and someone who needs to be told the state of the weather, it is simply something to say to establish a friendly attitude on passing or meeting someone. Similarly, if we ask someone 'How are you?' we do not expect or want a run down of their medical condition. Greetings are usually phatic and some situations almost demand the use of phatic. Entering a lift with a stranger for instance may feel uncomfortable unless one makes some small talk.

Phatic is paradoxically both unnecessary and essential; unnecessary because it makes no material difference if it is not used, essential because it makes life pleasanter. It is certainly one of the most common forms of speech used by almost everyone. For a form of speech that is so common, writers rarely use it in fictional dialogue, this is because dialogue tends to be pared down to essentials and to write phatic remarks every time characters meet would be boring for the reader.

See also DIALOGUE

Picaresque Novel

The picaresque novel is one which recounts the ongoing adventures of the central character who is invariably a rogue. There is no conventional plot but rather a series of episodes some of which may expose or satirize aspects of society. Episodes could be taken out of such novels without damaging the novel's coherence, something which would be impossible in the novel with a conventional plot.

The word 'picaro' means 'rogue' in Spanish and sixteenth-century Spain produced the first picaresque narratives or novels, for example, *Don Quixote* by Cervantes (1605 and 1615). French versions followed and early English fiction writers also produced picaresque novels, for example Daniel Defoe (*Moll Flanders*, 1722), Henry Fielding (*Jonathan Wild*, 1743) and Tobias Smollett (*Roderick Random*, 1748).

Although not popular now picaresque novels are occasionally written. A classic from the late nineteenth century is Mark Twain's *The Adventures of Huckleberry Finn* (1884) which he followed with *The Adventures of Tom Sawyer* (1886). Both of these follow the pattern of the picaresque novel in that they recount a series of loosely connected incidents in the life of the central characters and their friends. Twain also injects considerable humour into the stories together with a high degree of satire by viewing the often absurd and cruel behaviour of adults through the eyes of a child.

A later English novel which is in a modern, modified picaresque style is Kingsley Amis' *Lucky Jim* (1954). This comic novel recounts the adventures of the central character Jim in his first job as a university lecturer and Amis uses the novel to satirize some university types and practices. Although in diary form, the Adrian Mole novels by Sue Townsend could be called picaresque. The humour in these books compensates in a way for the lack of a plot and while Adrian is hardly a rogue, he is a luckless incompetent. The author also employs satire of a gentle kind.

While the writer of picaresque does not have the problems of creating a well-worked out plot, other skills are necessary. To involve the reader for the length of a novel with a series of episodes requires skill in creating an engaging character, as well as inventing interesting adventures imbued with humour and satire.

See also EPISTOLARY NOVEL; PLOT AND STORY

PLAGIARISM

Plagiarism is stealing another author's work. An act of plagiarism could be copying a whole work or simply copying sections of it. When lengthy extracts of another author's work are copied, plagiarism is easily identified and hard to deny by the plagiarist.

As well as involving cheating, plagiarism is an offence under the Copyright, Designs and Patents Act, 1988. This law protects an author's right to own and earn from his or her work and thus breach of someone's copyright constitutes plagiarism. It is a civil rather than a criminal offence but if it is found to have occurred, the offender may have to pay damages. The associated shame and loss of reputation might well be as bad as any financial punishment.

The Copyright Act discusses the use by others of short quotes, sometimes known as 'fair dealing'. Obviously the use of short quotations will involve acknowledging the source. The out-and-out plagiarist on the other hand will attempt to pass off the other author's work as their own. Ideas and facts are not subject to copyright and thus cannot be plagiarized but an exception to this would be if a writer came up with a completely new theory or idea.

Once a writer is out of copyright (seventy years after their death) they may be quoted with impunity. It would be unlikely for someone to copy a classic novel or extracts from one but there are a number of contemporary novelists who use the characters from classic novels in a new story. This is quite permissible and does not breach copyright. Characters created by Jane Austen, Emily Brontë and Arthur Conan Doyle among others have been used in this way and a successful series of novels has been written by George MacDonald Fraser using the character of Flashman from *Tom Brown's School Days*.

Works that are out of copyright may be published by anyone without acknowledgement or incurring a fee.

See also COPYRIGHT

PLOT AND STORY

Novels, short stories and plays are concerned with the interplay of characters, action, dialogue, thoughts and motivations of characters within a given setting. The structure of the actions or events has been called the plot but plot needs to be investigated further for two reasons. First, it is the element which probably gives writers more concern than any other and, second, there is no clearly accepted definition. Is it the same as story? If not, how does it differ? Views on plot have been discussed since Aristotle's time but it is probably useful to begin with some of the ideas of the novelist E. M. Forster. His theories concerning story and plot have been influential since they were first expressed in lectures given in Cambridge. They were later published in the book *Aspects of the Novel* (1927), which also discusses character, fantasy, prophecy and rhythm.

E. M. Forster on Story and Plot

If we have heard of an interesting incident concerning people in our neighbourhood, or about relatives or strangers and we tell the incident to friends who are unaware of it, we may refer to our narrative as a story. We would be unlikely to call it a plot. Our narrative would almost certainly be straightforward, without flourishes, and almost certainly in time sequence of the events as they took place. We may add a few embellishments such as what the people we are talking about are like and possibly how we feel about them. We would hope that our listeners would be hanging on to every word. Such a narrative (we might call it gossip) accords with E. M. Forster's definition of story: 'It is a narrative of events arranged in their time sequence . . . it can only have one merit: that of making the audience want to know what happens next.'

Forster goes on to contend that while this is 'the slowest and simplest of literary organisms' it is also, he claims, the element common to all novels. We would endorse Forster's claim that in story the reader must want to know 'what happens next'. If the reader puts aside the short story or novel unfinished, then the writer has failed.

Forster's ideas are more contentious when he defines plot and distinguishes it from story. He wrote 'A plot is also a narrative of events, the emphasis falling on causality. "The king died and then the queen died" is a story. "The king died and then the queen died of grief" is a plot. The time-sequence is preserved, but the sense of causality overshadows it.' He goes on to say that the story is a sequence of '. . . and then, and then, and then . . .' whereas the story with a plot invites the reader to ask why and the novelist to put an emphasis on the reasons or motivations why people do things. Forster, something of an elitist, refers to those readers who only want stories as 'cave men' and, even worse in his eyes, the 'movie going public'!

While not without interest and perhaps some merit, Forster's distinctions between story and plot rather fall down when one tries to find examples of the two kinds of fiction. It is true that the great novels and what may be called literary fiction deal with causality and motivation in characters but so also do most, if not all, popular and escapist fictions. The crime story would not really work if the criminals did not have motivations for their crimes and frequently the authors of such fiction explore these in some depth. We may sometimes question the validity of the psychology of characters in popular fiction but then we do that of more serious literature as well. Even the simplest story for infants often deals with not only what characters do but *why* they do what they do.

Perhaps the most valuable lesson Forster has for the writer relates to the way he emphasizes the importance of causality. The more sophisticated reader is more interested in why characters do things than what they do.

Forster's emphasis on time sequence is also not particularly helpful. The simplest fiction is likely to be told chronologically but so are many classics and popular fiction often uses flashback and fore-shadowing. A novel with a complicated time structure may, in fact, be disguising a relatively simple story that would have been apparent had it been told chronologically. Nonetheless, a manipulation of the time sequence may be used to highlight features that in a chronological sequence would have been missed by the reader.

Critical Ideas on Plot

More recent critical ideas on plot do not provide much practical advice for writers. Jeremy Hawthorne in his book *Studying the Novel* (revised edition 1979) states that plot involves '. . . some sense that the actions represent a whole rather than merely a succession of unconnected events'. It is true that almost any novel will have a unity or wholeness about its events. It is difficult to envisage a piece of writing that could be called a novel if it consisted of unconnected events.

Hawthorne, like Forster, puts an emphasis on time sequencing and the fact that fiction may manipulate time for artistic purposes. He states 'Plots are found in novels rather than in ordinary life; life has stories, but novels have plots and stories'. In other words the novelist is selective. In a novel, say, which spans a time period of five years, only a relatively few episodes in that time sequence will constitute what goes to make up a plot; inessentials will be omitted. Hawthorne also agrees with Forster about the importance of causality.

The Chicago school of critics (influenced by Aristotle, although not following him completely) emphasize that in a plot the author is arousing and controlling the reader's interest and his emotional responses to events and characters, even creating a kind of tension or anxiety which will be resolved at the end of the fiction. Some writers may wish to do this, perhaps most, but there is no formula for doing it.

Plot Structure

So far the different ideas on plot expressed by various critics have noted the importance of: (a) time structure; (b) causality and motivation on the part of the characters; (c) a unity of events which involves the omission of inessentials in the lives of the characters.

From the writer's point of view, a practical way of examining plot in fiction is to analyse specific fictions and in particular the central thing in most stories, the protagonist.

A basic premise is that a fiction, be it a novel, short story or drama invariably has a protagonist who at the beginning is found in a situation which presents them with a problem to solve, a goal to be achieved, an aim to be realized, a predicament to get out of or a purpose in life that is not easy to realize. These are generalities. The problem may be to save a marriage, to get out of one, to find something to do with one's life, to find a partner, to discover who has cheated you, to discover one's ancestry, etc.

If the story is to have a happy ending, the goal will be realized, the problem solved or the aim achieved. Thus, we have the beginning and ending of the structure of the story. The most interesting and longest part is the middle section – how the aim was realized, or the problem solved. This part will also show the protagonist beset by problems. If the goal were achieved too easily the fiction would lack interest. Conflict, in particular, is essential in this middle section. It is what gives the plot interest to the reader.

Some examples from both serious and popular fiction will illustrate the points made above. In all of Ian Fleming's James Bond stories, the hero is presented with a seemingly insuperable problem that usually boils down to how the world can be saved from the actions of a mad villain. The substance of the story or plot is the overcoming by the hero of the various obstacles put in his way by the villain and his gang. The obstacles and setbacks seem insurmountable but Bond always eventually overcomes them.

In the detective story, the detective's aim is to solve the crime, catch the criminal and again obstacles abound to frustrate his efforts. In the romance, the hero or heroine wants to win the woman or man, but the road to this must not be too easy if it is to be interesting.

Literally hundreds of fictions have been written with this basic plot structure. The art of the writer, of course, is to provide interesting characters and variations on this.

This basic plot does not just apply to popular or genre fiction. It is apparent in Shakespeare's plays. In *Hamlet,* the central character's aim is to avenge the murder of his father. Others wish to prevent him from doing so but the biggest obstacle is his own nature, his inability to take decisive action and his distaste for revenge. In *Romeo and Juliet* the protagonists wish to realize their love and the chief obstacle is the fact that their two families have been feuding for years and are known to oppose the relationship. In these two plays aims are not realized and tragedy results.

In Charles Dickens' *Great Expectations* the hero Pip has desired from childhood to love and marry the cold-hearted Estella. A very convoluted plot with numerous sub-plots leads him to be given hope that he might achieve his goal. Interestingly Dickens had intended that Pip should definitely not marry Estella but he was persuaded that the novel would be more popular if he did.

This plot structure can be represented diagrammatically as in the box.

START OF STORY
PROTAGONIST has:
GOAL – AIM – PURPOSE – PROBLEM TO SOLVE

AIM frustrated, difficulties arise
PROTAGONIST seeks to overcome obstacles/
other characters' actions
Conflicts abound

Seeming SUCCESS is met with further/temporary setbacks
OVERCOMES OR FAILS TO OVERCOME DIFFICULTIES

CLIMAX/RESOLUTION
TRAGIC or SUCCESSFUL/HAPPY or NEUTRAL/
INDECISIVE ENDING

In a short story the above plot may have to be simplified. In a long novel there could be a whole series of obstacles and setbacks before the climax and resolution.

Almost any novel can be looked at and it will display this plot structure or some variation of it. Sometimes it may not be obvious – for instance when it is hidden by a complicated time sequence. The purpose of the protagonist is not always apparent at the beginning.

Novels by all the major classic writers such as Dickens, Jane Austen, George Eliot and Thomas Hardy demonstrate this plot structure. So do novels by most contemporary writers.

Even in avant-garde work where it seems unlikely this plot structure can be discerned. For instance, in what appears to be a very original and experimental play, *Waiting for Godot* by Samuel Beckett, the two protagonists have an aim in life – they are waiting for Godot. The substance of the play in both acts is their frustration in not being able to realize this desire and ultimately the ending is tragic or tragi-comic because Godot never comes. In this play Beckett is playing with conventional plot.

At the other extreme the structure can be seen in this fable by Aesop, 'The thirsty crow'.

Aim	A crow, who was suffering intensely from thirst, saw a pitcher and flew to it in great haste, hoping to find water in it.
Obstacle	When he reached it, what was his disappointment on discovering that the pitcher contained so little water that he could not possibly get at it because of the narrow neck.
Struggle	After trying every way he could think of to reach
Setback	the water, but without success,
Renewed struggle	he at last hit upon a plan which he thought would bring the water to his reach. Collecting all the small stones he could find, he dropped them one by one into the pitcher,
Climax	until he had caused the water to rise into the neck of the pitcher, when he was able to reach it
Ending/ Triumph	and drink his fill.

A Plot is Like Life

It is of some relevance and interest to examine why the plot structure described above is so universal. The main reason is that it imitates the progress through life of most human beings. People at various stages of their lives have aims or goals they wish to fulfil or achieve. Fulfilling and achieving them is neither straightforward nor easy; there are usually obstacles, struggles and setbacks. Some of our aims we achieve, others we do not. Fiction, usually concentrates on one or a limited number of aims but in life, once we have achieved one goal, we tend to pursue another. The adolescent's aim may be fulfilled but the adult will have a new and different one. A common pattern of life goals for many people is something like this: desire to go to school, wish to succeed in exams and get to college, desire to get a degree or qualifications so that a chosen career choice can be followed, desire for a job and promotion, wish to fall in love and marry; get married, want divorce and get it (setback); remarry and so on. Even the retired person sets new goals: to travel perhaps or to take up a new hobby. At each stage in our life the present goal seems all-important. Older people will wonder why they were so concerned about school exams. Whatever goal the writer is dealing with, he or she must make it important for the reader even though they may not share that goal in their own lives.

An Alternative Plot Structure

A similar but alternative plot structure to the one described above can be represented as in the diagram. The numbered points are described in the following list.

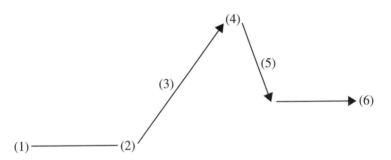

1   This is the exposition which describes the setting, situation and the main character(s).
2   This delineates the central character's problem or aim and the opposition to the easy realization of it.
3   This is sometimes called 'rising action' (hence the sloping arrowed line) which deals with the character's various attempts to deal with opposition or conflict. This stage will probably be the longest part of the story.
4   This represents the climax of the story.
5   This represents the 'falling action' or the resolution of the problems or aims. For the character it may be success or failure. This section will be quite short.

6   This is the conclusion or denouement. As in the other plot structure pattern it can be happy, sad, tragic, neutral or indecisive.

The thing the writer must remember is that plot structures and principles such as the ones described do not necessarily make the task easy or mechanical. The good short story or novel depends on the writer's injecting original and interesting characters, conflict, suspense and problems into the fiction.

See also ANACHRONY; CHARACTERS; CLIMAX; CONFLICT; ELLIPSES; PLOT (RECENT AND OLDER THEORIES); SUB-PLOT; SUSPENSE

PLOT (RECENT AND OLDER THEORIES)

In a recent book called *The Seven Basic Plots: Why We Tell Stories* (2005), Christopher Booker outlines what he believes are the seven plots found in fiction. Briefly, they are as follows:

1   *Overcoming the Monster* (the word 'monster' being used loosely to indicate an enemy of the hero or of society). This plot concerns the hero in conflict with the monster or evil and finally overcoming it. *Beowulf*, the James Bond novels, *Dracula*, and *Little Red Riding Hood* are examples.

2   *Rags to Riches*. In this plot the ordinary or the underprivileged have the strength to overcome their disadvantages and problems to make good. *Jane Eyre* and *Cinderella* are examples.

3   *The Quest*. In this plot a character goes on a long and difficult journey to find some 'treasure' which may be physical, human or spiritual. The *Lord of the Rings* trilogy and *Silas Marner* are examples.

4   *Voyage and Return*. This plot has similarities with *The Quest* but usually concerns the protagonist having to leave his or her native community to find something important and returning a wiser person or with some benefit for the community. Many Biblical stories are based around a voyage and return, from the story of Moses to that of Jesus.

5   *Comedy* is about a state of confusion which is eventually resolved for the main characters. Shakespeare's *The Merchant of Venice* and his other comedies are examples.

6   *Tragedy*. The protagonist is over-ambitious, proud or his or her aims are unworthy (e.g. a desire for power) and ultimately tragedy follows. Shakespeare's tragedies are examples.

7   *Rebirth*. This plot might concern a wrongdoer or misguided person realizing their error and setting out eventually on a new

life. One of the best examples is Scrooge in *A Christmas Carol* by Dickens.

Booker, in a coda, also suggests additional plots on *Rebellion* and *Mystery*, the latter to account for the relatively recent detective genre. *The Catcher in the Rye* and *1984* both contain the *Rebellion* plot.

Whether Booker's plot categories are more valid than the basic plot described in the entry for plot and story is left for the reader to decide. They may be seen as complementary. His book is essential reading for all potential fiction writers and even if his ideas taken together are rejected, as they have been by some critics, there is a wealth of information in the book. Many critics, for instance, would not refer to tragedy and comedy as plot types, tragedy and comedy can occur as an adjunct to any kind of story.

An older theorist of plots and the nature of fiction is the late Joseph Campbell in his book *The Hero With a Thousand Faces* (1948). Campbell also sees common patterns over the ages in fiction and specifically in the nature of the hero and the hero's journey. He relates this to ancient myths and also utilizes the work of the Swiss psychiatrist, Carl Jung. Campbell's ideas were famously picked up by George Lucas and used as a basis for plotting the *Star Wars* series of films. Hollywood film writers have since made use of his ideas in innumerable films, particularly blockbusters.

See also PLOT AND STORY

POINT

Point is the name given to the size of type used in books. Ten or eleven point is common in novels and many non-fiction books. Books for very young children are frequently in a much larger point. Computer word processing and desktop publishing software programmes have a facility for changing the point size at the touch of a button. Sometimes 'font size' is referred to, although the 'font' is really the style of print, for example Times New Roman, Ariel, etc.

POINT OF VIEW

The point of view in a novel is supplied by the narrator or narrative method used by the writer.

See also NARRATIVE METHODS

PORNOGRAPHY AND EROTICA

Erotica is a term used to denote literature and other arts concerned with sexual love and which has an erotic or sexually arousing effect. As far as literature is concerned, there will be detailed descriptions of a variety of sex acts and the sexual organs and other erogenous zones. Pornography has the same function and the distinction between the two is difficult to make. Erotica is usually used if there is some artistic merit in the work, pornography is almost exclusively arousing, or that is its intention. It has been noted that one man's or woman's erotica is another man's or woman's pornography, and vice versa. Jeremy Clarke described the difference wittily if not terribly helpfully when he observed '. . . in erotica you use a feather and in pornography the whole chicken gets roped in'. Pornography has rarely been acclaimed. This is suggested by the derivation of the word, Greek 'porni' for 'prostitute' and 'graphe' for 'writing'.

Erotica and pornography have always been popular with many people although others condemn them out of hand.

Shortly after printing began in the west in the fifteenth century, photography in the nineteenth century, the film industry started in 1895, and the internet began in the late twentieth century, pornography quickly became a substantial part of these media. Internet pornography has to a certain extent reduced the amount of literary pornography but a search of any large bookshop will almost certainly reveal that many erotic novels are published. Series of books exist (such as *Black Lace*) which provide an alternative to Mills & Boon romances. Many are targeted specifically at women. This is not because women are more interested in erotica than men; rather it seems to be that men prefer the visual images on the Net. Women often seem to like their erotica framed in a story.

The most famous erotic novel still extant from the eighteenth century is John Cleland's *Fanny Hill* (originally called M*emoirs of a Woman of Pleasure*, 1748–49). The play on the words in the heroine's name is reflected in the content of the novel which is a simple story of a young girl going to London, becoming a prostitute, falling for a client and eventually marrying. Her various sexual exploits are described in detail and make up the body of the novel. Cleland did not use a single crude or direct word about sex. The novel has been said to be a classic of the use of both euphemism and euphuism. It may be regarded as periphrastic. It demonstrates that erotica need not use crude language. It may also explain why it has become a Penguin Classic.

D. H. Lawrence's novel *Lady Chatterley's Lover* had been put on trial a few years before *Fanny Hill* but it was cleared of charges of obscenity on the grounds that the book had literary merit and was not solely concerned with sex.

The 1960s to 1980s saw many prosecutions of novels, plays and even a poem for obscenity but since the 1980s few novels have been prosecuted for obscenity. The main qualification for writing them is an ability to write sexual scenes which people enjoy and which are not embarrassing or silly. (There is an annual award organized by a literary magazine in Britain called the 'Bad Sex Award'.) The plots are minimal and straightforward and the story must be such that ample opportunity is given for characters to interact carnally and with considerable frequency and enthusiasm. Erotic fiction, in fact, has become almost respectable. Literotica, a course in writing erotic fiction was openly advertised in 2005. Not surprisingly 'sex scenes' form a part of many novels but the terms discussed apply only to those works in which sex and sexual description are the dominant content.

See also EUPHEMISM; EUPHUISM; OBSCENE PUBLICATIONS ACT

PRINT RUN
The print run is the number of copies of a book (or magazine) printed in one edition.

PROLETARIAN NOVELS
Proletarian literature is concerned to present working-class people sympathetically and usually aims to expose injustice in order to encourage change. Some critics argue that only working-class writers can do this sincerely and by the nature of their work most novelists are or become middle class. (In some countries this may not be the case.) It is significant that in the 1950s and 1960s in Britain a group of writers emerged who began by portraying working-class characters but invariably the solution to their problems was to become middle class or to have the trappings of middle-class living. The character may have changed but there was no change in society. The most obvious examples of this were the novels of John Braine (1922–1986). In his 1957 novel *Room at the Top*, the hero, Joe Lampton, as the title suggests, may have been working class but he wants to find room among the rich. (The sequel was *Life at the Top*). Braine himself began as a left-wing radical and following his own success he veered to the right

and became a vocal supporter of capital punishment and the then repressive government in South Africa.

Kingsley Amis's first novel *Lucky Jim* demonstrated left-wing credentials but Amis too moved to the right and his later novels frequently enraged the left and feminists alike. Stan Barstow and Alan Sillitoe were working-class writers who retained their integrity but not the success of their early work. Sid Chaplin was a miner's son, he become a miner himself, and subsequently a writer who sensitively portrayed the lives of miners and their families.

Many nineteenth-century novelists, of course, dealt with social themes and were sympathetic to the poor and disaffected. Dickens himself had been brought up in poverty and many of his novels portray injustices to the poor and children in particular. Dickens' attitudes were ambivalent, however. For example, he has little support for the idea of trade unionism in his novel *Hard Times*.

Other Victorians such as George Eliot, Elizabeth Gaskell, Charles Kingsley and Elizabeth Barrett Browning also showed sympathy for the disadvantaged in society but it would be more accurate to call them humanitarian rather than proletarian writers.

The climate of the present times and increased personal affluence for most people in western society means that there are few proletarian writers now. Some novelists, though, continue to place social problems as the central themes in their work. It is almost inevitable if the writer feels strongly about an issue. One problem that affected all the novelists mentioned and is important for all those who intend to explore social themes is the general unpopularity of didacticism. This is a possibility and may even be a temptation for the proletarian or social writer.

The following are major works by the writers mentioned:

Kingsley Amis, *Lucky Jim* (1954).
Stan Barstow, *A Kind of Loving* (1960).
John Braine, *Room at the Top* (1957).
Sid Chaplin, *The Day of the Sardine* (1961).
John Dos Passos, *The Big Money* (1936).
Maxim Gorky, *The Lower Depths* (1902).
Jack London, *The Iron Heel* (1907).
Alan Sillitoe, *Saturday Night and Sunday Morning* (1958).
Upton Sinclair, *The Jungle* (1906).
Robert Tressell, *The Ragged Trousered Philanthropists* (1914).

See also DIDACTICISM; REGIONAL NOVELS; STORY AND NOVEL CATEGORIES

PROOFREADER

A proofreader is the person employed by a publisher to read the proofs of a manuscript to check:

- Accuracy of spelling, punctuation and grammar.
- The factual accuracy and consistency of the text.
- The text fits into a distinct house style.
- The typesetter has followed the copy editor's instructions.

PROTAGONIST

The protagonist in a work of fiction is the main character. Protagonist is a more useful term in most cases than hero or heroine because it implies no particular characteristics or personality features. We expect heroic qualities in a hero; a protagonist may be heroic, cowardly, good, bad or indifferent.

The word *protagonist* was originally used for the leader of the chorus in Greek drama and then it referred to the lead actor. Occasionally there may be dual or multiple protagonists in a story. (*The Three Musketeers* by Alexander Dumas is an obvious case.) Most authors, however, favour a single protagonist. The 'agon' part of the Greek word means 'contest' and almost always the protagonist will be in contention or conflict with another character or characters or with some adverse set of circumstances.

Being the main character, the protagonist will probably have a complex personality and, possibly even contradictory traits; it is also usual during the course of the narrative for the protagonist to develop and be changed through his experiences.

The protagonist will be of more interest to the reader if he has a number of obstacles (or villains) to face – or, if you like, by an *antagonist*. In Shakespeare's *Hamlet*, Hamlet is the protagonist and Claudius the main antagonist. In *Othello*, Othello is the protagonist, Iago the antagonist. In *Dr Faustus* by Christopher Marlowe Dr Faustus is the protagonist; his antagonist is the Devil or his temptation to sin.

See also ANTAGONIST; CHARACTERS; CONFLICT; HERO; PLOT AND STORY

PSEUDONYMS

Pseudonym comes from the Greek, meaning false name. It is a fictitious name used by an individual as an alternative to his or her legal name.

The main people who use a pseudonym are those in the public eye, also writers (pen name) and criminals.

There are various reasons for taking a pseudonym, the main ones being:

- To hide one's real identity.
- To have a more memorable name.
- To have a more easily pronounceable name.
- To have a more attractive name.
- To disguise a foreign name.
- To suggest the opposite gender to the person's real one.
- To satisfy the desires of an agent or publisher.

Some writers have taken on multiple pseudonyms, usually for the different kinds of writing they do or the different publications for which they write. Daniel Defoe's real name was Daniel Foe but he also used over a hundred other pseudonyms. The nineteenth-century novelist, William Makepeace Thackeray used over thirty names. The prolific children's writer Charles Howard St John Hamilton was better known as Frank Richards, author of boy's stories, and Hilda Richards for his stories for girls. He also used at least four other pseudonyms.

In the nineteenth century, women writers were subject to prejudice and writing was not usually considered a suitable job for a woman. So the three Brontë sisters took names which were rather neutral and they hoped publishers would assume they were men. Charlotte called herself Currer Bell, Emily Ellis Bell and Anne Acton Bell. Mary Ann Evans used one of her husband's names and called herself George Eliot. After publication the true identity of the author usually came out.

The following are some notable writers who used pseudonyms. Their real name is on the right:

Anthony Burgess	John Wilson
Lewis Carroll	Charles Lutwidge Dodgson
Marie Corelli	Mary (Minnie) Mackay
Maxim Gorky	Aleksei Peshkov
O. Henry	William Sydney Porter
John Le Carré	David John Moore Cornwell
George Orwell	Eric Arthur Blair

PSYCHOLOGICAL NOVELS

Psychology is the scientific study of the mind, mental states and behaviour. The term 'psychological novel' is a rather vague one but it appears to be used of three distinct types of novel:

1   Novels which attempt to convey the inner workings of an individual's mind using a specific literary technique.
2   Novels which are more concerned with exploring a character or characters' deepest thoughts and motivations and which places character analysis as far more important than plot.
3   Novels which are more frequently called 'psychological thrillers'. These often contain at least one character who is suffering a psychological illness. At worst they may be psychopathic and they are frequently criminals such as serial killers with some morbid obsession.

All three types of novel obviously owe something to psychology which was of great interest in the early part of the twentieth century and continues to be so. Sigmund Freud (1856–1939) has been of particular significance. He emphasized the importance of the sexual impulse as a motivation for much human behaviour, even though some of his early disciples (Adler and Jung) and later psychologists have rejected this notion.

The authors of psychological novels are rarely, if ever, trained psychologists and may have little knowledge of the subject. Psychology has in a sense become part of the mindset of most people since the middle of the last century. Many people refer to conditions like Oedipus and Electra complexes, identity crisis and repression and use terms such as libido, ego, inhibition, as if they were familiar with academic psychology. It is disputable how accurately such terms are used.

Of course some people, including novelists, were quite aware that the inner life was as important as the exterior one of action before psychology became an accepted discipline. Shakespeare provides an in-depth examination of Hamlet's mind and motivations and the analysis of guilt in *Macbeth* is equally convincing. Some early novels, such as Laurence Sterne's *Tristram Shandy*, have characters who are deeply introspective in their first-person narratives. The German philosopher Karl Kraus (1874–1936) once remarked 'psychology is as unnecessary as directions on a poison bottle'. In other words, although professional psychologists might not agree, we are all amateur psychologists or at least students of human behaviour and motivation, we don't need special training.

The three types of psychological novel are as follows:

Novels of the Inner Life

The three pioneers of this kind of novel were James Joyce, Virginia Woolf and Dorothy Richardson. Woolf explained her view of what a novel should be about like this: 'Examine for a moment an ordinary mind on an ordinary day. The mind receives myriad impressions – trivial, fantastic, evanescent, or engraved with the sharpness of steel. From all sides they come, an incessant shower of innumerable atoms; and as they fall, as they shape themselves into the life of Monday or Tuesday . . .'

The truth of this is undisputable but equally obvious is a problem: does the reader want to know every passing thought, the trivial as well as the important? In fact, these novelists, although they may include material which is sparse in the more conventional novel, are equally selective.

James Joyce acknowledged that he was indebted to a French novelist, Edouard Dujardin (1861–1949) whose novel *Les Lauriers Sont Coupés* (1888) had used a kind of interior monologue that Dujardin described thus: 'The internal monologue, like every monologue, is the speech of a given character, designed to introduce us directly into the internal life of this character, without the author's intervening by explaining or commenting . . .' The author may not explain or comment, but he or she has chosen what to include and what to omit. Another precursor of the psychological novel was the Frenchman, Marcel Proust. The first of his 16-volume novel, *The Remembrance of Things Past* was published in 1912. It recounts memories of the protagonists past often evoked by a smell or other sensations.

One of the main writers to develop the techniques used by Joyce and Woolf was the American novelist William Faulkner, most notably in *The Sound and the Fury* (1929). Otherwise, these techniques are confined to sections in more conventional novels.

The Novel of Character

This type contains considerable character analysis. The character will be described in detail, his or her motives for action will be analysed in detail and the character will be (in E. M. Forster's terms) round rather than flat.

In general in these novels, characterization will be more, or as, important as action and plot. George Eliot (1819–1880) in her novels from *Adam Bede* (1859) to her masterpiece *Middlemarch* (1872) is generally recognized as one of the earliest exponents of an analytical approach to character delineation, not just of her protagonists but of minor characters as well. Henry James is also noted for his penetrating character analysis as well as being concerned with moral issues, in particular the contrast of innocence and experience.

It is perhaps invidious to suggest examples of novelists who are exponents of in-depth psychological characterization. There are so many.

The Psychological Thriller

The psychological thriller is, unlike the previous novels, part of a popular genre of fiction such as detective stories and police procedurals. It may also be the kind of novel where there is no mystery regarding the identity of the criminal but the interest of the story lies in the cat and mouse chase between the said criminal and the tracker, be it detective or otherwise. In some cases detection may not be involved. The psychology of the criminals in these novels is sometimes believable, sometimes dubious, and frequently the psychopath will indulge in ingenious games which in reality rarely occurs.

While the Russian *Crime and Punishment* (1866) may be the first truly psychological thriller, one of the first British examples is *The Strange Case of Dr Jekyll and Mr Hyde* (1886) written by Robert Louis Stevenson. This was written before the advent of medical psychology. The novel was one of Stevenson's most successful because he recognized a phenomenon of human personality which many people saw in themselves; that is, that we have two sides or personalities. One is rational and respectable which we present to the world and the other is irrational, harbours desires and violent impulses that we keep hidden or repressed. In this story, the effect of a drug brings out Dr Jekyll's alter ego Mr Hyde; the calm doctor is transformed into a psychopath. The transformation, at a naturalistic level, is unbelievable and exaggerated but the story contains a core of truth about human beings that remains as true today as it was in the late nineteenth century. Every day we see examples of the violent side of human beings being exposed and drugs are often a catalyst for this.

Recently the psychological thrillers by Thomas Harris have made a huge impact. His stories are about a psychopath, Hannibal Lecter. In the novels *Red Dragon* (1981), *The Silence of the Lambs* (1988) and *Hannibal* (1999), Lecter is a psychopathic killer but the novels usually also concern other psychopaths who Lecter helps to catch. They are characterized by gruesome violence. Hannibal is a cannibal and in one novel he actually feeds a victim part of the victim's own brains. (Medically, the brain is immune to pain.)

In Britain the chief exponent of psychological thrillers is Barbara Vine (pen name of Ruth Rendell), although some of Rendell's non-police procedurals are also psycho-thrillers. She deals often with murder but she is also interested in the effects of guilt, desire, greed and obsession. Most acclaimed are *A Fatal Inversion* (1987) as Barbara Vine and *Live Flesh* (1986) and *The Bridesmaid* (1989) as Ruth Rendell. Recent exponents of the psychological thriller are Joanna Briscoe (*Sleep With Me*, 2005), Julie Myerson and Maggie O'Farrell.

See also DETECTIVE STORIES; INTERIOR MONOLOGUE; STORY AND NOVEL CATEGORIES; STREAM OF CONSCIOUSNESS; SUSPENSE; THRILLERS

PULP FICTION

Pulp fiction refers to novel-length stories or short stories of a sensational nature. They are stories with plenty of action, clear heroes and heroines and often a woman in danger. They pay scant heed to social realism. The subject is usually a crime and the hero a detective, probably a private eye; but pulp fiction also embraces science fiction, Westerns and general adventure stories. One of the reasons for the title 'pulp' was the fact that these novels were published very cheaply and hence used cheap paper of the quality of newsprint. They would always have a garish cover and were always paperbacks.

Pulp fiction was an American invention for those (mainly men) wanting fiction, but with little interest in literature. A great deal of pulp fiction was imported into Britain but there were also British writers, the most notable being Hank Jansen who wrote dozens of novels. The writers never achieved acclaim; they wrote fast and usually under a number of names, one for Westerns, another for crime, another for science fiction. The books had a short shelf-life, rather like magazines. Pulp fiction as it was no longer exists, another victim of television. Some of Hank Jansen's titles give an idea of the nature of pulp fiction: *Sister, Don't Hate Me*; *Sweetie, Hold me Tight*; *Hotsy*. As the titles indicate there was a sexual content, but this was fairly tame by modern standards. The stories were usually first-person narratives, the hero or central character telling the story.

Quentin Tarantino's 1994 film *Pulp Fiction* interweaves three stories of the type found in pulp novels but the film has a wit and panache which the novels rarely attained.

See also ESCAPIST FICTION

PUN

A *pun* is a play on words usually for humorous effect. A pun can be created because some words, with the same spelling and pronunciation, have more than one meaning. Such words are called 'homonyms'. A 'homophone' is a word with a different spelling and meaning but the same pronunciation.

The 'homograph' is a word which is spelt the same as another but has a completely different meaning(s) and pronunciation.

Some examples:

Homonyms:	rest (the remainder/to relax)
	bay (a herb/a sea inlet/
	the cry of a hound)
	ear (hearing organ/ear of corn)
Homophones:	foul/fowl (nasty/bird)
	hair/hare (tresses/animal)
	bored/board (fed up/piece of wood/
	committee)
Homographs:	row/row (an argument/line of people, things/
	propel boat)
	lead/lead (metal/go out in front)

Although mostly used for humorous effect, the pun is not that popular and punning jokes are rarely regarded as great wit. For instance, this pun on the word rifle: 'The speaker at the convention on armaments lost his place and had to *rifle* through his notes'. This is likely to produce groans rather than laughter.

The pun is rarely used in fiction but writers such as James Joyce and Vladimir Nabokov have cleverly exploited it. A recent exponent of serious, if rather bizarre punning, is the novelist and short story writer, Mick Jackson. In a short story in *Ten Sorry Tales* (2005) two sisters living near the sea kill and kipper a stranger who has caused them displeasure and keep the semi-preserved corpse in their home. The narrator comments 'Edna said how nice it was to have a man about the house. Lol agreed but said that if they hoped to keep him they'd better consider how to stop him going off'. The pun lies in the dual meaning of 'going off'.

Readers who enjoy fiction for its literary value as well as its content will probably enjoy punning, but the writer should take care to be original, not to overdo it, and to make sure that it suits the mood of the story.

Purple Passage

A purple passage (sometimes called a purple patch) is a piece of writing that stands out from the rest of the text because it is particularly ornate or flowery in its use of words. Purple passages in prose are often deplored by critics because of their exaggerated language but there may sometimes be good reasons in the context of the story to highlight an incident by a change in the style of a language.

There is a famous passage in Emily Brontë's *Wuthering Heights* where Cathy tries to explain her undying love for Heathcliff. Some condemn it as purple prose; others regard it as a high point in Brontë's writing. The reader may judge:

> '. . . My great miseries in this world have been Heathcliff's miseries, and I watched and felt each from the beginning; my great thought in living is himself. If all else perished and *he* remained, I should still continue to be; and if all else remained, and he were annihilated, the world would turn into a mighty stranger. I should not seem a part of it. My love for Linton is like the foliage in the woods. Time will change it, I'm well aware, as winter changes the trees. My love for Heathcliff resembles the eternal rocks beneath – a source of little visible delight, but necessary. Nelly, I *am* Heathcliff – he's always, always in my mind – not as a pleasure, any more than I am always a pleasure to myself – but as my own being – so don't talk of our separation again – it is impracticable; and –'

Realism and Naturalism

For practical purposes there is not a great deal of difference between literary realism and literary naturalism. Writers in these traditions attempt to render the world and characters in as authentically lifelike a way as possible and supply factual descriptions and faithful representations of settings and human behaviour. They do not idealize, glamorize or romanticize and therefore frequently present the reader with the ordinary and the less dramatic side of life.

To achieve a semblance of realism, subject matter is important and realist novelists have often written about middle- and working-class characters rather than the nobility. The themes and subject matter are reflected in this choice and they mostly affect ordinary people: problems to do with love, marriage, employment, money and poverty.

The term Realism, with a capital 'R', is also applied to a movement which began in the middle of the nineteenth century as a reaction against a more romantic outlook. It could be argued however that a pre-nineteenth century novelist like Daniel Defoe was almost as much a realist as George Eliot, Mrs Gaskell, Jane Austen or Charles Dickens.

The Russian novelist, Leo Tolstoy (1828–1910) with *War and Peace* and Honoré de Balzac in France (1799–1850) with over ninety novels were part of the Realistic movement. Balzac, particularly, is notable for his use of detailed description of furniture, decorations, clothes, food, etc. to enhance the sense of the real, ordinary world. *La Comedie Humaine* was his name for a series of novels that he claimed amounted to a scientific study of French society of the time. Henry James (1843–1916) with his novels like *Roderick Hudson* (1876) and *The Europeans (*1878) and Mark Twain (1835–1910) were Americans associated with the movement.

Naturalism is a movement associated more with the later nineteenth century and in particular the French novelist Emile Zola (1840–1902). The Naturalists were influenced by the discoveries of Charles Darwin particularly the belief that natural selection was the means by which human beings evolved rather than the myth of creation. Zola saw himself in writing his novels as conducting experiments in human nature. He used his characters to show how they reacted in different circumstances depending on their heredity and environment and how this was likely to affect their emotional make-up. Whereas the realist writer observed and recorded, Zola and the naturalists did the same but also showed how external forces affected character. Heredity and environment, of course, were primary concerns of Darwin and his theory of evolution. Zola was inclined to place his characters in extreme situations in order to demonstrate his theories. He described this in a book called *The Experimental Novel* (1880). This extremism led to much criticism and some of his novels were temporarily suppressed.

These categories of fiction are still written and are popular today, but there is probably more variety of styles available to the writer and reader. In the heyday of realism, romantic novels were being written and were popular as they are now.

American naturalistic novelists include Jack London (*The Call of the Wild*, 1903), John Steinbeck (*The Grapes of Wrath*, 1939), and Norman Mailer (*The Naked and the Dead*, 1948).

Red Herring

It is said that in the seventeenth century hunting dogs were trained to follow the scent of a smoked herring which had been dragged through the woods or across fields on the end of a rope. (The herring was red because of the smoking process.) Later, they were used by the early equivalent of hunt saboteurs to put hounds off the trail. The smell was a diversion from the scent of the boar or fox.

A literary red herring is a means of diverting or distracting the reader from solving a mystery or crime too easily, something to divert their attention from the real criminal perhaps. The writer deliberately lays down false but plausible clues that make the crime or mystery more difficult to solve. Most crime writers use red herrings but they need to be used with care.

Another technique the writer may use is to introduce what seems to be a red herring but that later proves to be a genuine clue. Frequently a number of clues are provided, some genuine, some red herrings. The more there are the more the reader is likely to be distracted and unable to work out the solution. Where there are multiple suspects for a crime, some will produce genuine alibis, one may provide a red herring alibi but it may seem the most plausible one.

REGIONAL NOVELS

The term regional novel is sometimes used but it is not a very useful description because it gives no idea of the nature of the novel except where it is set. As every novel is set somewhere (unless the novelist deliberately makes the setting anonymous), it becomes even more problematic. However, those who use the term tend to mean that the setting is important to the story, it is usually provincial or rural. Novels set in London, however important that setting may be, would not be termed regional novels.

Thomas Hardy (1840–1928) is the most famous regional novelist having invented 'Wessex' based mainly on the county of Dorset in southern England. Some towns are given made up names but they can be easily identified. The largely rural life in Hardy's novels is undoubtedly important but one wonders if his themes and interests would have been different had he come from the north of England.

Arnold Bennett (1867–1931) set many of his novels in the Pottery towns of the English Midlands and the industrial setting is crucially important to his characters and plots – but he is not frequently referred to as a regional novelist. The American writer Harper Lee's prize-winning novel *To Kill a Mockingbird* (1960) about race issues could probably not have been set anywhere but Alabama in the deep south of America, but it is more accurate to describe it as a novel about racial prejudice rather than a regional novel.

Regional setting can have a bearing on a novel and the lives of its characters and it is something the writer should consider carefully. Few would claim, however, that setting or region is the most important element in a novel, but where it is crucial the writer should research the history and customs of the place and convey these in the story.

Writers such as Alan Sillitoe, John Braine, Stan Barstow and Kingsley Amis, at least in their early work, would be considered regional novelists. The critic D. J. Taylor has argued that in this century regionalism or provincialism in the English novel is increasing because writers do not now, for economic and other reasons, tend to go to London after their early success. On the other hand, there have always been regional and metropolitan writers and perhaps location is not a crucial issue.

See also ATMOSPHERE AND SETTING, PROLETARIAN NOVELS; STORY AND NOVEL CATEGORIES

REMAINDER

When a publisher decides that copies of a particular title will no longer sell and they want storage space, they may remainder that title. This means that they sell the surplus copies cheaply in bookshops that specialize in selling remainders. In the past publishers often chose to pulp unsold copies rather than remainder them.

RESEARCH

Readers expect the background to fiction to be accurate and authentic. A story by a reputable writer mentioned that a character had obtained three A levels late in life by studying with the Open University. The OU is a university, it does not teach A level subjects or even validate them. This is a small detail which had little effect on the story as a whole but incorrect details can have two effects: (1) they make the reader pause and question unnecessarily if they recognize the fault; (2) they can make the reader lose some confidence in the writer with regard to other details in the story.

It is up to the writer to get the facts right and there are a number of ways of doing this. Clearly if you write from your own background and experience, you will almost certainly get details of places, jobs and incidentals correct but writing only about your own background and experience is unlikely to be fulfilling or satisfying and even the jobs and hobbies of friends may not be known to you in detail.

The substitute for experience is research, and it is possible in some cases that research may take almost as long as the writing process even for fiction which on the whole usually requires less research than non-fiction.

The main means of research are as follows:

Reading   He may have been exaggerating slightly but Samuel Johnson said 'The greatest part of a writer's time is spent in reading, in order to write; a man will turn over half a library to make one book'.

Interviews   If you have to use characters whose work and activities you are not familiar with, there is no substitute for interviewing at the coal face. Most people are flattered by the invitation to talk about themselves.

Corresponding   If you cannot contact people personally who you may want to interview, try writing instead.

Places/Buildings   If part of your story is set in a town, city, village or a particular kind of countryside which you are not familiar with, visit it.

Films/TV   If part of a story is set in some foreign country, the cost of visiting may preclude a visit. Films and TV programmes about the place may be an adequate substitute.

Internet   The internet is a fund of information on nearly any topic but use only reliable sites.

Research of the kind described is probably impossible for what may be a more important element in the story: character portrayal.

See also CHARACTERS; WRITE WHAT YOU KNOW

REVENGE STORIES

Revenge is a means, we sometimes think, of righting a wrong. It is retaliation for harm done, getting even for what we take as an injustice or an injury. The injury may be physical, verbal or an action that we think demeans us or someone close to us. It may occur because we feel we have been cheated. The desire for revenge can cause a person to be angry; the sense of injustice can fester until it is expressed in violence.

It is the cause of some of the most powerful emotions. It can give satisfaction as Shakespeare suggests in Titus Andronicus:

> I am Revenge, sent from th'infernal kingdom
> To ease the gnawing vulture of thy mind
> By working wreckful vengeance on thy foes.

Revenge stories or dramas are said to have begun with the Roman dramatist, Seneca (4BC–65AD), although some critics trace them back to Greek drama. Seneca certainly influenced the flowering of tragic revenge drama in England in the period 1480–1530.

If we have a wrong done to us such as a violent attack, or suffer a robbery, or we have been cheated, in most cases we inform the police who, if possible will catch the criminals; a court case will follow and justice, we hope, will be done. Our revenge on the wrongdoer has been done for us by the law, more fairly and objectively than if we rushed to take personal revenge. In Elizabethan and Jacobean times there was no organized police force and no courts as we know them. Thus personal revenge was tolerated and thought to be justified. It was this situation that created the revenge story – along with a liking on the part of the audience for bloodthirsty action. In Shakespeare's *Hamlet* (1603) the protagonist takes revenge for the murder of his father; in *Othello* (1604) a husband mistakenly takes revenge on the wife he *thinks* has been unfaithful to him, and in the same play Iago takes revenge on Othello for reasons which are complex. Other Elizabethan dramatists who exploited the popularity of revenge tragedy were Thomas Kyd, Cyril Tourneur and John Webster.

Revenge stories are less common in modern times because of the law but they are still sometimes written and revenge often plays a major or minor part in stories of many kinds.

The British poet C. Day Lewis wrote thrillers under the pseudonym Nicholas Blake and one of his novels, *The Beast Must Die* (1938) concerns a father whose son has been killed by a hit-and-run driver. The father after a considerable time meticulously tracks down the driver, manages to get taken in by his family, and ultimately takes his revenge.

Although there is no category of novels today like the revenge plays of the Elizabethan and Jacobean age, revenge plays a part in many stories and it has considerable potential as an element of story because it combines action with deeply felt emotions. Francis Bacon in the sixteenth century said 'Revenge is a kind of wild justice, which the more man's nature runs to, the more ought law to weed it out'. Few would disagree, but the temptation to take revenge is not diminished by logic. Let us not forget that there can be satisfaction in revenge. Byron was not the first to point out that revenge is 'sweet'. The contemporary playwright, Alan Ayckbourn puts it even more strongly 'The greatest feeling in the world . . . Revenge. Pure, unadulterated revenge. Not weedy little jealousy. Not some piddling little envy. But good, old-fashioned, bloodcurdling revenge'.

For the writer of fiction, revenge has potentiality in stories for the creation of interesting characters and plots. The provocation to take revenge need not be as dramatic as the situations usually taken by the Elizabethan dramatists. Consider these provocations:

- A rival 'steals' a girl/boyfriend, wife/husband.
- A lesser qualified person gets a job you wanted.
- A person gets a job because they know the boss.
- You are cheated out of money.
- You feel life has dealt you a bad hand – others should suffer as well.
- Your good-looking friend always seems to get what you want.
- Your views are ignored even though they are better than those of others.
- Your boss exploits you.
- Everyone else gets the perks.
- Your ex-lover has taken advantage of you.

The list can be extended. Any of these could be the inciting incident in a story. The above are reasons for taking revenge; the writer must devise ingenious ways and means of executing it.

See also INCITING INCIDENT; STORY AND NOVEL CATEGORIES

REVIEW COPY
A review copy is a copy of a book that is sent out free by a publisher to newspapers and magazines (and occasionally radio and TV channels) in the hope of a favourable review.

REVIEWS
Most newspapers and magazines publish reviews or critical assessments of new novels on a regular basis. The potential writer of fiction should read these (and the novels) in order to find out the kind of novels that are being published.

RISING AND FALLING ACTION

The rising action in a fiction is the period or section after the exposition (which introduces the main characters, setting and situation) and leads up to the climax. The rising action is the most substantial part of the fiction in both length and importance and is usually the most exciting and interesting part for the reader. It is that part of the story which is concerned with the conflict between the main character(s) and whatever opposes their aims or goals. Each episode should increase the tension hence the term rising. Suspense is created for the reader in wondering what will be the outcome of the conflicts that occur. The climax or turning point in the fortunes of the protagonist is reached at the highest point in the rising action and then there is a shorter section of falling action leading to the denouement.

The foregoing may suggest very dramatic conflict and action but this is not necessary. The nature of the rising action and conflict will depend on what kind or genre of fiction is concerned. For instance, in a detective story, after the exposition which will usually concern the crime and the introduction to the detective, the rising action will concern the detective's attempts to solve the crime – finding clues, and testing their validity, eliminating red herrings and innocent suspects, possibly contending with further similar crimes and finally making a breakthrough which will be the climax or turning point. Then there will be the falling action about the run-down of the case and the denouement revealing the criminal and tying up loose ends. The criminal may be caught or die in a final showdown.

In romantic fiction, the rising action will be in a lower key. It will concern the ups and downs of the romance, concerns and conflicts with rivals, misunderstandings and problems, until at the climax the union is probably realized and the falling action and denouement may concern marriage or partnership. The examples here suggest positive ends, but this does not to have to be the case. The detective may fail; the romance may falter. Original fiction will vary the patterns suggested and the author's task in writing genre fiction is to devise original variations on common themes.

Serious fiction invariably follows a similar pattern. In Shakespeare's *Romeo and Juliet*, the exposition concerns the background to the feuding families, the Capulets and Montagues, and the meeting for the first time of Romeo and Juliet. The rising action concerns their developing love affair and the problems and conflicts they have to contend with. The climax (a double one) is tragic involving the death of both. The falling action includes comment by the Prince of Verona on the cause of the tragedy and the necessity for peace between the feuding houses.

Rising and falling action are vital to the plot of fiction.

See also CLIMAX; DENOUEMENT; EXPOSITION; PLOT AND STORY

RITES OF PASSAGE AND COMING-OF-AGE STORIES

It is necessary first to distinguish between the terms rites of passage and coming of age which, with regard to stories are sometimes used as if they mean the same thing.

A rite of passage is a ritual that marks a change in a person's social or sexual status. The main rites of passage discussed by anthropologists are birth, puberty, marriage, divorce, the menopause and death. Obviously the first and last of these and the rites associated with them (celebrations of birth, baptism, funerals) are mainly for the benefit of relations, friends and acquaintances. Puberty, the transition from childhood to adulthood has elaborate rituals in some cultures but less formal ones or none at all in technological societies in the west. Some people may celebrate leaving school but the milestone of the twenty-first birthday and elaborate celebrations has been eroded in the west with the acceptance of eighteen as being the age of maturity. The age at which a person can learn to drive, drink alcohol, legally have sexual partners and get married have also been reduced. Many people do not get baptised; secular and less formal funerals have replaced the religious rituals of the past. Orthodox Jews, on the other hand, keep up the rituals of the Bar Mitzvah and the Bat Mitzvah. Other minor rituals occur at birthdays, graduation and leaving home.

Arnold Van Gennep (1873–1957) identified three stages in the rite of passage: separation, transition and new integration. These can be illustrated with regard to marriage. Separation of the individual from the family takes place partially during the courtship of the couple; the engagement marks the transition and preparation for being married after being single; and new integration encompasses being married. In fiction (and possibly in reality) the process may not be without its conflicts.

Coming of age can best be regarded as one rite of passage everyone goes through and it refers to the transition from puberty or adolescence to adulthood. It is a time of conflict for most people and hence it has been the subject of many stories and novels. These conflicts, of course, are suffered by most people almost as a fact of nature but they can be exacerbated by particular external circumstances.

A classic twentieth-century rites of passage novel is William Golding's *The Lord of the Flies* (1954). The dramatic story about boys marooned on a desert island allows Golding to provide an allegory of the transformation from relative childhood innocence to adult cruelty. The novel ends 'Ralph wept for the end of innocence, the darkness of man's heart, and the fall through the air of the true, wise friend called Piggy.'

Coming-of-age stories are about some or all of these: growing up; learning about the true nature of the adult world; loss of innocence; the gaining of maturity; sexual awareness; growing understanding and tolerance; loss of idealism and seeing the world, warts and all. Obviously, conflict, the basis of plot, is embedded within these themes and it is probably what makes coming-of-age stories and novels popular with both writers and readers. In addition, some writers are able to draw on their own childhood experiences as part of their subject matter.

The following are examples of rites of passage and coming-of-age novels:

Wuthering Heights by Emily Brontë (1847). Wayward girl as a child finds soul mate and the love of her life but social conventions prevent their later union and tragedy results.

Great Expectations by Charles Dickens (1861). Orphan boy has trouble with guardian, falls impossibly in love, goes to the bad, but eventually makes good.

The Adventures of Huckleberry Finn by Mark Twain (1884). Boy thrown out of home by father learns about life, adult corruption, and tolerance during a trip down the Mississippi.

The History of Mr Polly by H. G. Wells (1910). Middle-aged man realizes he is in a dead end job and marriage and absconds from both to find fulfillment.

Coming Up for Air by George Orwell (1939). A man has a mid-life crisis and tries to recapture his past happiness only to find it no longer exists.

The Catcher in the Rye by J. D. Salinger (1951). Adolescent boy find adult behaviour and institutions phoney and tries to escape.

The Bell Jar by Sylvia Plath (1963). Fictionalized autobiographical account of a girl's nervous breakdown.

Oranges Are Not the Only Fruit by Jeannette Winterson (1985). Young girl has to escape from restrictive religious family in order to fulfil herself.

The Secret Diary of Adrian Mole, Aged 13 3/4 by Sue Townsend (1986). Over-ambitious youth finds attempts to find love and career thwarted in spite of idealism. Humorous take on his situation.

Cat's Eye by Margaret Atwood (1989). Complex story of adolescent girl's conflicts with friends and search for meaning.

Last Orders by Graham Swift (1996). Group of friends' lives are reviewed and changed by the death of a colleague.

Angus, Thongs and Full-Frontal Snogging by Louise Rennison (1999). One of a number of the confessional diaries of unfortunate adolescent, Georgia Nicolson. Hilarious take on adolescent growing pains.

Novels rarely fall completely into one category. While these novels are examples of rites of passage or coming-of-age stories, they could also, in most cases fit another category as well. For example *Coming Up for Air* could be described as a social realist novel or proletarian novel; *Wuthering Heights* as a romance and *Huckleberry Finn* as a social satire or humorous novel.

See also STORY AND NOVEL CATEGORIES

ROMAN-À-CLEF

A *roman-à-clef* (French for 'novel with a key') is a novel in which one or more of the main characters are closely based on real people, invariably famous people, and are recognizable as such although their real names are not used. An early example is *Les Liaisons Dangereuses* (1782) by Choderlos de Laclos. This is also an epistolary novel. Readers now would not recognize the historical figures behind the fictional characters but the novel and film versions of it remain popular.

A recent example of a *roman-à-clef* is *Primary Colors* (1998) about Bill Clinton's presidential election campaign in 1992. The portrayal of Clinton is both favourable (he is portrayed as a genuine man of the people) and critical (he is portrayed as a womanizer). The novel was published anonymously and enjoyed some notoriety. Later it was discovered that the author was a politico, Joe Klein.

Fictional names are always used in these novels but this would not avoid the possibility of libel suits if the real people were clearly identifiable and assuming they wished to bring a legal action. Clinton seems to have accepted the way he was represented.

The *roman-à-clef* is not the same as a non-fiction novel. In the latter almost all the events, situations and characters bear a very close relationship with real ones. Fictional names will be used in the *roman-à-clef*, whereas the real names may be used in a non-fiction novel. Clearly a great deal of research is necessary for writing both of these types of novels and they are probably inadvisable writing projects for the novice author. In the case of *Primary Colors* the author knew many of the characters.

The key referred to in the term *roman-à-clef* is the connection between real characters and events and those which are disguised in the novel.

Some other examples are as follows although in most cases the main point and purpose of the novel can be appreciated without realizing which of the characters are based on real people:

Point Counter Point	Aldous Huxley
Sons and Lovers	D. H. Lawrence
Women in Love	D. H. Lawrence
The Sun Also Rises	Ernest Hemingway
A Dance to the Music of Time	Anthony Powell

Recently some novels like *Primary Colors* have been published and have been successful because of publicity pointing out the connection with real politicians. Ideally the novel should stand up without these connections being made. Not everyone will know the key and in the case of the five novels listed above, they were published sufficiently long ago for any scandalous connections to have been forgotten.

See also EPISTOLARY NOVEL; LIBEL; NON-FICTION NOVEL

ROMANTIC FICTION

This entry is concerned mainly with modern genre romantic fiction. First, though, a few words about romance and romanticism are in order because they are terms that have a variety of meanings. Romantic can refer to a particular period in literary history and to a type of novel or poem (and, indeed, to the arts in general) that may or may not be within the recognized romantic period.

The romantic period is usually dated from the publication of the *Lyrical Ballads* by Wordsworth and Coleridge in 1798. (Some critics would date it somewhat earlier.) Their work and that of other romantics reacted against Classicism and Neo-classicism, favouring emotion over reason, imagination over formality. Nature was a popular theme and the supernatural Gothic stories are basically romantic. Romanticism was lively and extolled freedom rather than restraint. The Romantic period ended about the middle of the nineteenth century. Romanticism is often characterized by Wordsworth's remark in the Preface to the *Lyrical Ballads* that poetry is 'the spontaneous overflow of powerful feelings' although this apparently anarchic approach was modified by a later remark that it is 'emotion recollected in tranquillity'. Thus it was not a matter of letting words spill onto the page in an immediate response to some powerful feeling.

The definitions of romanticism are complicated by the fact that reference is often made to medieval romances which include Mallory's *Morte d'Arthur*, other stories of King Arthur, *Sir Gawain and the Green Knight* (fourteenth century) and stories of courtly love and chivalry.

Charlotte Brontë's novel *Jane Eyre* (1847) concerns a reticent, intense orphan who is no beauty and on the surface something of a mouse, although she has reserves of inner strength. She is employed as governess by Mr Rochester. He is moody, authoritarian, a man of sometimes violent temper. Jane falls in love with him but the romance is beset by problems and it is only years after she has left that they are finally reconciled and marry. It is the model for many later romance novels right up to the present although now the female character would be much more independent and forceful and there might be some sexual encounters which never appeared in nineteenth-century novels.

Before the Brontës Jane Austen had been writing her novels of romance and marriage but these were characterized by greater realism, wit, moral concern and a satiric outlook on the manners of the time. These features are not notable in the modern genre romance.

The modern popular romance has often been accused of being formulaic and it is difficult to deny that there are common patterns in these novels and a lack of originality in plots. This does not mean that they do not require great skill on the part of their authors. They are not all the same and to write different stories within a specified form is not easy and may well require as much thought and planning as any novel. Part of the formula is to have a happy ending but endings can only be happy, unhappy or indecisive so it is not a case of giving the author a particularly easy option.

The main characteristics of the romantic novel are as follows:

- A plot that follows the common pattern of the heroine having an aim that is to gain the love of a man. Numerous obstacles frustrate this aim until they are finally overcome and the romance is consummated in marriage or a partnership, usually the former.
- The whole story is concerned with romance and relationships although work and vacations may play a significant role.

- The ending is always positive and an impression is usually given that the happy outcome will be forever.
- The story is almost always told in the third person narrative form, usually from the point of view of the heroine although occasionally it is from the hero's point of view, or both.
- The whole story focuses on the couple. Sub-plots are infrequent but both man and woman will have friends, work colleagues and acquaintances.
- A rival will have a part in many stories, not necessarily an obvious one. In one novel the hero has a relative's child to care for.
- Although things may go wrong for a time, poverty, gloom and depression have no part in these stories.
- Locations are often exotic and fashionable. Some are specialized, e.g. medical fiction obviously will be set for a good part of the story in a hospital.
- To the publishers of these novels, escapism is not a derogatory term. They see themselves as supplying an escape for their readers from possibly a dull existence.

Women are said to read more than men and romantic fiction is aimed at them specifically. Many mainstream publishers publish romantic novels but undoubtedly the major publisher of romantic fiction is Harlequin, Silhouette, Mills & Boon which has editorial offices in London, New York and Toronto. Different categories of romantic fiction are issued monthly and each country has some specialisms, but the books are available almost on a worldwide basis. Other publishers tend to publish what in the trade are referred to as 'Single Titles', that is romances that are not part of a category, although some of these have sequels.

Mills & Boon publish category romances or 'lines' as they call them. These are novels which are easily recognizable from the cover. Market research has shown that some readers adhere to one category for a long time reading perhaps four medical romances a month.

In Britain the lines published at present by Mills & Boon are Modern Romances, Sensual Romances, Tender Romances, Medical Romances and Historical Romances. Details follow which are taken from the publisher's own descriptions:

1   *Modern Romances* must have strong, wealthy heroes who are ultimately tamed by an independent heroine. They must be sensual, fast-paced, escapist and emotional. They can be told from

the heroine's or the hero's point of view or from both. The settings are contemporary and fairly luxurious.

2   *Sensual Romances* have cosmopolitan settings and an independent heroine who is equally concerned about career, love and sex. A confident, sexy, easy-going hero complements her.

3   *Tender Romances* are less sexually explicit and the emphasis is on the emotional situations and the problems keeping the heroine and hero apart. Strong heroes are essential and of course the problems will be overcome.

4   *Medical Romances* usually demonstrate greater career equality between men and women and, of course, the setting is invariably a hospital although one character could be a GP and a clinic may be a principal setting. Characters can be doctors, nurses, midwives or paramedics. The job in these novels impinges on the romance.

5   *Historical Romances* can be about any period in history at all although for some reason the Regency period is the most popular. Historians would probably scorn these novels as history but some authenticity of historical detail is necessary. The emotional relationship is, however, the most important element and does not differ so much from more contemporary stories.

Fashions change and categories are changed from time to time. A relatively recent newcomer to the Toronto publications is the *Blaze* series that are the most erotic novels in the whole list. The heroine is frequently a single girl whose priority is not permanent partnership. The physical relationship is the most important. They are considerably more sophisticated than the old so-called bodice rippers, historical romances with an emphasis on the kind of sex suggested by the title.

Harlequin, Silhouette, Mills & Boon's publishing policy is very different from that of most publishers. Usually four novels in each category are published every month and these books, if they are not sold, are returned for pulping at the end of the period when the next monthly consignment will be sent to retailers. No backlist of books is kept. Old Mills & Boon titles can only be obtained on the second-hand market. Very occasionally a favourite author's novels may be republished in an omnibus of three novels. Clearly writers who crave lasting fame will not find it in this field.

Potential authors of escapist romances have one advantage over writers of other genre fiction. Mills & Boon provides detailed instructions of their requirements with regard to categories, length, character types and settings. Their best advice is to read the category that the potential writer is interested in. Many people are surprised when they first come to a genre romance. Some literary agents specialize in placing romantic fiction.

Romance and love relationships, needless to say, can be part of all other genres of fiction from science fiction to Westerns and also serious literary fiction.

See also PLOT (RECENT AND OLDER THEORIES); STORY AND NOVEL CATEGORIES

ROYALTY

The royalty is the share paid to a writer out of the proceeds resulting from the sale of his or her book. The royalty ranges from 5% to 20% depending on the status of the author and the expected sales of the book. The royalty may increase the more copies sold. Overseas sales may command a smaller royalty. If an advance payment is made to the author, no royalties may be received until this is covered.

SAGAS

Sagas are Norwegian and Icelandic stories from the twelfth and thirteenth centuries and while many have their roots in historical events they are largely embroidered tales. Sometimes they are based on older myths and legends and they concern kings. Heroism and revenge are frequent themes. Action takes precedence over character analysis and motivation.

The term saga is often used now to refer to popular, long novels concerned with family dynasties (family sagas) or stories of rural middle-class life (Aga sagas). This is not using the word saga completely inaccurately as some of the Norse sagas did concern families.

See also FAMILY SAGAS AND AGA SAGAS; LEGENDS; MYTHS

SATIRE

Satire aims to mock or ridicule vice and folly, sometimes the vice and folly itself, sometimes the people who perpetrate it. Satire can take the form of a novel, short story, poetry, essay, film, cartoon, play or TV show. Satiric magazines are available, the most notable one in Britain being *Private Eye* and in America *Mad Magazine* and *The Onion* (which is available online).

Targets of satire these days are frequently politicians and political policies, laws that do not seem sensible, social customs that seem nonsensical, the social class system, celebrities. Almost anything can be the subject of satire and has been. Anatole France satirized religion and French history in his novel *Penguin Island* (1908).

Notable satirical novelists of the twentieth century are George Orwell, Aldous Huxley, Evelyn Waugh and Joseph Heller. In *Nineteen Eighty-Four* (1949) Orwell satirized totalitarian political regimes and dictators and in his earlier *Animal Farm* (1945) he had targeted more specifically the regime and leaders of the USSR. Aldous Huxley in *Brave New World* (1932), one of his many satires, also attacked totalitarianism and in particular what he saw as a blind faith in science to bring about a desirable society where human problems would disappear. The American writer, Joseph Heller, in *Catch 22* (1961) mocks the idiocy of war and the military in its multiplicity of follies. Evelyn Waugh was principally a social satirist. A more recent social satirist is the novelist Martin Amis who wrote *Einstein's Monsters 1987* (short stories) and *London Fields* (1989). His target is the sheer sordidness of modern British life in the city and he attacks it with merciless bitter wit and verbal dexterity.

The satire or mockery of any subject can be serious, witty, humorous or downright farcical. Serious criticism, however, would not be labelled satire; there is always an element of mockery and possibly exaggeration in satire. It is rarely good-humoured. Orwell does not raise many laughs, Huxley was extremely witty, Waugh and Heller could be funny, witty, bitter and serious by turns.

It has been claimed that satirists are also moralists and there is some truth in this. In exposing what they regard as stupid and reprehensible behaviour or something like the folly of war, they aim to prevent something from re-occurring. Orwell was presumably warning that we should never put our faith in dictators even when they are or seem to be benevolent.

The satirist, in order to have any credibility, must be master of his or her subject matter and be able to find a suitable vehicle or story type for that subject. Huxley's *Brave New World* shows him to be well-versed in science and psychological theory and some of what he forecast in the novel and which seemed absurd in 1932 seems much less so today; the idea of test tube babies, for instance.

Satire can embrace many genres. *Brave New World* could be loosely called science fiction. Orwell's *Animal Farm* is in the form of a long fable or fairy story. Waugh wrote in a more realist tradition even though quite absurd things sometimes occur in his novels.

One of the problems some critics point out as a weakness with satire is that in satiric novels the ideas almost inevitably take precedence over the creation of character. Huxley's characters in *Brave New World* don't really need to be terribly believable because the novel is set in the far distant future where the world is very different from ours. Orwell overcomes the problem of believable characters in *Animal Farm* because his 'characters' are animals.

Satire has existed from the earliest times. *Lysistrata* by the fifth-century BC Greek dramatist, Aristophanes, is probably the first anti-war satire. Classical Latin satirists include Horace and Juvenal. The English novel began only a short time before Jonathan Swift wrote one of the most famous political and social satires, *Gulliver's Travels* (1726).

Is satire effective in its aims? Does it bring about the changes the authors clearly desire? This is a difficult matter to decide but perhaps regrettably they do not seem to have any direct effect, at least on the larger issues they take up. We still have the folly of war, politicians are no better or worse than they have always been, dictatorships still exist, and social injustice has not been cured. The human targets of satire rarely recognize themselves or their types in satiric work so they largely ignore it. Jonathan Swift was probably right when he observed 'Satire is a sort of glass wherein beholders do generally discover everybody's face but their own, which is the chief reason for that kind of reception it meets in the world, and that so very few are offended with it.'

The kind of reception it meets, he is implying, is indifference. That, however, does not make satire anything less than a skilled art which many readers find extremely rewarding.

See also INVECTIVE

SCIENCE FICTION

Science fiction is a genre that has alternative names and embraces a quite wide variety of story types. It is sometimes referred to as SF or Sci-Fi, or speculative fiction. The latter term is the widest and would include speculative or alternative history, such as Robert Harris's *Fatherland* (1992), in which the author speculates about what might have happened if Germany and the Nazis had won the Second World War and occupied Britain. Although Harris produces a scenario that did not happen, he uses the story to make comments on our existing society. More mainstream science fiction is usually concerned with the effect of science and technology on people and society now but also in the near or distant future. The definition of science fiction can be expanded by considering the following that cover many of the types of story told:

- The effect of science or specific technologies on our society.
- The effect of likely developments in science and technology in the future bearing in mind what already exists and can be developed.
- Imaginary societies with alternative science and technologies to our own, possibly with the intention of commenting on our own.
- Interplanetary travel.
- Interplanetary conflicts.
- Settlement on other planets and the problems which arise unexpectedly.
- Ecological problems caused by use of science and how they could change life on earth.
- Stories of very imaginative developments in science such as teleportation.
- Stories concerning mutants, robots and cybermen.
- Time travel.
- Adventure stories set in the future or on other planets.
- War stories set in the future or on other planets.
- Attacks on the earth.
- How computers or artificial brains will change the world in future.
- How advancements in media technology change our attitudes.
- How cloning may change human life in the future.

Some enthusiasts of science fiction divide it into 'hard' science fiction and 'soft' science fiction. The former is concerned largely with a background of speculation and technological developments that seem feasible in the light of present scientific knowledge. Novels of this kind tend to prioritize the science rather than characterization. Novels by Arthur C. Clarke, Isaac Asimov and Robert Heinlein usually fall into this category but not exclusively. Writers of hard science fiction are likely to have a fairly sophisticated knowledge of at least some branches of science.

In soft science fiction, characters are very important as is the effect of science on people and their feelings about advancements. Some use the term to indicate that the story is concerned with the 'soft' sciences such as psychology, sociology and philosophy rather than physics, mechanics and chemistry. For instance, B. F. Skinner's *Walden 2* (1962) posits the possibility of changing, even the perfecting of human beings by using behaviourist conditioning techniques. Skinner was himself a noted behaviourist psychologist and appeared to believe that not only was this possible, but it was desirable. Similarly Aldous Huxley in *Brave New World* (1932) imagines a society where embryos are conditioned in test tubes and further conditioned after they are born to be happy with their lot in life whether as a scientist or road sweeper. His novel uses a mixture of hard and soft science. Huxley wrote of test-tube babies long before this became a possibility. Anthony Burgess's *A Clockwork Orange* (1962) set in the near future looks at how criminal behaviour could be eliminated by conditioning miscreants to behave well. The novel discusses how this would diminish human freedom.

Clearly some novels fall between hard and soft science fiction and it is questionable how useful the terms are.

Although some critics would refer to books like Thomas More's *Utopia* (1561), Daniel Defoe's *Gulliver's Travels* (1726) and Mary Shelley's *Frankenstein* (1818) (which is also an example of Gothic fiction) as precursors of science fiction, the genre owes much to the late nineteenth-century pioneers, Jules Verne in France and H. G. Wells in Britain. At the latter part of the nineteenth century Verne produced novels about under-earth exploration (*Journey to the Centre of the Earth*, 1864), travel in space (*From the Earth to the Moon*, 1865), and the use of submarines (*20,000 Leagues Under the Sea*, 1870). H. G. Wells a few years later speculated on time travel in *The Time Machine* (1895), genetics in *The Island of Dr Moreau* (1896), and most famously an attack on earth by Martians in *The War of the Worlds* (1898). He wrote other science fiction before turning to more conventional novels.

A problem about science fiction is that it may date more quickly than mainstream fiction as science and events can overtake speculation. Most readers today find H. G. Wells's *The War of the Worlds* somewhat old fashioned and yet when it was written in 1898 it was the first novel about mass mechanized warfare affecting civilian populations. The refugees flowing out of London echo what happened only much later in European cities, and such movements had never occurred when Wells wrote the book. This was earlier than both the Boer War and the First World War where comparatively primitive methods of warfare pertained as opposed to what Wells envisages. He even uses what might be called 'accidental' biological warfare when the Martians are eventually seen off by a common human disease. *The War of the Worlds* is a remarkable novel and one which every aspiring writer of science fiction should read.

Curiously, science fiction which is in the future as far as subjects and themes are concerned is, for the most part, conventional with regard to style and construction. Plots follow classic patterns and writers tend not to experiment with language other than to make use of scientific terms – and sometimes to make up spurious ones. While space adventures require little scientific knowledge on the part of the authors, the more sophisticated stories do. Enthusiasm for science and the genre are essential.

Science fiction has never been one of the more popular genres in Britain but it is more popular and highly acclaimed in America. Many university English departments run courses on science fiction. Because it is speculative and not about things which exist, it is looked down on by some critics. This is curious in a way because all fiction by definition is a lie and the truths which emerge in mainstream fiction are no more valid that those that emerge from science fiction.

See also FANTASY FICTION; PLOT AND STORY; STORY AND NOVEL CATE-GORIES

SEQUELS AND PREQUELS

A sequel is simply a second novel (or film) that follows on chronolog-ically from an original novel using the same central characters and probably the same settings. Sequels are usually written because of the popularity of the original. *Harry Potter and the Philosopher's Stone* was the first Harry Potter book. Five sequels have followed with the promise of another. *Red Dragon* (1981) was the first thriller by Thomas Harris about the psychopath, Hannibal Lecter. Two sequels followed, *The Silence of the Lambs* (1988) and *Hannibal* (1999). Ian Fleming wrote a number of novels about James Bond but the novels that fol-lowed the first one are not strictly sequels. Subsequent books do not follow chronologically. It would be more accurate to call this a series of novels. Bond does not really age or develop. The same is true of the various Sherlock Holmes stories, although it is true that there is some attention to chronology in that earlier cases are mentioned in later books and in the final one Sherlock dies.

Sequels are not very popular in literature but are much more common in the film world. Film companies are always tempted to follow up and cash in on a successful film.

Prequels are the opposite of sequels in that a prequel is a novel that is set chronologically earlier than the original story. They are less common than sequels. An example is *The Magician's Nephew* (1955) by

C. S. Lewis which is a prequel to the more famous *The Lion, the Witch and the Wardrobe* (1950). The latter had five sequels.

SERIALS AND SERIES

Serials are long stories (often novel length) which are published in episodes on a weekly or monthly basis in magazines or newspapers. The number of parts may vary but it is usual for there to be between fifteen and twenty. Serial publication of novels was common in the nineteenth and the first half of the twentieth century and while some magazines still publish serials, it is now a fairly rare occurrence.

Charles Dickens and Thomas Hardy, among others, published most of their novels in serial form before book publication. Having this form in mind when writing them, it led to more melodramatic stories along with cliff-hanger endings to conclude serial episodes.

A series is also published in weekly or monthly parts in magazines and rather than being a divided up novel, it is a series of separate and complete stories using the same characters and general background. Television is now the main source of serials and series. Soap operas are examples of serials and programmes like *The Bill* and *Casualty* are examples of series. Comics for children contain many text and picture story serials and series but they have decreased as comics are less popular now than television and video games.

See also CLIFFHANGERS; HOOK; MELODRAMA

SERIAL RIGHTS

Serial rights refer to the subsidiary right to sell extracts of a book to a magazine or newspaper.

SETTING *SEE* ATMOSPHERE AND SETTING

SEVEN DEADLY SINS

Sin is not a commonly used word these days except by religious people and even they do not give it the emphasis it was afforded in the past. Nowadays, we are more likely to talk about weaknesses than sins, but these weaknesses are often the same as or similar to the ancient seven deadly sins. One or more of the seven deadly sins often provides the major problem for a character. One of the best examples is probably Christopher Marlowe's *Dr Faustus* (c. 1588). In the play the seven deadly sins are personified and paraded before Faustus in order to tempt him.

The seven deadly sins are listed here as possible starters for ideas. The reader might also think of recent stories he or she has read in which these sins or weaknesses are displayed by one of the main-characters. Alongside the sins are their opposites, sometimes referred to as the seven virtues. (Alternative names are given in some cases.)

Sins	*Virtues*
Pride (Vanity)	Humility
Envy	Kindness (Love)
Gluttony	Temperance (Abstinence)
Lust	Self-control (Chastity)
Anger (Wrath)	Patience
Greed (Avarice, Covetousness)	Generosity (Liberality)
Sloth	Diligence (Zeal)

Pride is usually said to be the cardinal sin which often leads to others. The original list of sins was devised by Pope Gregory the Great in the sixth century AD.

In 2005 the BBC organized a poll to find out what people today regard as the worst sins. Of the original list, only greed remains in the current seven. People were also asked which sin they would most like to indulge in and, rather illogically, lust was the most popular with both men and women, even though adultery was regarded as a major sin. The modern list of seven is as follows: cruelty, adultery, bigotry, dishonesty, hypocrisy, greed and selfishness.

A modern work of fiction might be more successful if one of these was used as the basis of a story rather than one of the original seven deadly sins.

See also HUBRIS; PLOT AND STORY; TRAGIC FLAW (HARMARTIA)

SHORT STORY

A short story is a brief prose fiction having similarities with the novel except in length. How short or how long is a short story? There is no absolute answer to this. Between 1,000 and 7,500 words is sometimes suggested; other critics would allow up to 20,000 words and some would allow shorter than 1,000 words. However, if the terms flash fiction and mini saga are accepted then they would cater for the under 1,000 word length. Certainly for a fiction of over 20,000 words, most people would refer to a novella or novelette.

Nowadays, for practical purposes, the magazines that publish short stories usually have standard lengths for their requirements, and potential authors would be advised to write to these lengths. Magazines will rarely consider much departure from their normally accepted lengths. Literary magazines are an exception to this and it does not apply to short stories that are published in book form where the length can be more flexible. But short stories in book form are almost always by established writers. Few book publishers will consider short stories from novice writers.

The short story has elements in common with the novel but with some modification. If there is an exposition, it will be very brief; some short stories plunge straight into the middle of the story, so to speak. Settings will be established with the equivalent of quick brush strokes rather than long descriptive passages. It will contain characters but fewer than in the novel; sometimes just one or two. It will often have a plot but no sub-plots. There will be rising action to a climax and a resolution or denouement. Often short stories have a theme or they make a simple point. Sometimes, so-called character stories will simply illustrate something about human nature. Usually the short story will cover a short or limited period of time for obvious reasons. Character development is unusual in the short story because there is not time for such development but many stories have been written which show how a character has been changed by some traumatic or unusual incident or experience. There are, it should be emphasized, exceptions to all of the above. Also like the novel, the short story can be realistic, satiric, tragic, humorous, romantic, fantastic and of any genre.

The worst kind of short stories are those written by novices and are, in effect, condensed novels; that is, there are too many characters, too much incident, too much plot, and therefore inevitably all these are dealt with cursorily and consequently lack interest for the reader.

The short story can be told in the first or third person and from almost any point of view. Sometimes experiments in point of view can work with a short story that would be virtually impossible at novel length. John Updike has a brilliant short story called *The Orphaned Swimming Pool*. It concerns the various occupants over a few years of a property that includes a swimming pool built by the first residents.

The swimming pool and its surrounds becomes a social centre for the community until the owners get divorced and move on. The empty house is still visited by swimmers and partygoers for a while until they tire of the frivolities. Some later occupants care for the pool, some neglect it. Eventually it is filled in because the latest occupants have a baby and regard it as a danger. In each case the characters of the owners are revealed in their attitude to the swimming pool. Updike also breaks the rule that a short story should only cover a short time. Rarely has so much been revealed in about 2,000 words.

The short story can deal with serious themes. A case in point is Franz Kafka's *Up in the Gallery*. The story is only about a page long and consists of two very long sentences. It is about an equestrienne in a circus. One sentence describes the glamorous horse rider and her acrobatic performance that is adulated by the audience and the enthusiastic ringmaster. The other sentence suggests the routine, gruelling life of the equestrienne, riding round the ring twice a day, every day, for as long as she can keep it up. Kafka manages to convey the tragedy that, in his view, underlies the glamorous surface which is seen by the casual visitor to the circus. At the same time, he uses the circus and its ring as a metaphor for the drudging lives of many other people. Again, a great deal is condensed into an extremely short story.

The short story can be tremendously versatile in its possibilities. As well as unusual examples such as those described above, there are character stories by James Joyce and Guy de Maupassant, well-plotted stories by O. Henry, twist-ending stories by Saki and Somerset Maugham and psychological character studies by D. H. Lawrence and Katherine Mansfield.

See also FAIRY TALES; FLASH FICTION; FRAME STORY; MINI-SAGAS; NOVEL; NOVELLA AND NOVELETTE

SHOWING AND TELLING

If a friend insists that someone he wants you to meet is almost always rude to people he meets, you may be a little wary or you may find it hard to believe. You will find it more believable if the friend gives a number of examples of his rudeness. This example is analogous to the two ways an author can convey a character or an event in fiction. The writer can report or tell the reader something about the character or the author can illustrate the point with a dramatized incident. He can show the character or event dramatically.

The boxes below gives some typical examples of telling and showing:

TELLING	SHOWING
1 The narrator tells the reader that Bill is a brave man.	1 An incident is described in which Bill saves a child on melting ice on a pond.
2 A married couple are said to be argumentative, always quarrelling.	2 An argument between the couple is provided in the form of a dialogue on a particular topic.
3 A character is described as witty, cynical or sharp-tongued.	3 The character's wit/ cynicism or sharp tongue is illustrated one or more times with witty remarks and cynical or sarcastic remarks.
4 The reader is told that an accident occurred involving a character.	4 The character recounts vividly to another exactly what happened to him/her.

In telling the author is the authority, sometimes also making or implying comments on the character or incident. In showing, the onus is on the reader to infer something about the incident or character.

It is fairly obvious that showing rather than telling is going to produce more interesting and vivid writing. If you doubt this, think what a film would be like if all the interesting action was described by one character to another rather than being dramatized and shown to the viewer.

Henry James is one of the greatest exponents of showing rather than telling and his novels illustrate how deep psychological insights into his characters can be conveyed to the reader through the actions of the characters and what they say. James, himself, rarely adds any comment; he does not *tell* us his opinion. It has to be acknowledged, of course, that an author is always in a sense manipulating the reader whichever method is chosen.

The main virtue of showing rather than telling is simply that it is more interesting for the reader. It is a method that conceals the author. As with all advice, there can be exceptions. Occasionally telling may be the most effective way of conveying something. Also in the first-person narrated story, the reader will expect the narrator/character to give opinions. We would be surprised, and indeed disappointed, if we got anything like objective and balanced views in the various diaries of Adrian Mole in the books by Sue Townsend.

Read these two passages:

> He was gaining on her and finally caught up. His arm stretched out and caught her as she screamed in fear . . .

> She could hear his thumping footsteps getting closer. The crunching sounds on the gravel sounded like minute screams. Then she felt something on her arm and at the same time smelt his hot, fetid breath on her neck. She struggled on in a last desperate effort to gain on him but she felt herself losing her momentum and balance as her arm was firmly caught. All she could do was scream . . .

Compare the passages and decide the virtues of each. It is important to remember that there is nearly always more than one way of conveying an incident or describing a character. The effective writer tries more than one and chooses that which is most appropriate for the purpose.

See also CHARACTERS

SIGNPOSTING

Have you ever been reading a novel and said to yourself 'Where the hell is this taking place, and who are these characters?' The author then is guilty of inadequate signposting. Readers like to know what is happening, who it is happening to and why and where it is happening. The writer establishing for the reader the location and characters in as natural a way as possible, this is signposting. It should not be overdone. If Jan and her family are having breakfast, we probably do not need to be told where they are. If a location keeps recurring because of characteristic events taking place there, then after the first one or two signposts, more will probably be unnecessary.

The writer has to use judgement to ensure when signposting is necessary and how detailed it needs to be. If the writer can get someone to read a draft of their story, they should be able to confirm whether the signposting is adequate or not.

You will have noticed in TV drama serials, especially American ones, that signposting frequently occurs, sometimes unnecessarily. Often the exterior of a building is shown before the viewer is taken to the interior – and it happens every time for that scene. In TV scriptwriting, these brief exteriors are called establishing shots and they are similar to literary signposting.

In its written form, signposting can be done indirectly. For instance, if the scene starts 'There was the hum of a dozen PCs and the less harmonious clattering of a similar number of printers . . .' that is probably enough to signpost or establish that the scene is in an office.

SIMILE AND METAPHOR

Similes and metaphors are probably the most common figures of speech or literary devices used in English poetry and they are also common in prose and spoken or written language. They are a means of describing something by comparing it to another.

The simile is very straightforward. Usually the word 'like' is used to compare things, 'His face was *like* an over-ripe tomato'. Another construction of similes is to use 'as', 'His face was as red *as* a tomato'. The comparison is direct.

The metaphor is more compressed than the simile. Its wording suggests one thing *is* another thing but we know that we should not take the statement literally. Robert Burns uses the simile 'O my love's like a red, red rose' to convey the girl's beauty. He might have used a metaphor and written 'O my love is a red, red rose'. We know she isn't literally and we know that he wasn't in love with a rose.

One of the most famous metaphors is in Andrew Marvell's poem *To His Coy Mistress*:

> But at my back I always hear
> Time's winged chariot hurrying near.

'Time's winged chariot' is death. Marvell is warning us to make use of time while we have it or, to put it in another metaphor 'to make hay while the sun shines'. The difference between Marvell's metaphor and the one about hay is that the first is original; the second has become a cliché. Many similes and metaphors become clichés (as black as coal), and the writer should always strive for original ones if the writing is to have impact. George Orwell gave the following useful advice: 'Never use a metaphor, simile, or other figure of speech which you are used to seeing in print'.

Some single words and expressions are used metaphorically and have become part of everyday language. For instance, if I refer to a 'bottleneck', quite different meanings will be apparent depending on whether I'm talking about wine or traffic. If it is traffic then the expression is being used metaphorically.

See also CLICHÉ

SKETCH, LITERARY

A sketch probably conjures up the idea of a rough drawing. The literary sketch is long established and unlike a story it lacks a plot. While rooted in fact it does not necessarily portray a purely factual account of its subject matter. It tends to be entertaining, often amusing and sometimes critical of modern manners. The sketch has been characterized as part short story, part essay. The length is usually one to two thousand words.

Charles Dickens' *Sketches by Boz* (1839) is a series of sketches on people and life in the mid-nineteenth century. Sketches usually appear in newspapers and magazines. Parliamentary sketches have become common in most newspapers today where the writer gives a very personal, amusing and sometimes cynical account of daily business in the House.

Character sketches obviously play a part in novels although character is usually revealed gradually in fiction by means of description, dialogue and action rather than in an extended description. Radio is one of the main outlets for short sketches and many are written by foreign correspondents to provide an insight into people, places and manners abroad.

The term sketch is also used for a short dramatic scene which may contain usually a couple of characters who illustrate peculiarities of character or manners and may perhaps make some amusing point. Harold Pinter wrote a number of sketches as well as full length plays.

SLANG AND SWEARING

In 1928 D. H. Lawrence wrote and tried to publish *Lady Chatterley's Lover* and it was almost immediately banned partly because of sexual descriptions but largely because of Lawrence's use of two four-letter words (fuck and cunt). The book was not published openly in Britain until 1962 after a lengthy court case. Since the 1960s swearing and four-letter words have been allowed although some newspapers still ban their use and publishers would tend to consider their target audience for a book to dictate whether they might be used. Considerable swearing, though, is now found in some literature for teenagers.

Similarly, swearing has increased over the years in films and on television after the 9 p.m. watershed. Before the 1960s it was never heard at all.

Most people use slang and many people swear. Inevitably, characters in fiction would be likely to do both and there is no reason why a writer should not let characters swear. But some pointers are worth noting:

- Many slang words date very quickly. If you use today's latest slang expressions, remember that they may have disappeared in months or a few years and your work will seem dated. (You may, however, wish to look up and use dated slang for a special purpose – say a novel set during the Second World War.)
- Some people swear every other word and it is extremely boring, it would be even more boring in a novel.
- Choose the language including bad language according to the life, social class, and job of the characters using it.
- Some readers and viewers object strongly to swearing. Judge your target audience and their likely reactions, and use or do not use it accordingly. A Mills & Boon editor of romantic fiction would be shocked to receive a manuscript littered with four-letter words because the writer had so misjudged the target audience.

See also DIALOGUE; STANDARD ENGLISH

SLUSH PILE

The slush pile is the novice author's nightmare and it is just as well that most of them do not even know of its existence. The fact is that there are more aspiring authors than there are published authors and most mainstream publishers are sent dozens of book manuscripts every week. The task of reading and assessing them all would be extremely time-consuming and expensive. So a pile is made – the slush pile – of unsolicited manuscripts and members of the publisher's staff read and assess them to see if they have some merit. Some manuscripts may only be skimmed or partially read.

To avoid your manuscript ending up on a slush pile, it is better to write to a publisher of the kind of book you have written, providing a brief outline of it and possibly a sample of the writing. They will then judge if they want to see the whole book and if they do they will look at it more quickly.

STANDARD ENGLISH

Standard English is a term with different meanings for different people and even for different linguists. As far as standard written English is concerned it is that English which keeps to the rules in currently accepted grammar books and the spelling given in current dictionaries. (Even here there are problems. Some dictionaries give one spelling for a word and another dictionary gives an alternative, although the cases where this occurs are very few.) Generally speaking, standard English will eschew dialect words and slang.

Most fiction writers use standard English because it communicates most easily with a wide range of people. It is the variety of written English that is taught in educational establishments. There are some exceptions. James Joyce in *Finnegan's Wake*, Irving Welsh in *Trainspotting* and J. D. Salinger in *The Catcher in the Rye* do not use standard English.

Writers who mainly use standard English occasionally deviate from it in order to create some special effect. Charles Dickens, for example, in this passage from *Bleak House* (1850) breaks a basic rule of grammar by omitting the verb from each clause. He does this deliberately in order to paint a more vivid picture of the fog:

> Fog on the Essex marshes, fog on the Kentish heights. Fog creeping into the cabooses of the collier-brigs; fog lying out on the yards, and hovering in the rigging of great ships; fog drooping on the gunwales of barges and small boats. Fog in the eyes and throats of ancient Greenwich pensioners, wheezing by the firesides of their wards; fog in the stem and bowl of the afternoon pipe of the wrathful skipper, down in his close cabin; fog cruelly pinching the toes and fingers of his shivering little 'prentice boy on deck'.

Fog is everywhere, just as it is in this passage.

Because English is now almost a world language, there are inevitably variations from the standard written in Britain. Thus there is also standard American English, standard Australian English, standard Indian English.

Standard English is not to be confused with Received Pronunciation (RP) which is the regionally neutral accent spoken by some people all over the country. It derives from the south-east, the seat of government and is sometimes referred to as the Queen's English or BBC English. It is an accent like any other but it tends to enjoy more prestige than the other regional accents because it is associated with educated people and those of high status, although not all those who are educated and of high status speak it.

Unless there are compelling reasons for writing in non-standard English, it is best to keep to the standard simply because most readers appear to prefer it and almost everyone understands it. The compelling reasons for not using it would be where a non-standard form of speech characterizes a narrator or character in the story and for special effects such as that exemplified by the Dickens passage.

See also DIALOGUE

STEREOTYPES

Originally a stereotype was the metal printing plate from which hundreds or thousands of identical copies of printed matter could be made and which would look identical. The word is now used mainly metaphorically. A stereotyped character is one that is over simplified and frequently appeals to prejudices some people have about certain groups of people. Those who stereotype regard the individuals who make up groups as all the same, like the copies obtained from a printing plate.

Stereotyped groups are often racial or social. It is sometimes suggested that all Asians speak English in a particular way, that young male West Indians invariably have dreadlocks or wear a particular kind of headgear, that working-class men drink beer, swear and wear flat caps, that upper-class girls are often found on horses, that gay men mince and speak effeminately and grandmothers are never not sitting in their armchairs knitting. In other words, if a writer creates stereotyped characters, they are not acknowledging that everyone is different.

Most stereotypes are negative. However, the traditional stereotype of the nurse is that she is caring; that of the policemen, that he is helpful so long as you are on the right side of the law. Positive stereotypes are as undesirable as negative ones; both refuse to portray people as individuals.

Advertisers sometimes make use of stereotypes of men, women and people of different ages. Most men's top shelf magazines portray women as sex objects.

Stereotypes should be completely avoided in fiction (and probably everywhere else as well). It is an easy and lazy way to create character. Note that stock characters are not necessarily stereotypical.

See also STOCK CHARACTERS

STOCK CHARACTERS

Stock characters are characters that recur again and again in particular genres of literature and are identifiable by common character traits, behaviour and manner of speech and the way they are regarded by and behave towards other characters.

It is said that in ancient Greek comedy the stock characters were impostors and braggarts, rustics, buffoons and the self-demeaning. Part of the comedy arose from the clash between these types. Even today many comedy double acts contain dominant and put-upon characters.

A modern example of the use of stock characters is the soap opera. Those who have watched more than one soap opera will notice that similar types appear in most of them. The main soap opera stock characters are:

The tragedy queen (or prince).
The bimbo.
The wise woman or guru.
The bitch.
The gossip.
The hard business person.
The rake or vixen.
The mixed-up teenager (male or female).
The teenage mum.
The one who tries but always fails.

There are many others and sometimes one rather unbelievably changes into another.

It is to be noted that a good writer (perhaps helped by a good actor) can take a stock character and make a convincing character out of them. Stock characters are modelled on real people as much as any fictional characters. It is just that one particular characteristic tends to be over-emphasized and repeated. If some fault lies with the soap opera genre it is that it tends to concern itself with a limited group of character types. This may be partly because audiences seem to enjoy the limitations.

Television, possibly more than novels, relies on stock characters. It is difficult to find a police series (and they are legion) without policemen and women who have not got domestic problems. Senior police officers nearly always unmercifully berate those of lower rank. A surprising number of police officers are criminals themselves. Perhaps TV should not be blamed, many of the police and detective series are based on novels.

Other stock characters appear in genre fiction. Any avid reader will have come across at least some of them:

The femme fatale.
The damsel in distress.
The impractical intellectual.
The mad or eccentric scientist or professor.
The faithful sidekick or servant.
The housewife lush.
The tart with a heart.
The old soldier (probably a Colonel) who deplores anything modern.
The dominant grandmother/mother-in-law/old aunt.
The reluctant hero.
The put-upon mother.
The stooge.
The rebellious teen.
The 'shoot first, ask questions later' character in a Western or police-man (e.g. Clint Eastwood).

It should be reiterated that the writer need not necessarily avoid such characters. All are based on reality. The art of avoiding a stock charac-ter is to see that they are fully rounded and with a variety of charac-teristics and behaviour patterns rather than just one. So the tart may have a heart but she will be many other things as well.

See also CHARACTERS

STORY AND NOVEL CATEGORIES

Genre is discussed in a separate entry but basically it refers to cat-egories of literature and in the case of fiction to different categories of novels or short stories. Listed below are the names of the separate entries in the Glossary of the various genres or categories of fiction that are defined and discussed.

Two points should be kept in mind when reading any of these entries. (1) The genre names are not absolute and unqualified. A detective story may also have elements of the romance or the revenge story in it; science fiction may have elements of horror in it. An his-torical novel could also be romantic and a detective story as well. There are no hard and fast rules about genre and the various entries discuss the category that dominates. Some examples of novels which cover more than one genre are: *War and Peace* (1869) by Leo Tolstoy, pri-marily a war novel but also a novel of Russian manners, a love story and a historical novel; *1984* by George Orwell, mainly a political novel but has elements of science fiction and is a love story; *Howards End* by E. M. Forster, a novel of manners and a romance. (2) The main categories of fiction are covered. Some additional genres are chase stories, kidnap and rescue stories, sex and shopping novels and caper stories. The first two of these, of course, could come under the category Adventure and quest stories, and the latter often refers to the more light-hearted crime or detective story.

The following categories have separate entries: Adventure and quest stories; Autobiographical novel; *Bildungsroman*; Campus novel; Chick lit; Detective stories; Dystopian novel; Existentialism (Existential novel); Family sagas and Aga sagas; Fantasy fiction; Gothic fiction, horror and vampire stories; Historical fiction; Lad lit; Mystery fiction; Non-fiction novel; Nouveau roman; Novel of manners; Picaresque novel; Pornography and erotica; Proletarian novels; Regional novels; Revenge stories; Rites of passage and coming-of-age stories; *Roman-à-clef*; Romantic fiction; Thrillers; Utopia (Utopian novel); War novels; and Western stories.

Most writers will find themselves drawn to a particular genre because of an inherent interest in it. Even with an interest and a background of reading the particular genre, it is quite likely that research will also be essential.

Story Concept

A story concept is a summary of the story in a single sentence that inevitably omits details of characters, plot and setting. The central characters may be part of a story concept. It is useful to think of a concept for any story because it provides the minimal skeleton on which to hang the details. It also indicates whether the writer has a viable story to tell and keeps him or her on track when working out the details.

Some examples of what may have been the concepts of some published novels are as follows:

The Catcher in the Rye by J. D. Salinger (1951) Adolescent male rebels against school, fellow pupils, family and adult values because he finds them all phoney.

The Silence of the Lambs by Thomas Harris (1988) Rookie female detective befriends and employs cannibal psychopath to catch another psychopath.

Jane Eyre by Charlotte Brontë (1847) Abused orphan gets job as governess to harsh man's illegitimate daughter, falls for father not
knowing he is married, but after further misfortunes marries him.
The War of the Worlds by H. G. Wells (1898) Martians invade earth,
devastate half the world that is only saved when the Martians die of
flu.

Those who know any of these novels will see how the detail is added to
create an interesting plot and story. Notice that each of these concepts
could be prefaced by the words: 'What would happen if . . .' In other
words the concept provides the basis of both the conflict and suspense
in the story.

Notice also how each has a subject (Adolescent male, Rookie female
detective, Abused orphan, Martians) which identifies the main character or characters, followed by a verb that indicates some of the conflict in the story or something which is done by the main characters(s),
e.g. rebels, befriends and employs. The story concept is a simple
device but a useful one.

See also PLOT AND STORY

STREAM OF CONSCIOUSNESS

William James the American psychologist and brother of Henry James,
the novelist, coined the term 'stream of consciousness' to describe the
ebb and flow of inner experience in his book *Principles of Psychology*
published in 1890. He used the word 'stream' after considering 'chain
of thought' and 'train of thought' because he thought these two
phrases suggested too great a degree of cohesiveness and organization
whereas stream echoes the rambling nature of thought. Literary critics
later took his term to refer to a style or technique of writing.

Literary critics frequently use 'interior' or 'internal monologue' to
mean the same as stream of consciousness and it is true that it is difficult to pinpoint significant differences in the techniques used by
writers such as James Joyce, Virginia Woolf, Dorothy Richardson and
the American novelist William Faulkner.

If there is a difference between stream of consciousness and
interior monologue then the latter refers solely to the rambling, dis-
jointed inner thoughts of a particular character whereas stream-of-
consciousness technique has slightly wider implications. For
example, the opening page of James Joyce's novel *A Portrait of the
Artist as a Young Man* attempts to describe vividly the life of the

protagonist when he is a baby. It is written in a mixture of first- and third-person narrative style whereas a character's thoughts would usually be in present tense. The passage vividly conjures up experiences of infancy like wetting the bed, seeing 'moocows', observing his relatives and them observing him, snatches of songs, a visit to a shop for lemon platt and a concentration on smells that an adult might not notice. He takes in and remembers odd snatches of conversation he has heard. What Joyce does is not so much describe infancy as recreate it for the reader to experience. It is much more vivid than a conventional description from an adult narrator's point of view. Joyce manages to get into the consciousness of the infant and the reader. The passage begins as follows: 'Once upon a time and a very good time it was there was a moocow coming down along the road and this moocow that was down along the road met a nicens little boy named baby tuckoo. . . . His father told him that story: his father looked at him through a glass: he had a hairy face.' In this novel, Joyce recreates the teenage hero's fear of hell not by straightforward description but by providing a lengthy description of his thoughts and reactions to a priest's sermon on the horrors of hell.

It is often difficult and perhaps unnecessary to make a clear distinction between 'stream of consciousness' technique and 'interior monologue'.

See also INTERIOR MONOLOGUE

SUB-PLOT

A sub-plot may have the same structure as the main plot but it is subsidiary within the novel. The sub-plot, or the characters in it, are likely to complement or contrast with the main plot. Novels need not have a sub-plot; longer ones often do. They are unlikely to be found in short stories because the length does not allow for them.

Jane Austen's novels, which frequently concern young women looking for love and marriage often include one or more couples to contrast with the developing relationship of the main couple. In Charles Dickens' *Great Expectations*, the main plot is about Pip's obsession with and search for love and marriage with a cold-hearted girl, Estella, but family life is also central to the novel and the reader is provided with at least four other contrasting families: the young Pip and his life with his carers, the Gargerys; his life within the cold confines of Miss Havisham's house; the strange home life of the lawyer, Mr Jaggers; and the warm, loving home life of Jaggers' office assistant.

There are also other love affairs and marriages to compare with Pip's 'relationship' with Estella.

See also PLOT AND STORY

SUSPENSE

In reality a suspenseful situation affords a person a subtle mixture of pleasure and discomfort. The child waits for Christmas and its presents with both frustration and pleasant anticipation; the adult awaits the outcome of a job interview with hope mingled with doubts. Readers of fiction are distanced from the situation full of suspense but nevertheless a skilled writer will engender a similar mixture of pleasure and anxiety for them.

More importantly for the writer, the creation of suspense must compel readers to read on because they desperately want to find out what happens next – who committed the murder and why, whether a marriage will take place, the child will be saved, the desired object will be found. In Robert Louis Stevenson's *Treasure Island* one of the most suspenseful episodes is when Jim has stowed away on a ship and hidden himself in an apple barrel. While there he realizes from overheard conversations that he is among pirates. The reader is on tenterhooks. Will they find him? What will they do? What can he do? Suspense often depends on the writer putting a character in a predicament, the way out of which is not obvious.

Suspense appeals to the insatiable curiosity nearly all human beings possess. The writer must create a sense of uncertainty and anticipation to feed this curiosity. It is a feature of both popular and serious fiction. The reader wonders how James Bond will escape from the tight spots he gets into but equally the audience wonder if Romeo and Juliet will achieve happiness together or whether Othello will find out the truth about Iago and thus desist from murdering his wife.

A reader's apprehension and concern can arise from some suspense situations. If readers find a character sympathetic, they will be concerned about the outcome of a suspenseful position that puts them in danger. Millions of children (and some adults) have shed a tear at the ultimate fate of Bambi, after hope that it would.

Suspense is an intrinsic element of story and is closely related to the construction of plot and conflict. Almost all conflicts have an element of suspense because the outcome of the conflict is unknown to the reader. It also arises from the nature of the characters and their response to particular problems. The writer must create suspense if readers are to carry on reading the story and they must ensure the suspenseful situation and its outcome are plausible within the terms of the story.

The outcome of suspense may be tragic, comic, ironic or happy. Suspenseful situations in fiction may be concerned with an episode that is resolved fairly quickly but there can be a series of such situations. In some novels, particularly detective stories, the suspense will be sustained throughout or until near the end. Time is often a crucial factor. Will the kidnap victim be rescued in time? Will the bomb be defused before damage is caused? Will she catch the plane?

It was pointed out in the entry on plot and story that a plot has a similar pattern to a person's progress through life and hence its appeal. The appeal of suspense is similar.

See also CONFLICT; IRONY; PLOT AND STORY

SUSPENSION OF DISBELIEF
Suspension of disbelief is a term which appears to have been first used by the poet, Samuel Taylor Coleridge. It refers to the fact that when reading a fiction, watching a film or a play, people suspend the fact that they know this is fiction, that these are actors or words written by one person. They lose themselves in the fiction. In a fantastic science-fiction story set in the future, the audience may know before and after reading it that it is not true but their enjoyment will be enhanced if they lose themselves in it and accept the fictional world. Authors aim to make us suspend our disbelief because when we do not we are more likely to dismiss the work.

If the audience suspend their disbelief they dispense with the critical faculties they would bring to bear on something real. For instance, the stage looks artificial but we accept it as a living room or a roadway.

The complete phrase used by Coleridge is 'willing suspension of disbelief', suggesting that the reader deliberately puts him or herself into a frame of mind to accept the work being read in spite possibly of inadequacies in it. Some readers may have had the experience of observing the reactions of two people who have been to see a film. One wanted to go; the other did not. The reactions of the first to the quality of the film are likely to be more favourable than those of the second person because the first would be more inclined to willingly suspend their disbelief. The second person would be more ready to criticize.

Clearly an author has no magic formula for making people suspend their disbelief and audiences and readers probably do it to very different degrees. Few adults get lost in a story or film in the way young children do. One only needs to watch a child looking at a story they like on TV or listening to someone read to them to notice from their facial expression that they have left the world of the present and have become immersed in a fictional world. *Doctor Who* and *Star Wars* fans appear to suspend their disbelief more readily than most people.

Whether suspension of disbelief is necessary for the enjoyment of fiction is open to debate.

SYMPATHY

It is sometimes suggested that central characters or protagonists should be sympathetic, that they must be admired or liked by the reader. It is true that a story with a likeable protagonist or hero will be appealing to readers, especially to readers of popular genre fiction, but such a character is not essential as an examination of a number of novels confirms. There are too many successful novels with unlikeable or villainous characters to indicate that sympathy is necessary.

It is probably true that the protagonist must at least have some characteristics the reader can relate to. A dislikeable character may have weaknesses with which readers can identify.

Some protagonists are anything but admirable and some do not have any traits that we can identify with. Raskolnikov in Fyodor Dostoevsky's *Crime and Punishment* chooses to murder old people simply to demonstrate his power over life and death and because he thinks he is a superior being and is clever enough to get away with it (he does not). In addition, he has few if any endearing qualities. We are entitled to ask, therefore, why *Crime and Punishment* has become such a successful classic, albeit not one with universal appeal. There are three possible reasons. Maybe readers see a darker side of themselves in Raskolnikov even though he may repel them. Perhaps more important is the fact that we are interested in extreme characters and their behaviour. It is something similar to our curiosity about real life crime and criminals. We want to know what makes them tick. Another possibility is that the villain gets his punishment and thus some semblance of stability is restored to society.

The likeable rogue is another protagonist who we not so much admire as simply find fascinating and often humorous. How do they get away with it? The novel genre has produced such characters since its early days, for example Henry Fielding's *Tom Jones* (1749). One of the most popular rogues in current literature is George MacDonald Fraser's Flashman. Harry Flashman was the unsympathetic villain in *Tom Brown's Schooldays* (1857) by Thomas Hughes. In Fraser's series of novels he gets applauded. We would probably despise these characters if we met them in real life; the distance created by the novel makes them more tolerable.

See also EMPATHY, PATHOS AND BATHOS

Syntax

Syntax is the branch of grammar which deals with the order of words, or the relationship of words, in sentences, phrases and clauses. Different languages have different syntactical rules. The rules of syntax are not a problem for most people because they are picked up in learning to speak, read and write a language. English syntax tends to follow the arrangement *subject, verb, object* in sentences, e.g. 'The dog ate the bone.' This is how most speakers and writers would express the idea although it is not wrong to say 'The bone was eaten by the dog.' No one, however, would say 'Dog the bone ate the'. In some sentences, a syntactical change might change the meaning and may express an untruth. For instance, the sentence 'John hates James' may be true and so is 'James is hated by John', but reversing the word order to 'James hates John' may be untrue.

For the most part the choice of meaningful syntactical structure or word order, causes no problem for the writer.

Tall Tales

Tall tales are exaggerated stories sometimes about famous and historical characters and sometimes about unidentified people. They tend to be passed orally from person to person and occasionally they get printed as fillers in newspapers or magazines. Their truth should always be questioned but they are not serious lies. Their purpose is to amuse and entertain and they are not usually taken too seriously. 'You're making it up!' is a common response to someone who tells a tall tale.

Tall tales play little part in written literature although Mark Twain made use of them as diversions related by characters in some of his novels.

The following is an example of a tall tale which has made the rounds over many years and in many versions:

> A hospital was phoned by a distraught mother who explained that she had caught her young son in the garden eating ants. She did not know how many he had eaten. The doctor advised that there was no need for panic. The ants would not be harmful and if he had eaten a lot, a bout of sickness might result which would be a good thing rather than something to worry about. The mother was duly reassured but added just as the doctor was about to ring off that she had given her son some ant killer just to be on the safe side. At this the doctor suggested that it might be a good idea, after all, to bring the child to the hospital as a matter of urgency.

See also JOKES

TAUTOLOGY

In literary terms tautology can be defined as saying the same thing twice in slightly different ways or using two words that have similar meanings. Examples of the latter are 'free gratis', 'lonely solitude', 'recent innovation'. Journalists, in order to fill the space allotted to them for a news story, often repeat parts of the story in slightly different ways. They tell the gist of the story in an initial paragraph and then recount it in detail and then sometimes sum up the same thing again in the final paragraph. They are using tautology to fill the space.

Tautology in fiction should be avoided, if it is used, there must be a very good reason for it. It should not, however, be confused with repetition which can have a useful effect. For an example of repetition as opposed to tautology, see the passage from *Bleak House* by Charles Dickens in the entry on Standard English.

See also STANDARD ENGLISH

THEME

The theme of a work of fiction is the issue, idea or topic which the author clearly thinks is generally important (or it is important to the author) and which he or she wishes to convey to the reader with the probable intention of persuading the reader to share his or her views on the issue.

The author's theme may have been the starting point for the work because the writer's interest in it may have led to the invention of a plot and characters to illustrate it. It should be noted, however, that this can be a dangerous or undesirable approach to story creation because it is possible that the whole work may become didactic or moralistic. Many critics would argue that it is better for the theme to arise naturally from characters and plot rather than the other way around. In some cases, though, it may be difficult to tell which came first and even the author may not be sure.

A theme usually provides a thread throughout the fiction, although it may not be obvious at every stage and perhaps not until the end. Some authors make their theme implicit and a few may make it very explicit. John Milton in his long poem *Paradise Lost* tells the reader quite openly that his intention is 'to justify the ways of God to man'. Clearly, if the theme is to have some importance, it must be sufficiently obvious to the reader at least by the end of the work – and preferably without the author spelling it out.

Fables are examples of brief stories which have an obvious theme, usually a moral. For example, *The Hare and the Tortoise* by Aesop preaches that 'slow and steady wins the race'. It is generally accepted that fables have morals or lessons but didacticism and preaching is not at all fashionable in contemporary fiction and has not been for some time. Themes do not necessarily convey moral points, of course. They may simply convey the author's views on the situation or some aspect of it.

The theme of a work of fiction is not the same as its subject. Thus, in Shakespeare's play, *Othello*, the subject is the problems besetting an older man who marries a young girl, the theme is the corrosive nature of jealousy.

Ideally, characters, plot and theme should blend inseparably and certainly neither the characters nor plot should be manipulated artificially or unnaturally in order to illustrate a preconceived theme. Thomas Hardy has been accused of allowing his belief that human beings were the victims of a malevolent fate or destiny to create stories where everything was stacked up against the central characters. As one critic put it, Hardy's characters are 'raped by destiny'. In his defence it should be pointed out that Hardy himself said that 'character is fate'; although there may be some truth in this, his own fictional characters are never able to change and they do seem to be destined for tragic lives or ends. Hardy's themes are not in any sense moralistic. Hardy is certainly not saying that if you behave well, life will be kind to you – rather the reverse.

The following is a list of themes, all of which have been used many times in works of fiction. The reader may be able to connect some of them with a particular novel, play, or short story.

- Nature and how human beings are out of tune with it.
- How we must work with nature if we are to survive.

- The many facets of the destructive power of time.
- Alienation of the individual from others or from society.
- Death or accident shows the absurdity or vanity of human ambition.
- Love can be destructive.
- Love is the only thing worthwhile.
- Live in the present: it's all we have.
- Growing up is inevitably problematic.
- War between the sexes is inevitable.
- Finding one's identity is important but problematic.
- Family life is both essential and destructive.
- Marriage is a natural and desirable state for human beings.
- Marriage is an unnatural and undesirable state for human beings.
- One's identity and life chances are conditioned by birth/money/job/friends/family.

The writer, however, would never choose a theme from a list such as that above. If the writer is to have a theme in their fiction, it should arise from some issue that they personally feel strongly about. Fiction does not have to have a theme. Some novels are mainly character studies; escapist fiction may simply tell a story with plenty of action.

See also CHARACTERS; DIDACTICISM; ESCAPIST FICTION; FABLE; MOTIF; PLOT AND STORY

THRILLERS

There is considerable overlap with regard to thrillers, detective stories and mystery stories. In addition, spy or espionage novels, horror and adventure stories may also be called thrillers. The defining characteristic of the thriller, not surprisingly, is that it thrills and excites through a mixture of action and suspense. The Protagonists in thrillers are mostly male. The names of the categories above signify some important differences which can best be understood by an examination of the elements in a work everyone would call a thriller: any novel about James Bond by Ian Fleming.

James Bond is not a detective, although he may in a limited sense use his powers of detection; the novels are not horror stories or mystery stories. There is usually no secret about who the enemy is. They are spy stories but Bond is more of an action man than the subtle and devious spy like George Smillie found in the novels of John le Carré. Bond is certainly an adventurer. The following elements are found in most Bond novels and most of them appear in the majority of popular genre thrillers:

- Fierce actions and fights.
- Gun play and other use of weapons.
- Exotic locations and usually a number of them.
- Surprises leading to suspense (e.g. the protagonist gets into an impossible predicament from which he has to escape – and does.)
- A villain of evil intent.
- Some sexual intrigue.
- The protagonist is macho, tough, sexy, clever and resourceful. He is a bit of a rebel in that he takes with a pinch of salt the advice of his superiors and prefers to work alone. Characterization is minimal, characters are defined by what they do and they are rarely introspective.
- Patriotism.
- Technology is advanced both with regard to weapons, transport and gadgets.
- Dangerous situations abound and may be caused by the enemy, nature, animals and time. Time often almost runs out when a bomb has been primed, for instance.
- Grief is never felt for the demise of enemies or minor characters and is even short-lived for the loss of friends or colleagues.
- The protagonist may have a sidekick although these can change in the course of the story. They may be female; the protagonist is usually male.
- Quite frequently a friend, or someone who poses as one, turns out to have been on the enemy's side all the time. Other reversals occur.
- There are numerous confrontations (and fights) usually leading up to one with the master-villain.

Currently popular thriller writers include Lee Child, Jack Higgins, Frederick Forsyth, Tom Clancy, Robin Cook, Stephen King (who writes some non-horror novels) and Brian Garfield. Garfield is the author of *Death Wish* (1972), one of a category sometimes referred to as 'vigilante thrillers'.

The techno-thriller is another subgenre being concerned, as the name implies, with detailed information and accounts of technical and medical matters in a thriller context. Some also have a military or war background. Robin Cook's *Coma* is about a maverick medical organization stealing bodies from hospitals for experimental purposes. Cook's own medical background makes a possibly far-fetched story seem plausible. One of his latest is *Seizure* (2003), the title gives the theme. Tom Clancy's *The Hunt for Red October* (1984) has a submarine and political defection background. He has written novels about drug-dealing and Irish terrorism. Terrorism of various kinds has potential as a subject for the thriller.

The spy novel can also be categorized as a subgenre of the thriller as the previous comments on the James Bond novels have suggested. More serious spy thrillers were written by Graham Greene including *The Quiet American* (1952), *A Burnt-Out Case* (1961) and *The Comedians* (1966). John le Carré's *The Spy Who Came in from the Cold* is an example of a spy novel regarded also as a serious literary novel. It is thoughtful and probably true to life. The protagonist, against the odds of the popular spy novel is lonely and alienated. It has none of the action and mayhem that is characteristic of the more popular spy thrillers by writers such as Ken Follett, Robert Harris and Robert Ludlum.

The pioneer thriller writers, a genre that really did not exist until the twentieth century, include the following:

The Riddle of the Sands by Erskine Childers (1903).
The Scarlet Pimpernel by Baroness Orczy (1905).
The Four Just Men by Edgar Wallace (1905). Wallace was the best-seller
   of the early twentieth century and wrote over 150 novels.
The Thirty-Nine Steps by John Buchan (1915).
Ashenden or The British Agent by W. Somerset Maugham (1928).
Blind Corner by Dornford Yates (1927).
The Mask of Dimitrious by Eric Ambler (1939).

The older novels are strong on plot but less violent than their modern counterparts.

Thrillers are presently extremely popular as has been shown and there is a huge range of subject matter embraced by the genre. All must contain as a major part of the story: thrilling action, suspense, cliffhangers, chills and spills, uncertainty and tension.

See also ADVENTURE AND QUEST STORIES; DETECTIVE STORIES; GOTHIC FICTION, HORROR AND VAMPIRE STORIES; STORY AND NOVEL CATEGORIES; SUSPENSE; WAR NOVELS

TITLE PAGE
A page at the front of a book giving the complete title, the author's name, the publisher's name and sometimes the place of publication.

TITLES

A title should be succinct, appropriate to the content and type of fiction, easy to say, never a cliché and possibly intriguing or mysterious. These rules are sometimes broken possibly because it is rarely easy to sum up a book in up to four or five words – this is about the maximum number of words for a title. The writer should examine current titles and judge which are appealing. Probably the technique most frequently used for novel titles is to use a few words from a quotation evocative of the main theme of the novel. Very often the whole quotation is used as an epigraph.

It might be worthwhile to look at the following titles of famous novels which were changed from the originals (given in brackets). Is the final title used an improvement on the original? Bear in mind that the familiarity of a title possibly makes it more appealing. Note how in two instances, clichés have been rejected.

Brick Lane by Monica Ali	(*Seven Seas and the Thirteen Rivers*)
David Copperfield by Charles Dickens	(*Mag's Diversions*)
Catch-22 by Joseph Heller	(*Catch-18*)
Jaws by Peter Benchley	(*The Summer of the Shark*)
The Magus by John Fowles	(*The Fox*)
A Portrait of the Artist as a Young Man by James Joyce	(*Stephen Hero*)
Pride and Prejudice by Jane Austen	(*First Impressions*)
Sons and Lovers by D. H. Lawrence	(*Paul Morel*)
Treasure Island by R. L. Stevenson	(*The Sea-Cook*)
War and Peace by Leo Tolstoy	(*All's Well that Ends Well*)

See also CLICHÉ; EPIGRAPH

TONE

Tone is the attitude of the author to his or her subject, characters and reader and is revealed by the writer's moral outlook. The tone will suggest to the reader optimism, pessimism, formality or informality, humour or seriousness, satire, irony or playfulness.

While an author may adopt a particular tone for a specific story or purpose, it is generally thought that a writer's tone infuses most of his or her work and is conditioned by personality and attitudes. For instance, the novelist Thomas Hardy is generally thought to express a rather pessimistic view of the human condition and this tone persists through nearly all his novels and poetry, a large body of work.

It is obviously important to adopt a tone which is suitable for the subject, although sometimes taking a tone contrary to that expected may produce interesting or dramatic effects. Joseph Heller's novel *Catch-22* is about the tragedy of war, but Heller adopts a humorous tone which brings out the absurdity of war.

TRAGIC FLAW (HAMARTIA)

The idea that the central figure in a tragedy has a tragic flaw (*hamartia* in Greek) originates from the ideas of Greek philosopher Aristotle (384–322 BC) discussed in *The Poetics*. He believed that tragic heroes should not be intrinsically evil but their downfall would rather be the result of a flaw in their character even though in other respects they may be benevolent and largely good or respectable. Aristotle believed that hubris or pride was the most serious tragic flaw. In his terms, of course, pride would be seen as most serious if it involved disobeying or insulting a god – making oneself better or wiser than a god. However, he also discussed in this context errors of judgement, mistakes and immorality.

Shakespearian tragedies contain characters with flaws which bring about their downfall, e.g. Hamlet's inability to make up his mind and to take action, Othello's pride and jealousy, Macbeth's undiluted ambition.

Modern tragedy, as in the novels of Thomas Hardy, frequently suggests that tragedy is caused not by a character flaw or inner weaknesses but by outside agents such as social or political conditions over which the individual has little control. In Hardy's novel, *Tess of the D'Urbevilles* (1891), Tess, the tragic heroine, has a child out of wedlock (a serious sin in the nineteenth century) and murders one of her tormentors. Hardy subtitles the novel *A Pure Woman* suggesting he believes her mistakes are made as much by her circumstances and the attitudes of society as by her own character flaws. It is true, of course, that many of Hardy's characters have serious personality weaknesses.

Weak characters and analysis of their weaknesses are a feature of much modern fiction but complex social and political issues are also the reasons for tragedy.

See also HUBRIS; SEVEN DEADLY SINS

TWIST ENDING STORIES

Twist or surprise ending stories are stories where the ending comes as a surprise to the reader or viewer. Even though it may be unexpected, the ending must be consistent with what has gone before and logical within the terms of the story.

Stories with twist or surprise endings tend to be avoided by literary artists but such stories are undoubtedly admired considering the number of novels, short stories, plays, TV plays and films which exploit the twist in the tail of the story. Crime or mystery stories, which are one of the most popular kinds of novel, are a particular genre of the surprise ending story because many of them do not reveal the criminal or the solution to the mystery until the last few pages.

Contemporary writers as acclaimed as P. D. James, Ruth Rendell and Reginald Hill are noted exponents of surprise ending novels. Roald Dahl's short stories for adults use this type of ending with ingenuity. Thomas Hardy is also a master of the form.

The surprise must be prepared for. The writer must not cheat by introducing new information which has been withheld from the reader deliberately to engineer the disclosure. Characters must be consistent. The surprise must not depend on characters behaving contrarily to the way they have been presented earlier. The writer may use red herrings to disguise an important fact but everything must legitimately lead up to the surprise which should be quite plausible.

There is no point in starting a story and hoping a good surprise will come to mind before the writer reaches the end. More than in any other kind of story writing, the writer must know where they are going from the very beginning. Only then will they be able to disguise, misdirect and insert red herrings in order to create the twist.

Before discussing techniques of the surprise ending it may be worth examining an example of the genre. Somerset Maugham was a master of it and his story *The Verger* is a good case in point. It is a story so well known that revealing its secrets does not spoil it. The special subtlety of *The Verger* is that the reader actually knows the surprise at one level and yet the story still delivers a surprise.

The story concerns Albert, a church verger who after fifteen years of loyal service is forced to leave his job when a new progressive vicar discovers that Albert is illiterate. This had not bothered the previous vicar and it did not stop Albert doing his job efficiently. After the Parish Council gives him news of his imminent dismissal, Albert despondently wends his way home and, as an occasional smoker, fancies a cigarette. He discovers that there is no tobacconist in the area. He decides to cut his losses with the church and with the help of his wife, he makes a career move. He opens a tobacco kiosk in the area where he could not buy cigarettes. It is so successful that within a year or two he has a string of tobacco kiosks. He organizes them; his wife does all the paperwork and accounts. Then one day his bank manager summons Albert to the bank. He has so much money in his current account, the bank manager suggests some more profitable investments. When the bank manager asks him to read and sign the forms Albert, to the surprise of the manager, has to confess that he cannot read and write. The banker asks him in amazement what he might have achieved if he *had* been able to read and write. Albert tells him 'I'd be the verger of St Peter's, Neville Square'.

The reader knows this, but the way it is put at the end is still a surprise and it clarifies a point or theme of the story: that educational achievement is not always a road to success. As well as a surprise ending story with a serious point, it also belongs to another popular genre, the biter bit. In this case it is the new vicar who in a sense gets his come-uppance.

There could be variations of the structure of the story described above. The following are some of the other types of surprise ending stories:

- A person turns out to be very different from the way he or she is perceived by another character. In this kind of story there must not be an uncharacteristic change in the nature of the character.
- Behaviour, which would be expected to lead to a satisfactory outcome, leads to the opposite. Or vice versa: a nasty trick in fact does some good for the person on whom the trick is perpetrated.
- Things that are aimed for or desired prove to be undesirable when they are achieved.

Irony, an outcome rather different from that which is expected, is a feature of the Maugham story described above. Thomas Hardy was devoted to the ironic story. These are some of the ironies which form the basis of some his and some other writers' stories.

- Actions done for good moral reasons lead to undesirable consequences.
- Bad turns lead to a good outcome for the intended 'victim' against all expectations.
- Sacrifice leads to unhappiness and bitterness rather than the reverse which was expected.
- A fantastic effort is expended to achieve what would have happened anyway.

Some other ways of achieving the surprise ending are as follows:

- The writer leads the reader to assume some logical outcome of a character's actions and then surprises them with a different but believable outcome.
- A character is portrayed as appearing to be mean, evil, treacherous or nasty but his actions are finally shown to have been for a good cause or reason.
- The apparently good, helpful or moral character is revealed at the end to have had selfish motives.
- In crime stories the apparently innocent character is revealed as the villain or vice versa.

The previous examples demonstrate how character is integral to the plot of the story which has a twist and suggests that characterization must be carefully created. The following also require careful characterization.

- The central character has an apparent goal or aim which his adversary takes steps to thwart, but these measures are revealed to be what the character really wanted the adversary to do.
- A character assumes an aim or goal in order to draw his adversary's attention from his real intent.
- A character falsely portrays character traits or aims to divert attention from his real nature or purpose which is shown in the end and is consistent with general character traits. (This is a difficult one to bring off successfully.)
- A character's behaviour appears suspicious or strange but is justified and explained at the end.

The above are skeleton outlines but all have been used in published stories. The art is to clothe them with convincing characters and situations. It would be profitable whenever you read a twist ending story or see a TV play with a surprise ending to make a summary of the plot and analyse how the surprise has been engineered.

See also IRONY; PLOT AND STORY; SUSPENSE

TYPEFACE

A typeface is a style of type. It is sometimes called a font. Many hundreds exist and sometimes a new typeface is designed for a particular purpose. Computer word processing and desktop publishing programmes usually contain many choices of typeface.

UNDERSTATEMENT (LITOTES)

Understatement (or litotes, to give it its literary name) is deliberate understatement in order to mean the opposite of what is said. Thus when we say: 'Not bad', we mean 'good'. It is a feature of some people's speech and usually indicates a kind of modesty. For instance someone who has just performed an amazing feat may say: 'Anyone could have done it'. Sometimes it is used to soften reality as in: 'She's not the most beautiful girl in the world' when the speaker means that she is not attractive. Another use of understatement is to indicate that something is less important than it really is.

Understatement is likely to be a feature of the dialogue and the personality of a character rather than the omniscient narrator of a fiction although a first-person narrator may use understatement, ironically enough, in order to emphasize something. Its use makes the reader think about what has just been said because of its apparent contradictory nature.

The opposite of understatement is hyperbole.

UNITIES (CLASSICAL UNITIES, THREE UNITIES)

Aristotle in *The Poetics* suggested that an ideal drama conforms to the three unities of time, place and action; that is, that the action would take place in a single day and at a single location. Some plays followed this dictum and in France in the nineteenth century there was a movement to suggest the greatest literary works would follow Aristotelian patterns. Few plays now conform to the three unities and few literary critics would endorse doing so. It is even less likely to occur in a novel or film. In fact, some people see that one of the merits of fiction is that it can cover considerable time periods and take place in a variety of locations.

Only rarely do dramatic and interesting events occur within the space of a day. The author of a fiction that covers a number of months or years will have taken out the highlights from the period and dispenses with the mundane events which are part of most of the characters' lives.

Only one film known to the author follows the unities. It is *12 Angry Men* (1957). This film concerns the twelve jurors following a trial in which one of them tries to convince the others that the person charged is innocent. The whole film takes place in one room and lasts as long as it took the jury to come to their decision (a matter of about 100 minutes). Clearly this is a dramatic situation that plausibly occurred within a limited time period. Most dramas take longer to unfold and most occur in more than one location. There have been some television plays which have conformed to the three unities but this may be because the television medium is more suited to the idea. Also in the past producers often had very small budgets that precluded an extensive and expensive range of locations.

The novel is unsuited to using the notion of the three unities. James Joyce's *Ulysses* covers just one day in the life of its protagonist but the novel is so long that it would be almost impossible for a reader to read it in a day.

See also HYPERBOLE

UTOPIA (UTOPIAN NOVEL)

Utopian novels form a small but distinctive genre of the novel and there are some important books in this category. The word *Utopia* was the name of a book by Sir Thomas More published in 1516 in which he envisaged a perfect commonwealth. He coined the word from the Greek *outopia* meaning 'no place' and *eutopia* meaning 'good place'. Utopian stories usually serve two functions. They describe the kind of society the author would like and criticize or satirize elements of the society the author lives in and which he or she thinks could be improved.

There were earlier ideas of utopia although the authors obviously did not use the name. Plato's *Republic* (fourth century BC) imagines a kind of communist state wherein goods are owned in common, controlled breeding of children occurs and slavery is accepted. The rulers of this land are philosophers (Plato was a philosopher).

Other early utopias include Francis Bacon's *New Atlantis* (1627), *Looking Backward* (1888) by Edward Bellamy and *News from Nowhere* (1891) by William Morris. The depiction of Eden in the Bible and St Augustine's *City of God* could be described as utopian.

More modern utopias can often also be classed as a branch of science fiction because the authors project ideas on current technology and electronics to envisage how they will transform society in the future. Some authors will imagine improvements, others a deterioration in society. H. G. Wells is one of the greatest exponents of the utopian novel in the twentieth century. He wrote several including *A Modern Utopia* (1908) and *Men Like Gods* (1925).

There were always those who doubted the possibility of achieving a utopia and anti-utopian stories were also written, e.g. *Gulliver's Travels* (1726) and Samuel Butler's *Erewhon* (1872). In the twentieth century, the majority of writers who envisaged the future wrote dystopian novels. These depicted vividly the horror which might happen in the future through the overuse and misuse of science.

A problem for writers of the strictly utopian novel is that it is quite difficult to interest the reader in a perfect world. Such a novel will be mostly description. The stuff of most fiction is when things do not go smoothly. Conflict between people is impossible if they are pleasant and well behaved. Thus Aldous Huxley in *Brave New World* (1932) envisages (although he does not approve of) a world which has been made pleasant for everyone through scientific progress and the application of genetics and psychology. In order to create tension in this perfect society the old world (our world) still exists and clashes with the brave new world and its inhabitants.

See also DYSTOPIAN NOVEL

VANITY PUBLISHING

Reputable mainstream publishers accept manuscripts because they think they have merit and will sell. In exchange they usually pay the author an advance and also pay for all printing and distribution costs. They have an established method of advertising, distributing and selling the books. They will also pay royalties to the author on copies sold.

Vanity publishers are not so discriminating in choosing books for publication because they demand payment from the author for all printing and production costs and they expect payment from the author for publishing their book. They make a profit; the author may not. They do not need to discriminate because they have no risks and nothing to lose. They may produce a catalogue of their publications but they often have no distribution system and take no responsibility for trying to sell the books so authors are left with most of the books to sell themselves. Some authors tout them around shops but this is obviously impossible on a countrywide basis.

Very occasionally a book published by a vanity publisher is taken up by a mainstream publisher but the author who uses a vanity publisher should accept that they are paying a considerable amount to see a book with their name on as the author. They will probably end up giving quite a lot of books away, possibly selling a few through local book-sellers, and almost certainly having a pile at home.

VILLAIN

It is pointed out in the entry on heroes that heroes must have weak-nesses as well as strengths such as courage and, resourcefulness if they are to be believable. The anti-hero is not exactly the opposite of the hero, although he or she exhibits negative qualities rather than heroic ones, neither is the anti-hero a villain. The villain is the oppos-ite of the hero although, perhaps strangely, the villain may exhibit resourcefulness and maybe even courage. The villain is the opposite of the hero in literature because they have different aims. The hero will be intent on achieving good for some individual, group or society and will not be selfish or egotistical. The villain aims to get power or wealth or both for him or herself and has no compunction in using and even killing others in the process.

Like heroes, villains come in many shapes and sizes. Clearly defined heroes and villains are portrayed in Ian Fleming's James Bond novels. James Bond encapsulates all the heroic virtues mentioned although he lacks the compassion that is often a characteristic of the hero. He is also regarded as sexist. The villains in the Bond stories tend to have common aims: to take over the world for their own aggrandizement, wealth and pleasure. Power is their aphrodisiac.

The Bond stories result from the antagonism between Bond and the various villains he encounters. His aim is to retain stability and democracy in the world; the villains aim to take over the world.

The James Bond example demonstrates the hero and villain writ large and probably very unrealistically. In most novels, plays, and films there is greater subtlety in the portrayal of both although there is no doubt that popular literature and drama often contain fairly clearly defined heroes and villains. Think of the many crime and detective novels. The detective or policeperson is the hero (although they often have weaknesses) and the criminal is the villain (although they often have attractive qualities).

In some stories the villain turns out not to be so villainous after all. In Charles Dickens' *Great Expectations*, Magwitch, when he first appears, seems to the boy Pip to be the most scary of creatures, an escaped criminal still with his chains and threatening to attack the boy if he does not bring food and a file. By the end of the novel Magwitch turns out to be a good man who had simply been brutalized by injustice and poverty. Other Dickens villains such as Bill Sikes and Fagin do not have many redeeming features. Shakespeare also has some arch-villains although they are subtly portrayed; characters such as Iago in *Othello* and Shylock in *The Merchant of Venice*.

The modern novel and play tend to deal in less sharply defined heroes and villains, the writers recognizing that people are rarely black and white. The villainy too may not be so clearly obvious. The villainous desire for power is more likely to be power over a spouse or member of the opposite sex or someone in the workplace rather than for world domination. Political power, of course, and the desire for it has been the theme of a number of successful novels and plays.

While heroes and villains, either obvious or subtle, are the staple of the modern story, it was not always so. Villains do not appear in classical literature but appear in the drama of the sixteenth and seventeenth centuries. Shakespeare, Christopher Marlowe and later Cyril Tourneur are some examples of the creators of striking villains in early drama.

See also ANTI-HERO; HERO; HEROINE; PROTAGONIST

VOICE (ACTIVE AND PASSIVE)

Active and passive voice are grammatical terms indicating the verb and the relationship between the subject and object of the sentence. In the sentence 'The fox killed the rabbit', 'fox' is the subject which acts on the object 'rabbit'. The verb is said to be in the active voice; the subject is performing the action, in this case killing. The subject is the actor. But the sentence could be written 'The rabbit was killed by the fox.' In this sentence, the subject is the victim of the actor or it is acted upon. So 'was killed' is in the passive voice whereas 'killed' was in the active voice. The meaning is the same in each sentence but there are important nuances of meaning. Take the sentence 'The man killed the child.' It is a stronger sentence than 'The child was killed by the man.' The latter leaves some doubt about the deliberateness of the act.

The writer will choose which voice to use depending on the context and the shade of meaning desired to convey to the reader. In most cases it will probably seem natural which to choose. Generally speaking the active voice produces a stronger statement. Consider these two head-lines and why a newspaper would choose one rather than the other:

BRITISH TROOPS KILL 20 INSURGENTS
INSURGENTS KILLED BY BRITISH TROOPS

For brevity, directness and clarity the active voice will often be pre-ferred, e.g. 'The boxer felled his opponent.' If the specific actor or doer of the act is unknown then the passive voice may be appropriate, e.g. 'The darts match was won by the best players.' The darts match in this case is more important and specific than best players.

WAR NOVELS

War is ever-present somewhere in the world; wars elicit strong emo-tions from love of country to hatred of the enemy; war is conflict. It is argued elsewhere that conflict is essential in fiction and therefore it is not surprising that war is the subject of many stories. The conflict comes ready-made.

War stories have been written by writers who have experienced warfare at first hand but some of the most acclaimed war novels have been written by people who were not involved. Pat Barker's trilogy *Regeneration* (1991), *The Eye in the Door* (1993) and *The Ghost Road* (1995) are good examples, They have depended on meticulous research and seem authentic to those people who have experienced war and its aftermath. One reason why non-combatants have been able to write successful war novels is that participants can only ever be involved in a small part of the vast theatre of war so unless the story is concerned with a limited aspect even the participant must rely to some extent on research.

Research is also the only way of getting material for past wars. Pat Barker's trilogy concerns the First World War and very few people who were involved in it are still alive.

One of the first great war stories still extant is the epic poem *The Iliad* attributed to Homer and dating from the eighth century BC. It is about the Trojan wars that occurred a few centuries earlier than the poem. One of the most notable things about this story is that the author glorifies war and soldiery. The characteristic of almost all modern war stories is that the authors are almost all anti-war or at least neutral on the subject, regarding it at best as a necessary evil.

The only partial exception to this is exemplified by those writers who make war, or a background of warfare, a setting for showing the heroism of their protagonists or, indeed, their cowardice. Bernard Cornwall in a series of novels about his hero Richard Sharpe has been very successful and so has George MacDonald Fraser with his novels about the coward and womanizer, Harry Flashman, a character he took from the novel *Tom Brown's Schooldays* by Thomas Hughes. Sharpe is involved in India, the Napoleonic Wars in France and Fraser manages to place Flashman in places as far apart as the Battle of Little Bighorn for Custer's last stand and the Charge of the Light Brigade and other situations he manages not to get too involved in. His priority is conquering women rather than countries. Both of these series are really examples of war or historical stories as escapism and adventure although both authors are meticulous about background detail.

Most war novels, and certainly the literary war novels of the twentieth century have been vigorously anti-war and dedicated to showing the suffering and pain involved for combatants and civilians alike. Probably the first great war novel after the First World War was by the German, Erich Maria Remarque, *All Quiet on the Western Front* (1929). Remarque emphasizes the futility and sheer waste of that war and the complete lack of glory involved. The protagonist, talking to recruits when he is on leave, adapts the slogan 'Sweet and decorous is it to die for one's country' which is found on many war memorials. He tells the boys and men 'It's dirty and painful to die for your country'.

The Second World War has inspired many novels, the most acclaimed coming out of America. Herman Wouk's *The Winds of War* (1971) and *War and Remembrance* (1978) were best-sellers and their sales were boosted later when they were made into TV series.

Norman Mailer's first and most acclaimed novel *The Naked and the Dead* (1948) has been cited as probably his best work. It grew partly out of his own experiences during the Second World War.

Joseph Heller's *Catch-22* (1963) enjoys most prestige as an anti-war satire, the title of which has become something of a catch phrase. The central figure in a fairly large cast is Yossarian, a bombardier in the American Air Force. He and his fellow airmen are based on an island off the Italian coast and he has flown many combat missions (as Heller did). Scared out of his wits, he tries to get grounded by feigning insanity. The Catch-22 of the title is this. Air Force regulations say a man is insane if he willingly goes on dangerous combat missions but if he requests to cease duties he must be sane and thus he must continue flying missions. The novel is a tour de force of characterization, humour, bitter satire, detail about life as a combat flier and the sheer absurdity of the whole enterprise. In spite of some complexity, the plot is simple. Yossarian has an aim, he wants to get out of danger and combat missions. In other words, he is human.

Every war has produced its literature and the books range from satirical and humorous to the tragic and pitiful, from stories of individual courage and tragedy to panoramic sagas like Leo Tolstoy's *War and Peace* (1863–1869). While not the most popular genre of fiction, war stories have a continuing appeal to a substantial readership and there is a wide range of possibilities with regard to war and setting. The greatest appeal of many of these novels is that they can combine world-shattering events with individual human stories and cover the human emotions from exhilaration to bleakness. They can be straightforwardly historical to sharp satire. Whatever the background, accuracy and authenticity is vital and therefore research is paramount. Success has been achieved by both those writers with personal experience of their subject matter and those who rely on research. War novels can be a type of adventure story but perhaps writers should remember a comment of the French author and aviator, Antoine de Saint-Exupery (1900–44) 'War is not an adventure. It is a disease'.

See also STORY AND NOVEL CATEGORIES

WESTERN STORIES

The Western story or novel has periods of popularity and times when few are written and read. The early years of this century have been a fallow period in Britain. Even in America it is not one of the most popular kinds of genre fiction, having been replaced by the more general adventure story of which it is a subgenre. Nevertheless, a revival of popularity in both Western fiction and films is not an impossibility. This may be because its appeal is to do with universals such as the pioneering spirit and the opening up of frontiers as well as the more basic appeals of action, gunfights, punch-ups and warfare. It is a genre which has usually dealt in absolutes: good versus bad, right versus wrong, goodies and baddies, cowboy and outlaw, farmers and industrialists, cowboys and Red Indians. The last of these is one reason for the decline of the Western. In the Western's early days the Red Indian was seen as the enemy. Justice, along with the modern sense of political correctness, has seen the Red Indian renamed 'Native

American' and regarded as a victim of the exploitative white man. The Western was deprived of one of its most common antagonists.

Western novels divide into two basic kinds: (1) those which have an authentic background of the pioneering days in America (and also, of course, the American Civil War); and (2) escapist fiction which romanticized the West and created a myth about cowboys, outlaws, Indians, trappers and gold miners. It is not that these did not exist, it is just that hundreds of novels and films gave them undue prominence when the reality for the early pioneers was that life was largely hard graft uninterrupted by frequent gunfights.

While the period thought of as the heyday of the Wild West was probably about 1850–1900, earlier novels presented a more accurate picture of the West and escapist novels are mainly a product of the twentieth century. For accuracy one can go to James Fenimore Cooper whose novels *The Pioneers* (1823) and *The Last of the Mohicans* (1826) portray Western life as it was for many.

The mythic Wild West, where fact and romantic fiction blur, made more impact on readers and film-goers than the real west. To show how fact and fiction merge, the reader may wish to consider these eight familiar names which have appeared in many fictional representations of the West: Billy the Kid, the Sundance Kid, Hopalong Cassidy, Shane, Annie Oakley, Deadwood Dick, the Cisco Kid and the Lone Ranger. Which four are real people and which four are fictional characters? (See end of entry for the answer.)

The mythic Western was encouraged by writers like Zane Grey (1875–1939), a dentist who took to writing Westerns and had written sixty by the time of his death. He was claimed to be the most popular post-First World War writer in America. His most famous novel is probably *Riders of the Purple Sage* (1912). Another writer of Westerns was Louis L'Amour (1908–88), his most well known title is *Hondo* (1953). Most prolific of all the popular writers was Max Brand (1892–1944) who published in the region of 500 books, most of them Westerns. His most famous work is *Destry Rides Again* (1930).

Even popular escapist Westerns must, to satisfy their readership, have some authenticity with regard to locations, weapons, character types and events. The latter, which have been central features in many novels and films include the Lincoln County War, the Johnson County War, the Gunfight at the OK Corral and the Battle of the Alamo. The Western writer must research as meticulously as the general historical novelist. Providing this background is kept in mind, the plot of Western stories is similar to that of Adventure and quest stories.

The readership of Westerns is worldwide even though, for obvious reasons, it has been most popular in America. Similarly most writers of Westerns are American but not exclusively so. Some respected writers in other genres have written Westerns, most notably Elmore Leonard who is usually known for his gritty, character-driven crime fiction. Aspiring writers of Westerns should note, however, that few British publishers consider Westerns at present.

(The four historical personages mentioned above are Deadwood Dick, Annie Oakley, the Sundance Kid, and Billy the Kid. The others are fictional.)

See also ADVENTURE AND QUEST STORIES; STORY AND NOVEL CATEGORIES

WRITE WHAT YOU KNOW

Write about what you know is very common advice given to aspiring writers. It is advice to be taken with a pinch of salt. Those who rec-ommend writing about what you know do so for perfectly sensible reasons. If you know your subject, you can concentrate on the process of writing. In addition, if you are sure that your information and knowledge is accurate, you will be confident in your writing and less prone to criticism from readers who may notice inaccuracies.

A distinction needs to be made here between what may be referred to as background detail and characterization. The former would include things like knowledge of a place, an historical period, a job or profession, a hobby, a sport and so on. If any of these are relevant to the story, then the writer's knowledge of them is important. Character is a more vague and subjective matter. Writers must know their char-acters well and understand what makes people tick. They should have created profiles of all the major characters in a fiction and provided them with a background. Understanding and knowledge of people and their motivations is quite unlike understanding and knowledge of, for instance, a profession. It is not something we can learn except in a very general way over the course of our lives. Some people are per-ceptive about others, some are not. Perhaps a good writer has to be, or should be, the former.

So should we just write about what we know? It would be better advice to say that we should get to know what we want to write about. Thus if you include a lawyer or doctor in a story, it is incumbent on you, the writer, to research these professions and try to talk to members of them. Only then will you be able to write about them convincingly. Basically, prior knowledge is replaced by or supplemented with research; and some professional writers spend almost as much time on the research for a novel as they do on writing it. The American popular novelist Arthur Hailey wrote a series of novels based in and around great commercial institutions. One is called *Airport*, another *Hotel*. Hailey had not worked or spent huge amounts of time in these places but he spent considerable time researching how they worked, the people who worked in them and their clients. His books, whatever their other faults, were never accused of being inaccurate with regard to detail.

Another important qualification to the advice write what you know is this. If taken at face value, it may be inhibiting to the writer. If we take as examples the genres of fantasy and science fiction, these may seem beyond our abilities because we haven't experienced fantasy and we may not know much about science. Did J. R. Tolkein know the world he created for *The Lord of the Rings*? Rather, he used his imagination, as all fantasy and science fiction writers must, although for the latter some scientific knowledge may be useful. But many of the great science fiction writers of the past such as Jules Verne and H. G. Wells were not scientists. Imagination, along with an appreciation of current trends in science, was more important to them than academic scientific knowledge.

In the context of writing about what one knows, Robert Louis Stevenson's novel *The Strange Case of Dr Jekyll and Mr Hyde* is interesting. This novel was written in 1886; it is still in print and it has been filmed many times. It was written before psychology and psychoanalysis but Stevenson had noticed, possibly in himself, that most of us have a social, well-balanced side and also a darker side that we largely repress. What would happen if this darker side were unleashed? From a simple observation about which he really knew very little and by using his imagination, Stevenson created a classic which has considerable psychological authenticity. It has had tremendous popularity probably because it exhibits a truth we recognize. Most of his readers are probably glad that Stevenson did not just write about what he knew.

See also CHARACTERS; RESEARCH

WRITER'S BLOCK

Writer's block is a condition suffered by some professional writers as well as those who write occasionally. Put simply it is a psychological state in which the writer is unable to begin or continue with a piece of writing. The condition is usually temporary but can persist for a considerable period of time, even years.

Many writers have difficulty in getting down to writing or getting started but writer's block is more than this. The American novelist and short story writer, Donald Barthelme, observed 'Endings are elusive, middles are nowhere to be found, but worst of all is to begin, to begin, to begin'. This vividly describes the problems of the writer and they probably beset most except those lucky few who have no difficulty with beginnings and cannot wait to get to the end. Writer's block is more serious and it refers to the impossibility of beginning or continuing with a piece of work.

Most writers specialize and if they suffer from writer's block, a possible solution may be to try some other kind of writing. But there is no suggestion there is an easy solution. Clearly some writers cannot do what previously they had found relatively easy.

Curiously, writer's block is a complaint with no equivalent in other jobs and professions. People may get sick of their jobs, but you do not hear of doctors who suddenly can no longer prescribe or diagnose and never has a plumber been known to lose the ability to change a tap washer or clear an S bend.

Writer's block after a period of considerable writing industry should not be confused with the less serious problem of just not being able to get down to the job of writing; that fear of the blank sheet of paper. This problem can usually be overcome by taking some practical steps in order to get started. Some questions can be addressed 'Have I got a subject which fires my imagination and which I really want to write about?' If the answer is no, then perhaps it is a good thing that writing has ceased and the writer should look for a subject which does fire him up. If the answer is yes, consider the following 'Have I done sufficient research so that I have all the material I need to hand?' If the answer is no, the solution is obvious; if it is yes, the next question is 'Is it the beginning that is the problem?' If it is, there is no need to worry about the beginning; a nondescript opening which can be revised and honed later should be written. Alternatively, the middle of the story could be written and the opening returned to later.

Another possible reason for not being able to put pen to paper may be a lack of planning. Character profiles could be created. Brainstorming could be tried.

Writing is largely a solitary activity but it might be a good idea to talk to other people about the story or project. They may be able to contribute something that will spark activity.

Another strategy may be to write the substance of the story or project in the form of a letter to a friend or known person then see if it can be turned into a story proper.

Changing the point of view might help. If a first-person narrative was used, trying it in third person may prove easier. If the central character was to narrate the story, it could be told from the point of view of a subsidiary character.

Shelving the project that is causing the problem and trying to write something completely different could get the writing muscle working. The original intention can be pursued later but, if the worst comes to the worst, abandonment may be the only solution and it might be best to start something different.

Occasionally writer's block is caused by physical conditions. Experiment with a different place to the usual writing situation. Ensure, of course, that the place is comfortable and quiet or, alternatively, choose to write in a different, possibly noisy place. Respond to a challenge.

See also INSPIRATION

Further Reading and Useful Websites

Books

Books on language basics

Blamires, Harry, *The Penguin Guide to Plain English*. Penguin, 2000.

Crystal, David, *Rediscover Grammar*, rev. ed. Pearson Longman, 2004.

Green, Jonathan, *The Cassell Dictionary of Slang*. Cassell, 1998.

Gulland, Daphne M. and Hinds-Howell, David G. (eds), *Penguin Dictionary of English Idioms*. Penguin, 1986.

King, Graham, *Collins Good Punctuation*. Collins, 2004.

Strunk W. Jr and White E. B., *The Elements of Style*. Longman 1999.

Writers should have as large a dictionary and thesaurus as possible. There are many published reputable ones including Oxford, Collins, Longman Pearson, Bloomsbury.

Books on publishing

Writers who wish to publish should consult one or both of the following books which are published and revised annually (see the entry on *Marketing*).

The Writers' and Artists' Yearbook. A & C Black.

Stock, R. (ed.), *The Insider's Guide to Getting Published*. White Ladder Press, 2005.

Turner Barry, *The Writer's Handbook*. Macmillan.

Literature surveys

For a survey of nineteenth- and twentieth-century fiction the following books are useful. They contain lists, biographies and essays on specific genres:

David, Deirdre, *Cambridge Companion to the Victorian Novel*. Cambridge, 2000.

McLeish, K. and Rennison N. *Bloomsbury Good Reading Guide: What to Read and What to Read Next*. Bloomsbury, 2003.

Rogers, Jane, *Good Fiction Guide*. Oxford, 2005.

Entries on many individual authors, both living and dead, can be found on the internet by putting the author's name into a search engine.

Fiction techniques
Books on fictional technique and basic themes which have appealed to readers over the ages are as follows:

Bell, James Scott, *Plot and Structure*. Writer's Digest Books, 2005.

Bernays, Anne and Painter, Pamela, *What If? Writing Exercises for Fiction Writers*. Harper Collins, 1991. (This is a useful book on techniques, especially for those who may have problems getting started.)

Bolker, Joan (ed.), *The Writer's Home Companion: an Anthology of the World's Best Writing Advice from Keats to Kunitz*. Hold, 1997.

Booker, Christopher, *The Seven Basic Plots*. Continuum, 2004. (This is a massive book on plot and although some critics reject Booker's claims about the seven basic plots, this volume is useful and interesting reading for any writer of fiction.)

Campbell, Joseph, *The Hero with a Thousand Faces*. Princeton University Press, 1972. (This is the book which has influenced many successful Hollywood screen writers, but it has application for any writer of fiction.)

Hawthorn, Jeremy, *Studying the Novel*. Arnold, 1985, rev. 1997. (This is a critical study but it also provides useful information on genres.)

Polti, George, *The 36 Dramatic Situations*. The Writer Press, 1984. (This is mostly regarded as old fashioned and over complicated but it may provide writers of fiction with ideas. Much of the content is available on the internet.)

Websites

The National Association of Writers in Education: www.nawe.co.uk (This association aims to support the development of creative writing in all educational and community settings. It is mainly for teachers, students and writers but anyone may join. There is an annual fee.)

The Arts Council of England: www.artscouncil.org.uk (The Arts Council promotes and supports all the arts and awards some grants to individuals. There are also arts councils for Scotland, Wales and Northern Ireland.)

Department of Culture Media and Sport: www.culture.gov.uk (This is the government department devoted to the arts and sport.)

British Science Fiction Association: www.bsfa.co.uk

Crime Writers' Association: www.thecwa.co.uk

Horror Writers' Association: www.horror.org

Romantic Novelist's Association: www.ma-uk.org

National Association of Women Writers: www.naww.org

Society of Authors: www.societyauthors.org

(Some of these associations above require that members have published in the appropriate genre.)

The Arvon Foundation: www.arvonfoundation.org (The Arvon Foundation organizes week long residential courses for writers.)

Software for producing small print runs of books: www.ragtime-online.com

Writers' Services: www.writersservices.com (This site contains over 1000 pages of advice for writers on many subjects.)

Openings: www.openinghooks.us (A site which contains many novel and story opening sentences. It is amusing and stimulating.)

www.writing.com is an online community of writers and offers the opportunity to publish work.

www.andromeda.rutgers.euc is an American site which guides the searcher to many other sites on writing topics.

www.ukauthors.com is a site which publishes stories on line, author interviews and other information for writers.

www.zott.com is an American site for mystery writers. It contains information on topics such as firearms, poisons and forensics.

Simply entering 'resources for writers' in a search engine will produce many other sites or more specific entries may be made such as apostrophe, speech punctuation, etc. The BBC site www.bbc.com is not only a comprehensive site for much factual information, but entering 'Writing' in the search box will lead to the latest advice for writers.